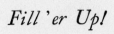

Fill 'er Up!

Books by Bellamy Partridge

Sube Cane

Cousins

Amundsen: The Splendid
    Norseman

A Pretty Pickle

Pure and Simple

Sir Billy Howe: Life of the Gay
    Revolutionary General

Long Night

Horse and Buggy

The Roosevelt Family in
    America

An Imperial Saga

Get a Horse

Thunder Shower

Country Lawyer

Big Family

January Thaw

Excuse My Dust

Big Freeze

The Old Oaken Bucket

Salad Days

Fill 'er Up: The Story of Fifty
    Years of Motoring

With Dr. Otto Bettmann
As We Were

Fill 'er Up!

THE STORY OF FIFTY YEARS
OF MOTORING

BELLAMY PARTRIDGE

McGRAW-HILL BOOK COMPANY, INC.

New York   Toronto   London

FILL 'ER UP!

43612

Dedicated to

the pioneers who founded the American Automobile Association
and to the millions of members of AAA clubs everywhere whose
unfailing cooperation for half a century has contributed greatly
to the improvement of motoring conditions at home and abroad

BY WAY OF *Introduction*

AND *Acknowledgment*

The entire history of motoring is still within the memory of living men. One would have to be eighty-five years old to have heard the pop of the first gas engine, but only sixty-seven to have seen that engine propel the first vehicle by gasoline. To have ridden in the first American-made car one would have to be only fifty-nine.

This first American car was built by two bicycle mechanics, brothers named Duryea living in Chicopee Falls, Massachusetts. It ran, but it never went anywhere except to the Smithsonian Institution. Built entirely by brother Frank, the second Duryea car was the winner of the first American automobile race, a 52-mile road contest held at Chicago in 1895. Frank Duryea, the driver, has been kind enough to furnish me with firsthand material about the origin and building of the car and interesting features of the race not previously available in print.

But the story of motoring cannot, like the story of the telephone or the thermometer, be wrapped up in a neat package. It is scattered over two continents. Many people had a hand in it, and although it was in America that it reached its highest development, first as a pleasure car and eventually as an indispensable vehicle for the culture and growth of our particular brand of civilization, it is not to be forgotten that it was in Europe that the motorcar was conceived and born.

We had the gasoline, but until a German doctor devised the proper engine for it we threw the fuel away as useless. When, however, we learned how to get the power out of our gasoline, the craze for motoring swept over the country like a tidal wave.

The motorcar made its first appearance as a plaything for the rich, since they were the only persons who could afford one. But it also had a wide appeal for those who were not rich, and when they could not buy a car they tried to build one; not, however, with any idea of going into the business. The vast majority of our early cars were made just for fun.

Henry Ford claimed that his interest was always in building cars to sell. This was probably so, for by the time Henry's first car was ready to run, European automobiles were being offered for sale in America, and the Duryea brothers in their one-room factory had already built and sold thirteen cars. But it is nevertheless true that most of the monkey-wrench mechanics and crackpots who were building cars in the back yards of America had no idea of selling them.

That first Duryea car came into a world that was singularly placid and content. It was a world of horses, of family prayers, of dinner at noon. It was a period of peace, marble-top furniture, and the mustache cup. The mothers and grandmothers had not yet taken up smoking and wearing pants. Children did as they were told, or took the consequences, for there were then no "teen-agers" in the present implication of the term.

We were still basically an agricultural country where prosperity was measured by bumper crops instead of belching smokestacks. The telephone had come, but had not yet enslaved us; and the phonograph with its wax rolls was a poor competitor for the magic lantern as parlor entertainment. Motion pictures had not reached the dignity of the nickelodeon, and the radio was still two decades in the future.

Our way of life was enjoying a leisure and a tranquillity that would never come again; but it was like the stillness before the storm, for the machine age was just around the corner, though nobody seemed to believe it. Even after the Chicago race there were big, important newspapers in the country which solemnly insisted that the horseless carriage could never supplant the horse. This turned out to be a rather poor guess, for within the next seven years our automobile factories were building more than 200 different makes of cars, while the annual registration had risen to 23,000.

The fifteen years after the Chicago race were the golden age of the motorcar. With the horseless carriage regarded as a vehicle for pleasure only, motoring was filled with romance and adventure. There was the charm of novelty, the tang of danger, the irresistible attraction of uncertainty, the tempting call of the open road, and, if you got there and back—the supreme reward of accomplishment; yes, and perhaps a little boasting. There were few motorists who did not feel that the pride of ownership was well worth all the headaches that went with the early cars.

Nobody whose first ride occurred soon after the turn of the century will ever have another to equal it. I remember taking an old lady for her first ride in my canopy-top Rambler. As we came to the crest of a hill and started down without slackening our pace, I could see her tightening her grip on the seat. Then I heard her gasp and exclaim, "Why—it's just like flying!"

It certainly was. I felt the same way on my first ride, and so long as I live I'll never forget it. My own children, and all the rest of their generation, have missed something by being toted around in a motorcar since birth.

For fifty years I have been the owner and driver of automobiles, and for fully half that time I have been collecting and saving little bits and oddments of motorcar history, catalogues and clippings, anecdotes and hearsay, comments and argument, and fragments which might otherwise have been lost. Then there is a diary and the pictures of my transcontinental pathfinding expedition of 1912.

In addition to this long-time accumulation of notes and reminders I have been fortunate in having access to the vast reservoir of new or unused material in the files and records of the American Automobile Association, for which I wish to express my appreciation and gratitude.

Then, too, I have had the willing cooperation of librarians in many of the large cities from coast to coast; and I have consulted with automobile companies, large and small, as well as with motor clubs, publicity departments, archivists, mechanics, car washers, truck drivers, and those philosophers who operate our taxicabs. Of them all I found the truck drivers the most standoffish until I explained that I was gathering material for a book. Then they were very likely to invite me into the cab, and in a number of cases I found that they, too, were thinking of writing a book. There is something about the automobile fraternity that makes people friendly and well disposed; and to all who have given me a helping hand I offer my sincere thanks.

Grateful acknowledgment is also made to Houghton Mifflin Company for permission to reprint the quotation from *Combustion on Wheels* by David L. Cohn.

Bellamy Partridge

Easton, Conn.
  1952

Contents

"Fill 'er up!" is a thoroughly American phrase. It suggests endless abundance and openhandedness. It is characteristic of a continental people whose life is geared to the car—a free-and-easy people to whom mobility is of the essence of living. . . . It is a phrase that could have been invented by no other people. There is no beauty in these words, yet they unlock for us the beauty of this continent which has just become ours, which we have scarcely seen, and which few of us will ever see in its entirety, the land being so vast and the time so short. (From David L. Cohn's book *Combustion on Wheels*.)

1 *Crackpots and Tinkers*

There was loud hammering in the back yards of America. Hammering and thumping and filing. There was also a lot of ear scratching and head shaking. What to do next—how to go about it. There was no blueprint, no plan. Nothing but an idea. How to put a light power plant on wheels so that it would propel a vehicle along the roads without any pushing on the part of a man or pulling on the part of a beast.

It was not a new idea. Human beings had been puzzling their heads over it for five thousand years, perhaps ever since the invention of the wheel. Antiquarians have expressed surprise that the American Indian, lazy as he was, never thought of the wheel. The fact is that the redskin seldom moved, had little to carry, and when he did his squaw was on hand to do all the work. Our squaws aren't like that any more.

That the wheel was the product of laziness seems pretty certain; it would carry the burden by rolling it along, but even the wheel had to be pushed or pulled. This brought an animal into the picture—an ass or a yak, possibly a buffalo, perhaps a horse or even a cow. Anything with four legs instead of two. But four-legged creatures were also lazy. They had to be urged along with a shout, a whip, or a goad; and they used to tire easily, especially if hauling a heavy load.

It was not until after the interesting experiments of James Watt with his old-fashioned teakettle that there was any considerable relief in sight for the beast of burden. Then Nicholas Cugnot, a Frenchman, built a three-wheeled road vehicle powered by steam. This was in the year of our Lord 1770.

The Cugnot contraption was a cumbersome three-wheeler

weighing many tons, with no room for either passengers or freight; and still the monstrosity started a new fashion of road transportation, especially in England, where steam seems to have gone to everybody's head. Inventors began to turn out huge steam buses which threatened to banish horses from the stage business; but the stagecoach people turned the tables by jamming through a law requiring power-driven road vehicles to be preceded by a man on foot carrying a red flag.

This infamous "red flag law" should be remembered, for it not only put the steam coaches out of business, but it also obstructed the development of the motor vehicle in Britain for a generation; and later it crossed the Atlantic to America where it was used in an attempt to flag down the oncoming motorcar.

Propulsion without labor seems to have been instinctive with man. It was this that put him astride the floating log; later it landed him on the back of a horse, and finally in a carriage. Having achieved the carriage, he tried to get rid of the horse. In 1748 a Frenchman devised a carriage run by clockwork. A Londoner in 1825 invented a wagon drawn by kites. Here in our own country sail-driven vehicles were tried without any notable success. Humanity was trying hard but not getting anywhere.

When self-propulsion came, it followed a roundabout course. Gasoline was produced as a waste product in Pennsylvania in 1863. Four years later a German doctor named N. A. Otto invented a four-cycle internal-combustion engine run by illuminating gas. We now come back to America where in 1874 George Brayton came up with a two-cycle motor powered by gasoline. Having seen that engine, George B. Selden of Rochester, New York, on May 8, 1879, applied for a patent on a "safe, simple, and cheap road locomotive, light in weight, easy to control, possessed of sufficient power to overcome an ordinary inclination."

That was that. America was not going to be heard from again in the motor vehicle field for thirteen years.

And in the meantime Gottlieb Daimler, a German, made the Otto engine run on gasoline in 1885, and that same year Carl Benz, another German, drove a three-wheeled vehicle powered by the Daimler engine. It was the first motor vehicle to be driven by gasoline. Benz hurried over to France, where he had heard of a firm interested in building motor vehicles and leased the French rights to his invention to Panhard-Levassor, who thereupon began the manufacture and sale of gasoline automobiles.

Both Benz and Daimler realized that they were on the trail of something important, and in 1888 both applied for American patents on their cars. Patents were forthwith granted to both— with the Selden application of 1879 still pending and very much alive. This looked like a promising situation for a big lawsuit; but for more than a decade no lawsuit over the patents was filed —and when it was, neither Benz nor Daimler was named as a defendant.

All these goings on at the Patent Office had little effect on the average American at the moment. The bicycle craze was at its peak, and he was skimming around on his bike and was much more agitated over the Sunday runs of his bicycle club and the question of smooth cinder paths over which to make the wheels run more easily.

It is hard to understand why America should have taken so little interest in the motorcar up to this time. News must have been constantly filtering through to this country by way of the press and the stories brought back by returning tourists of cars flitting about in the European cities. Several factories were in production in France alone, and the output in 1890 is said to have run into the hundreds.

Of course there was some tinkering going on in this country, but it was scattered and sporadic. As early as 1878 the legislature of Wisconsin was trying to develop a "cheap and practical substitute for the horse." So they must have been hearing things even in the Northwest. The lawmakers offered a prize of $10,000 to the winner of a steam-wagon race from Madison to Green Bay and return, a distance of 200 miles. Only two contestants qualified, and the winner, moving about as fast as a snail can go, was two weeks in covering the distance. The horses of Wisconsin must have had a good laugh.

Not long after this, a young man named Ransom E. Olds was clattering about the streets of Lansing, Michigan, in an iron-tired vehicle driven by steam, and a three-wheeler at that. His father, by the way, was a manufacturer of gasoline engines. Other inventors throughout the country were experimenting with steam cars, and some were even trying to drive cars by electricity, though without any great success, since a good storage battery had not at that time been made.

It seems odd that, with the success of the gasoline motor in Europe, more American inventors had not begun to experiment with it. This fuel had been cheap and plentiful since the development of the Pennsylvania oil fields. It had, in fact, been a drug on the market which the refineries would gladly have given away. But in spite of its uselessness they had to keep on producing it, since it was a residue of the process of making kerosene. Because it was explosive and dangerous to store, most of it was run off into the watercourses, where it killed the fish, destroyed riparian vegetation, and polluted the water for drinking purposes. It also gave off an unpleasant emanation throughout the countryside and, until the coming of the internal-combustion motor, was considered to be the problem child of the oil business.

It may have been that the hostile attitude of the insurance companies retarded to some extent the development of gasoline as a motorcar fuel. Ignorance or carelessness in handling it had been the cause of a number of serious fires, and insurers were restricting both its use and storage on premises covered by their policies. I distinctly remember hearing an insurance agent say, when explaining the great hazard of having gasoline around, that the dang stuff was especially dangerous since it could explode without even being ignited. And red printed slips were delivered with every policy warning the holder against the use or handling of so hazardous a substance.

However, there were certain hardy souls in America who were ready to take their life in their hands if they could only make a motorcar that would run on the much-abused fuel. They were scattered around in various places—Olds in Lan-

Winner of the first automobile race, from Chicago to Evanston, Illinois, Thanksgiving Day, 1895, was J. Frank Duryea, who, with his brother Charles, designed and built America's first successful gasoline auto. Car shown was a successor to their first car, produced in 1893.

William K. Vanderbilt, Jr., donor of the trophy competed for in the fabulous Vanderbilt Cup races held on Long Island, 1904 through 1910. Last and greatest of these races attracted 500,000 spectators. He is shown in a car which set a 1904 speed record of a mile in 39 seconds.

Speed meant little in this tight spot. It took an old-fashioned team of horses to get this Metz racer across a stream along the route of an early open-road race. Before the coming of supervised track racing, speed enthusiasts usually took to winding country roads for their fun.

In the Ormond Beach races of 1906, a number of the drivers, unable to distinguish between the beach and the sea in a heavy rain, drove their racers right into the ocean. It took a team of horses, a sturdy four-by-four, and strong men to retrieve the vehicles after the race ended.

sing, Haynes in Kokomo, Ford and King in Detroit, Winton in Cleveland, and the Duryea brothers in Springfield, Massachusetts.

Some of them had experimented with steam and found it wanting; and now all of them had turned to the Otto type of engine as probably the most suitable motive power for a road vehicle. Haynes had received his training with a gas company, Ford and Olds were machine-shop men, Winton was an ex-steamship engineer, and the Duryea boys were bicycle builders. All had caught the motorcar fever and, in the early nineties, were hammering doggedly in their back yards on what they hoped would turn out to be a horseless carriage.

The Duryea brothers, Charles and Frank, were not, as some have supposed, a pair of cantankerous New England Yankees. They originated in the Middle West, having been born on a farm in Wyoming, Illinois. After they finished their schooling, Charles, the older brother, went into bicycle work in Washington, D.C., where he was designing a lightweight machine to be known as the "Sylph." In 1888 Frank joined him there, and later they moved to Chicopee Falls, Massachusetts, where Frank worked as a toolmaker for the Ames Bicycle Company.

Charles, the designer, who was much more of a reader and dreamer than his brother, became interested in self-propulsion and in 1892 had an idea for building a motorcar. He had a set of plans prepared and with only these and his own enthusiasm interested E. F. Markham, a local man, to such an extent that Markham put up $1,000 to get the idea on its way. The investor was promised a one-tenth interest, and if he should advance enough to finish the machine, a one-half interest.

As a starting point Charles bought an old phaeton buggy and, since he was not a skilled mechanic, he hired his brother Frank to take over the construction of what they were now calling their "horseless wagon." Instead of starting with their power plant, they began with the axles, the steering gear, the frame, everything except the motor. That came last. Charles had a very indefinite idea of how a motor should be made. He had designed no carburetor, no exhaust pipe or muffler. He had planned a cylinder and a cylinder head with an ignition tube screwed into the top, but the burner for heating this tube had been left to later experiments. And in the meantime the months had been slipping away. They had started work about April 1, 1892, and soon September was looming, the time when Charles had agreed to take up some bicycle work in Peoria, Illinois.

He wanted very badly to try out the engine before he went away. If it would run and the job looked like a success, he might alter his plans considerably. But the trouble was that the chassis was nowhere near ready to have the motor installed. It would take days and perhaps weeks to get it ready, and since Charles was insistent upon a test they mounted the engine between two sawhorses and proceeded to try it out. From a drugstore they obtained an alcohol lamp and a perfume atomizer. The idea was to heat the tube with the alcohol lamp and spray gasoline into the cylinder through the intake valve—and give the flywheel a whirl. If it gave a kick they would know they were on the right track.

But, alas, it failed to give a kick or a cough or a wheeze— and Charles went off to Peoria a disappointed man, leaving his brother and the unfortunate moneylender out on a limb.

By this time, however, both were so involved in the job and so obsessed with the idea of making the wagon propel itself that they decided to carry on without brother Charles. The experiments with the engine had convinced Frank that with a proper burner he could make the motor run—but at just this time he came down with typhoid fever and was carried off to a hospital where he remained for a month, and even after he came out a long period of recuperation was necessary.

Work was resumed on the burner about the first of January, 1893. And having finished the burner, Frank designed and built a carburetor with a gravity flow, and built and attached a gasoline tank. Now he not only succeeded in getting a very definite kick out of the engine, but with some adjustments and refinements he had it running with so much regularity that it got out of hand and slammed into the wall of the shop. And if run for any length of time it became very hot, so he had to design and build a water jacket.

Although it would run, it was not ready for the street, and by the time Frank was ready to give the machine an outdoor test a great many things had happened to delay that important occasion. In the first place, Frank had to take time out to court and marry a wife, which kept him occupied until the month of May; then, too, he had almost completely rebuilt and redesigned the motor, and all the time he had to maintain diplomatic relations with Markham, who was still furnishing the money to carry on but was now near the end of his resources. So it happened that before he was ready for the test the summer was past, the harvest was ended, and the tree in the dooryard was covered with little crab apples.

Then came that day in September when they stood the vehicle up on its rear end to take it down on the elevator. It was parked behind a building until after dark when Mr. Markham's son-in-law, Mr. Bemis, brought a harnessed horse which pulled the machine to his barn on Spruce Street. When everything was ready the two men pushed the wagon out into the dirt road which ran past the house.

Trembling with excitement, Frank walked around to the rear of the wagon and grasped the flywheel which, like the rest of the mechanism, hung in the open below the seat, and gave it a whirl. Nothing happened and he gave another whirl—several others. Suddenly the engine started with a bang and a cloud of smoke. Stumbling with excitement, Frank hurried into a position where he could handle the steering tiller and applied the clutch.

The wagon moved—it went forward—and kept moving until it had traveled some 25 feet. Then it stalled. When cranked again, it started readily and moved until it had covered some 200 feet. After that, it was retired for the evening. The experiment was epoch-making. It was the first American-made gasoline car to run, and Charles Duryea, from whose idea it had sprung, was not there to see it go.

The story of the test was in the Springfield *Union* the next day, which was September 22, 1893. It began as follows:

> The first tests of the motor carriage built by J. F. Duryea
> and E. F. Markham have been made and although the
> carriage runs very well it does not give perfect satisfaction
> to the inventors, and some changes will be made in the
> mode of transmitting power from the motor to the main
> driving shafts.

The alterations were made and resulted in tests that were satisfactory to both the builder and his backer, and after that the wagon was occasionally seen on the streets of Springfield.

Charles had departed from Springfield in September, 1892, and Frank did not again see his brother until a month after the test when the brothers met at the World's Fair in Chicago. When Charles was leaving Springfield he had urged Frank to come with him, assuring him that if he did he would "wear diamonds." But Frank had refused to go. His interest in the wagon had gone too deep for him to walk off and leave it.

After going to Peoria, Charles had taken no part in the financing of the project. He had for all practical purposes thrown it overboard. But he listened eagerly as Frank gave him all the details of the test, and took the position that since the original idea was his, the result of it still belonged to him, though he magnanimously allowed Frank to come in as a partner, and Frank let him get away with it.

Soon after this, Frank began planning an entirely new car —on his own—and when later in the year the now famous Chicago race was announced he worked night and day to finish a car which he thought would have a chance of winning. Neither Charles nor Markham had any part in the planning or the financing of the Chicago car. The plans and drawings were worked out entirely by Frank, and on the strength of them he was able to obtain enough financial support to carry the project to a successful conclusion. His new backer was a promoter named H. W. Clapp who had taken an option which enabled him to form a company to build and market the car should it prove to be successful.

Clapp turned out to be a real promoter, and as soon as Frank had the new car tested and running around the streets of Spring-field he started a selling campaign. By the summer of 1895 he was taking orders for cars nearly every day, though they had no idea at the time what the price was going to be. Since the original car was no part of the deal and had been entirely by-passed, Clapp suggested eliminating both Charles and Markham from the new company, but Frank would not have it that way. Both were included as stockholders, and though they were equally inactive in company matters they were well compensated in the end.

2 *The Chicago Race*

America had long been a country of horse races, many of them impromptu affairs which came up suddenly on the road when one driver attempted to pass and show his dust to another. And if one had a really fast horse, the County Fair was a good place to let people know about it. With the coming of the bicycle craze a new type of racing was inaugurated and became immensely popular. But until 1893 nobody in America had even thought of the possibility of a race between horseless carriages.

The reason for this was that until then nobody in this country had constructed a horseless carriage that would really run. Any such vehicle seen on the road was almost invariably stopped for repairs. And the inventors experimenting with them were regarded either as a joke or a crackpot—they might as well have been seeking perpetual motion.

In France, however, the situation was quite different. The good roads presented a constant challenge, and the early inventions leading to self-propulsion had fallen into the hands of forward-looking individuals of sufficient financial backing to give them adequate and intelligent development. By 1894 the motor vehicle over there had reached the point where competition between makers was the next logical step in orderly progress. And the race from Paris to Rouen—well, it just came naturally.

The reaction of America was decidedly skeptical. The thought of an 87-mile road race by horseless carriages sent the eyebrows soaring. Preposterous! That was the word. The American press was almost unanimous in its skepticism—that is, if it carried the story at all. Not so with the inventors, for in the next few months after the Paris-Rouen road race more than 500 applications for patents on self-propelled vehicles were filed in the United States Patent Office. And there was one newspaperman who saw nothing preposterous in the idea of a motor vehicle race, not only in France, but in America as well.

The blueprint of such a contest was ready-made for him. The French race had been sponsored by a newspaper and had offered a large enough purse to be a real incentive. So the young journalist, Frederick Upham Adams, took a long chance and presented the idea to H. H. Kohlsaat, owner of the Chicago *Times-Herald*, the newspaper by which he was then employed.

Adams found Kohlsaat not too enthusiastic about the idea and he had to work hard to sell it to him. And he had to keep selling it over and over again until the racers were actually on the road. The opposition papers, especially in Chicago, jeered loudly and wanted to know where horseless carriages were coming from to put on such a race.

Adams realized from the first that there were not enough horseless carriages in America to warrant the staging of a worthwhile sporting event. But he had hopes of attracting foreign entries, and he was optimistic enough to believe that, if given a year in which to build their machines, American ingenuity would furnish him with a wide choice of entries. However, he insisted on a liberal purse.

Though Kohlsaat still regarded the event as a little shaky, he came through with a $5,000 purse, $2,000 going to the winner and lesser sums going to the runners-up.

Announcement of the race, made soon after the Paris-Rouen contest, was followed by a continuous stream of articles taking a very roseate view of the future of the horseless carriage and the importance of its development in America. Soon after this Adams made a tour of the country, hunting up the various horseless carriages that had been built or were under construction, urging that they should be ready in time for the race which had been set for the Fourth of July, 1895. He even ran down all the crackpot inventors he could find and tried to interest them in the fat purse.

If Kohlsaat had been fearful of a lack of entries, the results of Adams' efforts should have calmed his fears, for applications for entry blanks came pouring in from all directions. More than thirty were received from Chicago sources alone, and a dozen more from places scattered throughout the state of Illinois. Six applications came from Indiana and seven from Ohio. Pennsylvania was represented by six applications and New York by five. From Connecticut came two and from Massachusetts three, one of which was from the Duryea Motor Wagon Company of Springfield. Only four applications came from Michigan, not one of them from a source that had any part in the future of the automobile.

Several of the applications came from engine makers, and a few from builders of carriages. One was from a power-generating company, and another from a fireproof-covering firm. Three were from bicycle companies, one from a refrigerator manufacturer, and one from a maker of wheel chairs and perambulators.

The majority of the applications, however, came from individuals living in widely scattered villages, all the way from Center Point, Iowa, to Skowhegan, Maine. One application was from Sistersville, West Virginia. Two were received from Pine Bluff, Arkansas. All told there were nearly ninety applications, though when the race was finally run only six machines managed to stagger up to the starting line.

The year 1895 came in with the usual whoops, hollers, and headaches. To most people, it was just another year, but to Frederick Upson Adams it seemed to offer great possibilities. Still, as the winter tapered off into spring and the spring into summer, prospects for holding the race on the Fourth of July dimmed alarmingly. Entrants who had responded with such eagerness to the original announcement were now sketchy in their reports of the progress being made on their machines, and Adams and Kohlsaat adjourned the contest to early November, hoping that in the meantime something would happen to save the day.

And something did. It was another road race in France, this time from Paris to Bordeaux and return—a distance of nearly

800 miles—won by Panhard at the magnificent speed of 15 miles an hour. This woke up America like a slap in the face. The crackpots rushed back to their workbenches, and new entries began pouring into the office of the *Times-Herald*. To give the contestants more time to finish their machines, a further adjournment to Thanksgiving Day was announced. This gave the opposition newspapers in Chicago a field day, and they devoted columns to their sarcastic predictions that the race would never be run.

However, as the chilly weather of the fall came on, horseless carriages for the race actually began to appear in Chicago so that the drivers could familiarize themselves with the course and make their final preparations at the scene of the contest. The R. H. Macy entry had started from New York under its own power to make the drive to Chicago; but it had run into bad roads along the Hudson Valley and after being buried under a snowstorm in Schenectady was sent the rest of the way by freight.

As fast as the machines came in, Adams put them on display in a vacant store on Wabash Avenue, and to keep the interest alive he announced a preliminary bout for a $500 bonus. Of the twelve entries in town only six were able to reach the starting line. It shook down to a race between Duryea and Benz. The Benz won, but both cars were quite seriously damaged.

Largely for purposes of publicity but also to relieve Mr. Adams of monotony in the continual use of the word "horseless" in his outpouring of promotion matter, another prize of $500 was offered by the *Times-Herald*, to be awarded for an entirely new designation for the self-propelled vehicle.

Not only Mr. Adams, but many others were finding the word distasteful and could see no reason for attaching the name of an animal to a vehicle which in all probability was about to displace him.

Five hundred dollars for a name? That seemed like easy money, and most of the literate people east of the Rockies and west of the Alleghenies sent in what they hoped would be the prize-winning designation. The offices of the *Times-Herald* were almost buried under the avalanche of letters. Other newspapers

poked fun at the contest, and the whole country became so
horseless-conscious that the magazine *Horseless Age,* just then
being launched, made an attempt at exculpation and justification
for using the word in its title.

Every possible combination of the words *wagon, carriage,*
and *buggy* was proposed, and the word *motor* was rehashed and
reassembled *ad nauseam.* The word *cycle* was a special favorite, both as a prefix and suffix, and fragments of the word *automobile* were exceedingly popular. Repetitions were innumerable, and the prize, when awarded, had to be split three ways. The
winner—MOTOCYCLE! It was a complete flop. Even the *Times-
Herald* abandoned it after the race was over.

The word was a mistake, but Adams would not admit it.
He was not the fellow to sit behind the closed doors of the editor's sanctum holding Kohlsaat's hand. No doubt he said what
he could to cheer up the boss, but early and late he was rushing
around exuding optimism and trying to make a nationwide success of the motocycle contest.

Somehow he managed to keep the crackpots and inventors
swinging the hammer and hauling on the monkey wrench until the last moment, hoping against hope to have entries ready
for the starting gun. On the eve of the contest he called them
together for a final showdown, and out of hundreds of hopefuls
on his list he was able to exact a definite promise from only eleven
of the candidates.

Naturally Kohlsaat was down in the mouth at such a poor
showing and Adams had to work hard to keep him from throwing the contest overboard. If Kohlsaat had known what the
weather was going to be he would never have allowed himself
to be dissuaded.

The snow had already begun to fall when the meeting broke
up, but the temperature was warm and the weatherwise were
predicting hopefully that it would turn to rain. Which only
shows the unpredictability of the Chicago climate, for when
morning came the earth lay soggy and saturated under an 8-inch
blanket of snow which had drifted badly before turning into
sleet and slush. According to the rules of the contest, the start

was scheduled for 7:30, but by 8:30 only seven vehicles had arrived, the Pennington entry having been hauled there on a dray drawn by horses, to help a stock-selling campaign in which he was involved. It never ran.

In Charles Duryea's story of the race, written for *Horseless Age*, he tells of rising at six o'clock, swallowing a bite of breakfast, and setting out for the starting point at the Midway Plaisance. A half-hour's run down the Cottage Grove car tracks brought him and his brother Frank to the Midway not far from the erstwhile famous Streets of Cairo, a remnant of the Chicago World's Fair.

As they turned in, a kindly spectator called to them, "One is just ahead! It's been stuck in the snow for the last twenty minutes."

Looking ahead, they could see the machine being pushed by friendly pedestrians. But Frank Duryea, arguing that if they couldn't get through now, they certainly couldn't later, put on the power and went plowing through to the starting line. One by one other entries came struggling in and made ready to start.

In order they were:

The Electrobat of Morris & Salom, a battery-driven electric.

The Duryea, a gasoline wagon of Duryea Motor Wagon Company.

Benz, a gasoline wagon of German make entered by H. Mueller Manufacturing Company.

Benz, same type, entered by De La Vergne Refrigerating Company.

Roger, gasoline wagon of R. M. Macy & Company, also made by Benz.

The Sturges, an electric wagon of Harold Sturges.

Elwood Haynes had entered his gasoline car, but at the very last it had broken an essential part and the entry had to be scratched. It was a good machine, and if it had remained in the race the outcome might have been closer.

The Electrobat was out of the race even before starting, as it had been unable to assure a supply of batteries at the various relay stations, and had appeared only as a gesture of good will. Kohlsaat was not present at the start. He couldn't bear it and preferred to pace the floor at home. Adams was on hand with a long face, but fully determined that the show must go on.

He gave the word, and at 8:55 the Duryea, driven by brother Frank, with Arthur White as umpire, received the flag and started off. Its smooth pneumatic tires splashed up the slush and slewed and swung; then it started to move forward—slowly at first, then faster, and soon it had passed through the crowd and was lost to sight. The others went off at one-minute intervals. The De La Vergne, the second to go, proceeded only a block before it was stalled in the deep snow. The Macy car, coming up behind, was also stalled, as well as all the others except the Mueller Benz which did not get off until an hour later. One at a time the stalled machines were pushed by the good-natured crowd and started on their way.

Charles Duryea remained only long enough to see that they were off before catching a train for the Loop District of the city. There his company had made arrangements for a splendid team of horses and a light sleigh with which to trail his brother, so that he could be on hand for any emergency that might arise —and plenty did. He had figured that if Frank could hold to a speed of 4 miles an hour he would be at Van Buren Street at ten minutes after ten.

But Frank did better than that. He came splashing along less than an hour after the start. The waiting crowd cheered, and Charles waved with his hat to show Frank that he was there. After the machine had passed, he unobtrusively fell in behind and followed with his team and sleigh. The wagon, as the Duryeas called it, was running beautifully, but it still had a long distance to go, since the course followed the shore line to Evanston. There, after checking in, it was to return along Clark Street to Roscoe, where it turned inland for a short distance, and thence on through Humboldt Park and Washington Avenue to the starting place.

Frank had just crossed the Rush Street bridge when trouble descended upon him. The steering apparatus broke and the car was out of control when he brought it to a stop. Charles was right there to give advice, though according to the rules he could do none of the work.

With a monkey wrench Frank quickly removed the broken part and saw at a glance that it must be taken to a shop for repairs. Ordinarily this would have caused no great difficulty, but because of the holiday most of the shops were closed. That was where the team came in handy, for after racing all over the neighborhood Charles located a shop that was open, and Frank quickly made the repair, with a loss of only fifty-five minutes. But, in the meantime, the Macy wagon had passed and was now thirty-five minutes ahead, and an unidentified contestant was coming up only a few blocks in the rear.

Unfortunately, at just this time, the Duryea ran into an area of deep snowdrifts and the horses had to be slowed down to a walk to keep them behind. This, Charles thought, would be a good time to rest the horses and have some lunch. So he found a place to stable and feed the horses and ordered a hearty meal for himself. And here Charles lunched in comfort while Frank went struggling along through the sleet and slush without even a sandwich to stay his hunger.

Rested and refreshed, Charles ordered up the horses, consulted the route map he had clipped from the paper, and took a short cut to the next relay station which he reached just before Frank came laboring in with the news that he was in the lead with a clear road behind him for at least a mile. Charles suggested a ten-minute stop for a rest and a sandwich. The rest period was quickly over, and after Frank had resumed the grind Charles figured out another short cut to spare the horses.

This time something went amiss. Frank wandered off the course and lost his way, and while he was in unfamiliar territory the car broke down with a defective sparking apparatus. When Frank failed to arrive at the relay station as expected, Charles began speeding his horses up and down the connecting streets looking for him. At last, with a sigh of relief, he saw the Duryea standing by the curb and, nearby, Frank squatting over a charcoal fire, fanning the flame to heat one of the electrical connections so that it could be bent sufficiently to make a repair. Additional time lost, one full hour.

To their astonishment when they finally reached the next relay they found they were still in the lead.

The Duryea brothers had now come to one of the most delightful phases of the contest. All day the sidewalks along the route had been crowded with cheering spectators, but the traffic in the streets had remained light. By mid-afternoon, however, an improvement in the weather had begun bringing out the equipages of the smart set who wanted to enjoy a taste of the very excellent sleighing afforded by the first snow of the season. Young people home for the holiday from school or college provided an air of gaiety in the parks and along the boulevards of the West Side announced as the route to be followed by the racers.

The jingling of sleigh bells and the prancing of high-stepping horses had already given the city a real carnival air—when suddenly from nowhere the Duryea appeared, its unmuffled engine popping loudly and its warning bell clanging for the right of way. Sleighing parties quickly drew their teams aside and halted their prancing steeds to watch the strange vehicle pass. They had undoubtedly expected another racer to come careening along in pursuit. But when they saw that the Duryea was followed only by a team and a sleigh, they caught the idea and whipped up their own horses to follow along and watch the fun.

As Charles Duryea describes the occasion, "An army of sleighs and rigs followed, and occasionally one would get in front and in the way. There was much enthusiasm and many snowballs. We knew that the cavalcade was [packing the snow and] making a good road for the next fellow, but that did not worry us for we believed that we were going faster than he could anyhow."

What a picture this would have made for Currier & Ives! What a charming memory of the "gay nineties." The cheering crowds, the prancing horses, the pretty girls with rosy cheeks, tucked into the robes of the plumed sleighs. Then there was the music of the jingling bells, and the flying snowballs probably aimed at the umpire's derby hat. And out in front of it all the fussy little wagon without any horse, showing the way from a leisurely and peaceful life into a period of machinery and speed, war and income taxes, communism and atomic fission, bobbed hair and the cocktail lounge.

When no other racers appeared, the sleighing parties dropped out and turned back. Streets narrowed and the lines of pedestrians became thinner. The little machine finally ran into a "trackless waste of snow," to quote Charles Duryea once more. And here the horses went ahead to break open the road.

Progress was slower now. The engine was working harder when suddenly strange grinding noises were heard beneath the floor boards. Frank quickly stopped the car. A hasty examination disclosed that a chip, flaked from one of the driving gears, had wedged between two of the teeth. Once located, the trouble was easily cured by removing the chip. Daylight was fading and still the end of the race seemed far away.

At 7:18 in the evening the Duryea crossed the finish line. The only other car to finish, a Benz, did not check in until past midnight, according to Charles, though others clocked him in only an hour behind the winner. But Oscar Mueller, the driver, was not at the helm of the Benz. He had collapsed from exposure and excitement, and his umpire, the imperturbable Charles King, had brought the faltering vehicle over the line.

3 *The Afterglow*

After seeing the start of the motocycles, Adams hurried to the Kohlsaat residence on Lake Shore Drive to be with the boss while the racers were passing.

The cars were a long time in coming, but at last the waiting journalists heard a motor pounding in the distance. It was the Macy entry. This would have pleased R. H., who always liked to be out in front. The Macy had passed the Duryea while Frank was mending the faulty steering gear; but Kohlsaat and Adams did not know this and thought the Macy entry must be the better car.

Kohlsaat was vastly relieved to see the car. It was a life-saver to him, for it meant that after a year and a half of ridicule and sarcasm his motocycle racers were actually running the course, and he was giving Chicago and the rest of the world what he had promised—the first American race of motor vehicles.

One writer describes Kohlsaat as being jubilant; and another reports that he turned from the window and silently shook hands with Adams. This seems like quite a concession from the undemonstrative editor; but it was, after all, a big moment in the life of Chicago. His elation, however, was short-lived, for almost immediately he began to speculate on what might have happened to the other contestants. Where were they? Why had they not come along? Was the race actually in progress, or had it already broken down to a single surviving contestant?

The answer was finally furnished by the clumsy Sturges electric which came wallowing along through the snow like a weary hippopotamus. It was having battery trouble and soon after passing Kohlsaat's house it retired from the race. The Electrobat had already dropped out, and after another long wait the first of the Benz cars went slowly past, its belt clutch slipping and the engine bellowing with power that was not getting through to the wheels.

Last of all, thirty-five minutes after the Macy entry, came the Duryea. The engine was running sweetly, and though its steering mechanism was obviously giving trouble it was taking the heavy going far better than any of the others and appeared to be making up some of the lost time.

Roaring into Evanston well ahead of the rest, the Macy entry looked like a sure winner, but soon after it had refueled and checked out, it tangled with a streetcar and dropped out with a demolished front end, leaving only the Mueller Benz and the Duryea to fight it out between them. It was not, after all, very much of a fight, for in spite of all its misadventures the Duryea crossed the finish line in as good condition as when it started.

After the formality of checking in, the umpire, fed up with the vagaries and eccentricities of the motocycle, suggested taking over the team and driving slowly back to the livery stable under real *horse* power. His offer was accepted, and Charles, who had not yet learned how to drive, climbed in beside his brother and together they drove the motocycle back to Sixteenth Street, Frank remarking on the way that it was the only machine that was neither pulled nor pushed but had come all the way through under its own power.

And so it was that the Duryea won the first prize of $2,000 with an American entry, and Germany had to be content with second place and $1,500. The Macy entry received $500, and a like amount went to the Sturges, possibly for effort or perhaps just on general principles. The Electrobat received no money but was awarded a gold medal of a sturdily built lady in scanty draperies standing on a base marked VICTORY. Even the Haynes received $150, although it was not even present at the race.

The press coverage of the contest was nationwide, with edi-

torial comment that would have compared favorably in the
matter of space with an incident of international importance.
Quite naturally the chief basis of comparison was between the
motor vehicle and the horse. This line of contention had already
been well established and the commentators found plenty to
say on either side. The Chicago *Tribune,* leader among the scof-
fers, could see the race only as a demonstration that, for practical use, the horseless carriage was a flat failure and the race a
complete washout.

Of course the *Times-Herald* played up the contest as an
event of world-shaking importance. The paper could not have
spread itself any more had Chicago been the target of an invasion from Mars. Between these two extremes were the fence-
sitters who wanted to wait and see.

Since the race had been run in Chicago, instead of New York,
the metropolitan press felt called upon to be casual in its coverage. It was in fact so casual that it almost missed the boat. The
Herald was content to run a 4-inch story in a single column on
an inside page under the rather skimpy head:

MOTOCYCLES COMPETE

Duryea's Machine Covers the Fifty-four Mile Course
in 10 Hours and 23 Minutes over Bad Roads

It gave a much better location to a contest in Cleveland between Robert G. Ingersoll, the noted infidel, and a large group
of combined Methodists and Presbyterians who, at a huge mass
meeting, prayed fervently for his conversion. No money prizes
were involved, but Ingersoll won in a walk.

The account in the *Times* was even less impressive and somewhat more brief, whereas the story in the *Tribune* was carried
over to another day. The small town newspapers all over the
country were much more alive to the widespread interest in
the motorcar, and also made a more generous allowance for the
atrocious conditions caused by the storm which had almost entirely by-passed the Atlantic seaboard and laid all its disagree-
able emphasis on the Great Lakes region.

It was quite apparent that not one of the metropolitan papers so much as dreamed that in a short time all of them would be carrying thousands of lines of motorcar advertising as well as devoting entire pages and often whole sections to the interests of motorists and motoring.

Throughout the country all sorts and conditions of men were asking themselves and each other if the crackpots were so cracked after all. And if they could have remembered the names, they would soon have been hearing more of a number of unknowns who were present at the Chicago race in one capacity or another. There was Elwood Haynes who would have had his car in the race but for an accident. There was Charles B. King who had nearly finished the first motor vehicle ever to appear on the streets of Detroit and who had come over to see the race and to officiate as an umpire. And there is a little story about another Detroiter who did not come to the race but who is reputed to have said some twenty years later that he never wanted anything so badly in his life as to go to that race, but couldn't find anyone to lend him the carfare.

The words are ascribed to Henry Ford, but it seems almost certain that they are apocryphal. In his book *My Life and Work*, written in collaboration with Samuel Crowther, he says on page 34:

> Others in this country and abroad were building cars by that time, and in 1895 I heard that a Benz car from Germany was on exhibition in Macy's store in New York. I traveled down to look at it but it had no features that seemed worthwhile.

A little further down on the same page he says:

> During all this time I kept my position with the electric company and gradually advanced to chief engineer.

It seems logical to believe that if he could go all the way to New York to look at a car, he should have been able to go across to Chicago for something that he wanted very badly to do. Certainly with a job as chief engineer of the electric company he should have been good for a loan of fifteen or twenty dollars.

Another ambitious young inventor who was in Chicago the day of the race and was in all probability looking over all the assembled motor vehicles with care was a fellow named R. E. Olds who came from Lansing, Michigan. Nobody knew who he was that day, and as a matter of fact he wasn't much of anybody. Just another one of the young crackpots who tried to finish his car in time for the race and couldn't quite make it.

As Ford has said, others were building cars at the time, plenty of others, but America was still without a motorcar factory. Perhaps the Duryea Wagon Company came as near qualifying as any other firm, though it was a company in name only, with a small one-room shop, and was hard pressed for operating capital. Charles Duryea, in his article for *Horseless Age* written immediately after the Chicago race, says that he and his brother would have been glad to enter "one of our later wagons now nearly complete."

This was the first that had been heard of any later models of the Duryea, though only a glance at the car used in the race is necessary to show that this is not the original Duryea carriage tested on the dirt road in Springfield in 1893. The original machine was built on a phaeton body, with the engine and all the works dangling underneath the seat; whereas the racing car— old Number 5—is constructed on the lines of a side-bar buggy with a sturdy piano-box body in which the engine is neatly enclosed, and the dashboard is completely redesigned with lines like the visor of a cap.

"It was designed two years ago," Charles writes, "and built as an experimental job, in a cut and try manner. Changes and modifications have been made in it until it is a patched job throughout." This car is known as the 1895 Duryea. The old phaeton, known as the 1893 Duryea, is now in the Smithsonian Institution. The two have often been confused.

The gallant little racer was never again in competition after the Chicago race. It was shipped back to Springfield. Another Duryea was exhibited all around the country as the "identical horseless carriage that won the Chicago race"—a slight bit of exaggeration on the part of Barnum & Bailey. The motorized vehicle, then regarded as a freak, now furnishes the entire transportation for that same Greatest Show on Earth, with Ringling Brothers included.

The Duryeas went right on building cars, and on Memorial Day in 1896 the brothers had four entries in the starting line of a contest, this time a reliability run, sponsored by *Cosmopolitan* magazine. The nine contestants gathered at City Hall in New York and drove in single file up Broadway to Kingsbridge, where they took off for a run to Irvington-on-Hudson, and thence back to the Ardsley Country Club, a distance somewhat less than 20 miles.

Compared with the Chicago race, this was a thoroughly silk-stocking affair. Chauncey M. Depew, John Jacob Astor, and others of their ilk were in charge of arrangements, and after seeing the contestants off at Kingsbridge Mr. Depew placed the facilities of the New York Central at the disposal of the committee and whisked them up the river by special train. The special cut loose and made the run in fourteen minutes. But the contestants, though they were not supposed to be racing, began to arrive at the Country Club before the committee, seated on the veranda, had finished the first round of refreshments.

With Frank Duryea at the tiller, his entry won everything in sight, which was quite a victory when one considers the various aspects of the contest. Speed was rated at 35 per cent; simplicity of construction at 30 per cent; ease of operation at 25 per cent; and cost, which to the nabobs was of the least importance, at 10 per cent.

The Duryeas did not do so well in their next race, which was the first track contest for automobiles to be held in this country. They entered the same four cars in a meet held at Narragansett, Rhode Island, a few weeks after the *Cosmopolitan* contest. But the Duryea cars were balky that day, and the race was won by a Riker Electric Stanhope. Other cars were also balky, and the contest proved to be so dull and the breakdowns so numerous that the impatient spectators began to shout, "Get a horse!" This immediately caught on as a popular joke and developed into the derisive taunt which has been hurled at the stalled motorist ever since.

Of course the Duryea brothers were disappointed but not discouraged; for that same reason they sent Frank to England to compete in a 50-mile race from London to Brighton. Here Frank found himself facing the best of the European racers. He had no fear of the German machines since his victory over the Benz in the Chicago race of the year before, but he was apprehensive of the Panhard-Levassor which had easily won the Paris-Rouen and the Paris-Bordeaux races. He need have had no fear, however, for he won the contest easily at a speed of 12.5 miles per hour.

By this time the name of the Duryeas was so well established and their production so well assured that they started advertising in *Horseless Age,* which was quite the thing to do. They stress the fact that their machine is an all-weather vehicle for general use, and as for fuel economy they claim the car will go 100 miles on five gallons of gasoline. They have dropped the crude word "wagon," now substituting "finest specimens of the carriage maker's art," and add with elegance that their vehicle has none of the "carriage-without-a-horse" appearance.

At the time there was no better car made in America, and if the brothers could have worked together they would have been one of the greatest of the pioneer motorcar builders. But with the coming of prosperity old jealousies sprang up between them. Frank wanted full credit for all he had contributed, which was probably nine-tenths of the invention, six out of the seven Duryea patents being in his name. Charles, on the other hand, claimed the entire invention as his own.

The situation was complicated by the fact that both had gone too far along the road to success to yield to a possible compromise. Each considered himself too important and too well known in the trade to concede any of the claims being made by the other. There was glory enough for both if they could only have seen it that way. However, quarrels between relatives, especially brothers, are deeply felt. And so with opportunity pounding on the door the quarrel continued. Bitterness grew and finally reached the point where both would rather lose all than give in to the other. And with success smiling benignly upon them they blew up, dissolved their company, and went their separate ways.

Both continued in the motorcar field and tried to capitalize on the name. Frank organized the Stevens Duryea Company where he designed and built one of the fine cars of America under the name of Stevens Duryea.

Charles remained in Peoria where he turned back the pages and began the manufacture of a three-wheeler. The world did not want a three-wheeler and naturally the company failed. Once more Charles had to get away from it all, and he moved to Reading, Pennsylvania, started the Duryea Power Company, and made another attempt at the three-wheeler. When this blew up he moved to Saginaw and made still another attempt. With all the other builders making what looked like an automobile, he reverted to the days of the horse and built what he called a "Buggyaut" which he powered with electricity. That was his last attempt as a motorcar builder, but he lived on until 1938, bitter and lonely, and still trying to convince the world that he alone was the inventor of the first American horseless carriage.

Frank sold out his stock and retired from Stevens Duryea in 1915. There was nothing crabbed or bitter about him. In an interview in 1943 he remarked casually that the Duryea car was his invention, all except the steering tiller which his brother designed. He talked amiably about the past.

"My brother and I were just a couple of bicycle mechanics," he said, "like the Wright Brothers, who hit on something at a time when the world was ready for it."

He lighted one cigarette from another as he chatted on. "Our original car [note the word *our*] was planned to weigh 250 pounds and sell for $400."

Well, why not? The best buggy in the world could be bought in those days for less than $100, and a good horse would not cost a great deal more. And say a horse would eat a ton of hay in the winter months—that would be another $15, or give him two tons and call it $30. What could you buy today in the way of transportation for $230?

It would seem that the temperament of Charles Duryea was not entirely out of character with a man of ideas. Inventors have long been known as grouches and grumblers. Michelangelo (who invented the wheelbarrow) was a crabbed fellow noted for his irascibility. Morse and whole generations of telegraph operators after him have been grumpy, and Alexander Graham Bell was a difficult fellow to get along with. Elias Howe quarreled with everybody, and Thomas A. Edison, in spite of his genial appearance, could be petulant and touchy. Elwood Haynes was surly and controversial, and Henry Ford was noted as being sharp tongued and sarcastic. Alexander Winton tangled not only with Haynes and Ford, but with many of his early customers who were dissatisfied with his car.

Winton seemed to enjoy a good argument, and his battle with Haynes was for the credit of having been the first to sell an American-made car; the truth was that the honor, if such it was, belonged to neither. His quarrel with Ford was the result of his claim that the Winton car was the fastest thing on wheels, and Ford answered that in a characteristic manner.

4 *The Genius*

The question has many times been asked whether Henry Ford was a genius. That's almost like asking about the chicken and the egg. Henry was cranky enough to be a genius, but that takes more than merely being cranky. The greatest geniuses in history were born poor, and most of them did not qualify as geniuses until after they had been dead for a century or two. So we have some time to await the verdict of posterity in Henry's case.

Taken at a glance, Henry was a very ordinary fellow, born and reared in the rustic surroundings of an everyday Michigan farm. He had a country-school education, and at seventeen started out in life with a dinner pail in his hand like any country-bred boy apprenticed for a three-year stretch as a machinist in an engine factory. Henry's father didn't like to see him go; he wanted Henry to stay on the farm. But even then Henry was stubborn and set in his ways. So his father very sensibly gave in, and Henry worked out his apprenticeship and received his card. He was a good worker, though he liked to wander around the shop and see what other workers were doing. It was not that he was lazy, but he had unusual curiosity.

His taste ran to fine machinery, and while still an apprentice he spent his evenings repairing watches in a jewelry shop. In time he regarded himself as an expert watchmaker, and he got the idea that he could build a serviceable watch for thirty cents. If he could have done this nobody would have doubted that he was a genius. But after thinking it over with care, Henry gave up the idea on the ground that watches were not "universal necessities" and therefore people generally would not buy them.

29

This fortunately left an opening for the Waterbury Watch Company and later for Ingersoll.

Henry's first regular job after his apprenticeship was over was repairing steam traction engines, the clumsy old vehicles which used to rumble slowly along the dirt roads hauling a water tank, a load of coal, and a threshing separator behind. Quite naturally the idea of making a steam road carriage came to him and just for the fun of it he built one that would actually run. For two years he kept experimenting with various types of boilers, and although he found steam power flexible and efficient it required too much weight for a road carriage. He tried building them lighter, but this was dangerous, and not wishing to have his head blown off he abandoned the idea of using steam in place of a horse, and began to look for some other source of power.

Just by luck he was asked to repair an Otto gas engine, and so had an opportunity to see how it was made and how it worked. A little later he made one for himself to see if he "understood the principles." It had a 1-inch bore and a 3-inch stroke and developed about enough power to operate an egg beater or perhaps an airplane model.

Henry says he gave this away to a young man whose name he can't remember, and that the little motor was afterwards destroyed—anonymously, no doubt. And in the meantime Henry had given up his steam repair job and had returned to the farm. Not because he wanted to resume farming, but because he wished to continue work on a new motor he was building on the Otto principle.

Back on the land, however, Henry's experiments were not entirely in the mechanical field. He had found a new attraction in the neighborhood, a girl named Clara Bryant who was the daughter of a prosperous farmer living not too far away. Henry's father was delighted. He thought that if he could get the young fellow married to a local girl he might after all make a gentleman and a farmer out of him. So he offered the enamored swain 40 acres of timberland if he would promise to give up being a machinist.

In his anxiety to get married, Henry accepted the offer in

what he describes as a provisional way. This means that he took the 40 acres, married the girl, and then went right on with his experimental work with the Otto-type engine. He set up a portable sawmill, stripped the 40 acres of timber, built himself a snug cottage, and when a little later he was offered a job with the Detroit Electric Company, he took it. The job as engineer and machinist paid him $45 a month, and since this was more money than he was making on the farm he could see no reason why he shouldn't accept it. What Henry's father thought of the new arrangement does not appear; but perhaps he himself was enough of a Yankee to understand this kind of reasoning.

Henry and his wife rented a house in Detroit where he set up a workshop in the back yard. Here, during his spare time, he continued his work on the motor which at first he had intended to mount on a bicycle. It eventually became apparent, however, that the cylinder block, clutch, tank, and various other parts would be too heavy for a bicycle, so he changed his plan, added two more wheels, and made it into a "quadricycle."

"This first car," Henry wrote some years later, "had something of the appearance of a buggy." The picture does not bear out this description. It looks much more like a four-wheeled bicycle built for two—not tandem, but sitting side by side. It was mounted on 28-inch tires, steered by tiller, and had a gasoline capacity of three gallons.

Just when this machine was finished and running has long been a matter of doubt. In *My Life and Work* Ford says it was in 1892. His figures are not only confusing, they are impossible. I do not mean to insinuate that Henry Ford would prevaricate, but I do believe that he was not above a little dissembling, rather than let his publicity department down. With all the firsts that he had to his credit, his press agents could not bear to have others holding the honor of having built the first American gasoline car. For years there had been a mad scramble for this honor, with obscure inventors, long-haired cranks, and bespectacled crackpots all claiming to have built secret cars years before and presenting vague and varied credentials to prove their priority, all of which were quite obviously spurious.

So long as the Duryea brothers remained in the picture, the claimants kept in the background, but as the brothers began to quarrel between themselves and dragged their internecine strife into the open, filling the newspapers with charges and counter-charges, and issuing affidavits and printed pamphlets accusing each other of fraudulent statements, misrepresentation, and even falsehood—claimants began swarming up out of the grass like mosquitoes.

This question of priority was again taken up in 1949 by the *Chronicle* of the Automobile Manufacturers Association which, after considering all available information, awarded definite priority to the Duryeas in the year 1893. The Haynes is placed in 1894. Charles Brady King comes third, in March, 1896. King says it was a year earlier, but no matter.

"Henry Ford," the *Chronicle* states, "successfully operated his first motor vehicle in Detroit on June 4, 1896. It had a two-cylinder engine developing four horsepower." These findings are substantially in agreement with those of the Smithsonian Institution where the original Duryea and Haynes cars may now be seen. Ford's earliest car is in the Ford Museum.

Ford and King were close friends. They loaned each other tools and exchanged parts, and Ford may easily have been present at the midnight ride of Charles King when he proved that his car would run. Ford may even have been an occupant of the car. Curiously enough, Ford's initial test was also made in the darkness of the night. He cranked up for a trial spin at two o'clock in the morning while his wife stood watching, huddled under an umbrella, for it was raining. The car would run, but he had to go around the block to get it home, since it had no reverse to assist in turning it around in the narrow streets of the neighborhood. His only light was a kerosene lantern hung on the dash. I have always wondered why he was not arrested for disturbing the peace at that time in the morning, for without a muffler those old-time engines used to make as much noise as a machine gun.

Of his early use of the car by daylight, Ford writes in his autobiography: "It was considered to be something of a nuisance, for it made a racket and it scared horses. Also it blocked traffic. For if I stopped my machine anywhere in town a crowd was around it before I could start it up again. If I left it alone even for a minute some inquisitive person always tried to run it. Finally I had to chain it to a lamp post whenever I left it anywhere."

But inquisitive persons were not the only ones he had to reckon with. He was bellowed at by draymen and cursed by teamsters and others with scary horses. His machine, like all the old-time cars, had a way of breaking down in the worst possible places and he was soon in trouble with the police, probably for obstructing traffic. There were, of course, no speed laws in those days, no one-way streets, no parking limits, and Henry is at a loss to explain just why the police bothered him. "Anyway," he writes, "I had to get a special permit from the mayor and thus for a time enjoyed the distinction of being the only licensed chauffeur in America."

Here, no doubt, is another *first* to be hung on the wall of the Ford Museum. And still another *first* was the sale of the gasoline buggy in 1896 to Charles Ainsley of Detroit for $200. The car was not built to sell; it was intended only as an experiment. But Ainsley wanted to buy, and Henry needed the money to start another experiment.

The second experimental car was much like the first but was lighter. He still clung to the belt drive, perhaps on the theory that what was good enough for Benz was good enough for Ford. "Belts were all right," Henry explains defensively, "except in hot weather." Curious reasoning, this, when cars of that period were driven only in summer.

Henry's decision to retain the belt drive was typical of him. And after the statement about the hot weather he added, "That's why I later adopted gears." So he did, but it was years later.

All his life Henry Ford was stubborn about making changes in his design. The Ford was the last car in the country to abandon the planetary transmission, and his cars were still using mechanical brakes long after the safety and superiority of the hydraulic brake had been thoroughly demonstrated and universally adopted. He clung to the Model T until it was completely outmoded in everything but price; and he refused to modernize his Model A until after Chevrolet had outbuilt and outsold him and had crowded him from the pinnacle of leadership, a position that he was never able to regain.

Another *first* was stacked up when Henry bought back the car from Mr. Ainsley—the first used-car sale. And he made money on the deal, for he paid Ainsley only $100 for it.

As Henry peers back into the past, it seems to him that he was even then "looking ahead to production," but of course he had to have something to produce and all his spare time went into the building of a second and a third car. He was still with the Detroit Electric Company, the president of which had little sympathy with his experiments with the gasoline engine. It was not that he objected to the car—only to the motive power.

"Electricity, yes, that's the coming thing," said the president. "But gas—no." And that was that.

But as usual, Henry was stubborn. He had carefully considered electricity as the motive power of a car and had discarded it completely, not only because of its limited radius but because of its inefficient proportion of weight to power. He predicted that the electric car would never be a success. Time has demonstrated that it was a good guess, but it did not satisfy the owners of the Electric Company, and they intimated to Henry that he must make a choice between his job and his gasoline automobile.

There is a fable that when Henry met Thomas A. Edison at one of the meetings of the Electric Company and was telling Edison of his experiments with the automobile, Mr. Edison patted Henry on the back and encouraged him by saying, "The horse is doomed."

Henry makes no mention of this incident. "I had to choose between my job and my automobile," he says. "I chose the automobile."

He quit his job on August 15, 1899, to go into the automobile business. Since he had no "personal funds" he thought it might be "something of a step"—and it was.

There was at this time no considerable demand for automobiles. They were still regarded as being in the class with the bicycle, a plaything on a more expensive scale. Only the crackpots—and the farsighted economists—believed that the motorcar would ever be a commercial success. The bicycle, it seemed, had run its course. It was supposed to have passed the saturation point and was already on the slide. But Henry had gone into this gasoline-buggy thing, and he was determined to see it through.

Times were not too good. Crop prices were low and money was not only tight, but scarce. Just why Henry should have been so optimistic over his future is hard to understand. He had a car, and it seemed to him that all he needed to start in the automobile business was money, a medium of exchange that he knew very little about. It happened, however, that in Detroit at just this time there was a group of men of speculative turn of mind. These men had money to invest in the automobile business and were looking for a man with a car and sufficient know-how to organize and operate a factory.

This looked like a natural for Henry. He joined them in forming the Detroit Automobile Company; but they outmaneuvered him from the first. They gave him the title of Chief Engineer, but only a few shares of stock and no authority whatever. All they wanted was to make money, while Henry wanted to make a good car. Henry kept on trying until March, 1902. Then he resigned and was succeeded by Henry M. Leland. The company was reorganized as the Cadillac Motor Car Company.

Henry rented a little one-story brick shed and resumed his experimenting. By this time he had made in all about twenty-five cars, most of them for the defunct Detroit Automobile Company. But during his period with this company, times had been changing rapidly. The public had come to understand that the automobile would really go, and now they were becoming very curious to know how fast it would go. Henry Ford was not a sporting man. He had never taken any interest in races and probably had never seen one, but experience had convinced him that speed was now the popular measure of success for a motor-

car. He felt that the industry was being impeded by this craze
for speed, but he was certain that if he could build a car fast
enough to defeat all comers the world would beat a pathway to
his door.

He accordingly associated himself with Tom Cooper, a retired bicycle racer of some means, and C. Harold Wills, a slide-
rule engineer and able designer, and set about building what
he hoped would be the fastest car in the world. Other motorcar
builders were trying in the same way to attract capital; Alexander Winton of Cleveland had become a daredevil racer who
went about the country challenging anybody and everybody who
thought he had a fast car to meet him on the track.

Ford's first racer was a light two-cylinder car, and in his first
contest with Winton the Ford car won easily, leaving Winton
half a mile behind, his car shattered and smoking from the excessive speed. This should have settled the issue, for it gave
Ford wide publicity and enhanced his standing as an automotive
engineer. But when he learned that Winton was building a new
racer for a return engagement, Ford and his two associates
dropped everything else and began the construction of two of
the greatest racing chariots the world had ever seen. It was indeed the most famous and the most publicized pair of racers of
the period.

One was called "999" after the noted locomotive of the Empire State Express, and the other, built as a stand-in to be ready
in case of accident, was called the "Arrow." It was, of course,
the "999" which received most of the publicity. These two cars
were built with four gigantic cylinders and were rated at 80
horsepower in a day when the average car rarely went above 10
horsepower and never beyond 12.

When Ford tried out the cars he reported that the roar of
the cylinders was "enough to half kill a man." He added with
his usual hyperbole that going over Niagara Falls would have
been but a pastime after a ride in one of them. There was only
one trouble with these demons of the race track—neither Ford
nor his cobuilders dared to let one of them out to anywhere near
its capacity. But Cooper, an old hand at the racing game, knew

The "smoke eaters" of the day line up for a 100-mile "inaugural" race at the Indianapolis Speedway in 1909. Later the track was bricked over and the famed 500-mile Memorial Day race, under AAA supervision, was begun in 1911. It attracts many thousands of spectators each year.

Hill-climbing was a popular motor sport early in the century, serving often as a form of reliability testing of the then-new vehicles. Here a 50-horsepower Simplex sets a winning pace in a colorful race run on Sport Hill, near Bridgeport, Connecticut, in the spring of 1909.

A.C. Buffalo

First AAA long-distance tour was back in 1904, when these club members made a run from New York to St. Louis for the Louisiana Purchase Exposition. This trip was the direct predecessor of the famed Glidden Tours of 1905 to 1913.

Col. Charles J. Glidden, wealthy New England industrialist and donor of the bitterly contested Glidden Trophy, with friends and relatives in a British Napier. The trophy which he donated was once motordom's most prized award, competed for by owners and manufacturers alike.

Mud, mud, and more mud! How the Glidden Tour Pathfinders got out of
this mess is not on record. More than once, though, it proved all part of a
day's work to these men. It was their job to map out the route of the tour,
often along uncharted and near-impassable roadways.

Confetti-strewing along the route was a vital precaution during those
early Glidden Tours. Running well in advance of the Glidden Tourists,
members of the pilot parties marked the roads and turns of the route with
reams of shredded paper, to guide those following in their path.

It was oxen to the rescue here. Even the hardy Glidden Tour Pathfinders
had to resort to old-fashioned methods when their cars became stalled in
the mud of early roads. Shown above is Dai H. Lewis, man at right in
poncho, pioneer AAA Pathfinder, attempting to pay the farmer.

Typical of roads over which early motoring enthusiasts had to travel, the
stretch above was encountered during the first Glidden Tour in 1905. In
those days—before AAA Emergency Road Service—motorists had to
pitch in and dig each other out of the muddy traps encountered.

a man who wasn't afraid of anything in the way of speed. He was a champion bicycle racer and his name was Barney Oldfield.

In response to a telegram, Barney came on from Salt Lake City. Like almost everyone else, he had never driven a motorcar, but he was willing to learn. In a week's time he could drive better than any of them and was ready to take the monster over the course. The machine steered with a two-handed tiller and was especially difficult to handle on the turns. Barney would have liked a week or two of practice, but, because of the secrecy with which such things were handled at the time, he was allowed only a few practice runs at hours when no spies or railbirds were hanging around the course. And when the race was started neither the driver nor the owner had any idea how fast the car could really go.

As Ford was cranking the engine for the start of the race, Barney, with a stump of cold cigar clamped in his teeth, is said to have remarked grimly, "This chariot may kill me, but they will say afterward that I was going like hell when she took me over the bank."

Later in life this would have made quite a picture—Henry Ford cranking a car for Barney Oldfield. The drivers of Ford cars would have liked it.

The circular track at Grosse Pointe where the speed contest was held had been built for horse races and was surfaced with soft dirt far more suitable for horses' hoofs than the tires of fast-moving cars. There was no scientific banking such as we have today, and the driver of a powerful car was taking his life in his hands at every turn, especially with the tiller control. Being a 3-mile race, there was little time for jockeying.

Barney had figured that the winner must start with a rush, get out in front, and stay there no matter what happened. He had been warned to look out for the Winton "Bullet," also a specially built racer, so he kept an eye on it from the start. But the "Bullet" was no match for him and he quickly took the lead. The "999" was never headed, and Barney won by half a mile, leaving the "Bullet" and an assorted field eating his dust, of which there was a great plenty.

The big Ford racer had done what it was intended to do. It had advertised the fact that the Ford was the fastest motorcar then built. And it had also started the career of Barney Oldfield as a race driver. I saw him in a road race in California a few years later. He still drove with the stump of a cigar in his teeth, and as the breathless crowd stood watching him thunder past he scared up a jack rabbit, pursued it along the course, and overtook it as if it had been standing still—which it soon was.

Ford was jubilant over the result of the race which had not only put his car at the head of the speed kings, but had silenced the vociferous claims of the Winton rivalry. "A week after the race," Henry writes in his autobiography, "I formed the Ford Motor Company."

This is big talk. Ford did nothing about initiating the Ford Motor Company. It came to him on a silver platter. Nor was it a week—it was nearer a month after the race when he was approached by Alex Y. Malcomson, a prosperous Detroit coal-dealer, with a proposition to go into business together. Malcomson had been watching the automobile situation for some time, and he had been watching Ford. This looked like the right time to come into the field, and Ford looked like the right man. Malcomson would attend to the finances and hold the purse strings, and Ford would produce the cars. As vice-president and general manager Ford was to start with a salary of $3,000 a year.

The company organized with a capital stock of $100,000, of which each of the cofounders held 25½ per cent of the shares. Others came in, getting stock for loans or services. Albert Strelow, a carpenter, was given a small block of stock for a frame building in which to open the factory. The next outside investor to be taken in was John S. Gray, a Detroit banker and a friend of Malcomson's, who for a loan of $10,000 received a 10 per cent block of stock and was put on the board of directors.

Since Malcomson was unable to spend much time at the company office, he arranged to send in one of his own employees, a smart young fellow named James Couzens, to take over his part of the work as secretary and business manager. Couzens was placed on a salary and was given 2½ per cent of the company's stock. There were lawyers and others who were cut in on a small percentage of stock, and the company began business with a cash capital of $28,000.

It was Malcomson who, following in the footsteps of Olds, arranged to have Dodge Brothers as the principal suppliers for the new Ford cars, allotting to each brother 5 per cent of the capital stock and electing John Dodge to the board of directors. Dodge Brothers was to build the motors and other essential parts in its own shops, thus conserving floor space for the newly formed company. This turned out to be a very profitable arrangement for all concerned.

Malcomson had really been keeping tabs on the Olds Motor Works which was already established and doing a good business. Ransom E. Olds had finally finished the gasoline car that he failed to get ready for the Chicago race, and had built a second one. Not having much success in raising sufficient capital for a factory in Lansing, he had been looking around a bit. In Detroit he met a retired copper man with plenty of money and two unemployed sons. The sons had caught the automobile craze, and with this fact in mind Olds began to feel out the old gentleman as a prospect for some financial backing. He must have been a persuasive talker, for the father finally agreed to set him up in business if he would furnish jobs for the two boys.

That was how the Olds Motor Works got its start. The first car, however, proved to be too expensive for the market and finished the year with a considerable loss. But Olds had learned his lesson, and for the second year he designed a little curved dash runabout to sell for $650. But before they could get it on the market, the factory burned down. This happened in March, 1901, and left the company with everything destroyed except a single curved dash runabout which, during the excitement of the fire, somebody had the good sense to push outdoors.

They had money enough to start over again, but they had no drawings, no designs—nothing to start with but the one salvaged little roadster. So with commendable foresight they got back of the little car and put into it all the energy they could muster. They not only had it ready for the Madison Square Garden

Automobile Show in November, but as a publicity stunt they had Roy Chapin drive one of the little cars from Detroit to New York in time for the Show. At the present time this seems like a silly thing to do, but it was then supposed to prove something and the success of the trip made quite a stir. The car was capable, it was attractive, it was cute, and it was cheap. It caught on in a big way.

But the mud-covered driver, when he came jouncing through 34th Street and pulled up in front of the old Waldorf-Astoria, was shooed away by the doorman and had to sneak in the tradesman's entrance and go up in a service elevator to reach the room where Olds was pacing the floor as he waited for news of the whereabouts of the little curved dash runabout.

It had not been supposed that the little car would have any appeal for the city trade. It was too small, too insignificant, too cheap to attract any attention from a market accustomed to seeing nothing but impressive foreign-made jobs. But curiously enough it took the town by storm, and for the first time in history one individual dealer signed an order for a thousand cars. And Olds was back in business again.

At the factory everything was forgotten but the little curved dash runabout, and by the end of the year, with Dodge Brothers making practically everything but the name plate, cars were coming out of the shop at the rate of fifteen a day, and Ransom Olds had become the first mass producer of motorcars in the world.

There was, however, no low-price market for his product. At this time only people of large means were regarded as the market for cars. If Ransom Olds had been as shrewd and as far-seeing as Henry Ford he might have developed a market among the artisans and people of small means which could have made him, instead of Henry, a billionaire. But Olds, like every other dealer, thought the big money was to be made out of the higher-priced cars, and thus he missed the boat.

Ford, on the other hand, had not yet gone into production, but with Malcomson at his back, and young Couzens at his elbow he was on his way. He, too, had learned his lesson, and with Dodge making most of the parts—which were now being delivered to the Ford Plant in hay wagons—Ford could devote almost his entire attention to assembling, and it was here that the man's genius started to show through. His first big step toward preeminence was taken when he began bringing the work to the men—instead of the men to the work.

For years Henry Ford insisted that he borrowed the idea from the Chicago packers' overhead trolley used in dressing a beef carcass, but it should not be forgotten that he followed the Olds method of assembly for years before he thought of putting in the moving assembly line on which he rode to fame and fortune.

The first Ford built by the new company was called the Model A, but this is not to be confused with another Model A which appeared after the retirement of the famous Model T. This first Model A had a two-cylinder motor and sold for $850 without the detachable tonneau for which an additional charge of $100 was made. It was an immediate success and brought buyers and salesmen flocking to the factory doors. By working at top speed, the production ran over one thousand seven hundred and brought in a gross business of nearly a million and a half dollars the first year.

Ford, too, misjudged the market. He almost made the same mistake Olds had made. The man of small means was looking up to him; but Ford did not realize what was going on and he began thinking of putting out a higher-priced car.

But by this time other cars were coming into the market, and the demand was so great that it was said any car with four wheels under it could find a ready buyer. The Duryea had now reached the production stage. The Winton, though faulty, was getting its share of the business, along with many complaints. It was after buying a bad Winton that J. W. Packard said he could build a better car—and he certainly did. The unbelievable Stanley twins had brought out their first steamer and had driven it to the top of Mount Washington to test its ability. All kinds of cars were breaking out like the measles in unexpected places.

At the turn of the century almost any town of importance could boast of its automobile factory, or at least of an inventive genius who was in a receptive mood for capital with which to launch a factory for building a car he had almost completed, or had started, or possibly had thought of. During the first five months of 1899, according to *McClure's Magazine*, "companies with the enormous aggregate capitalization of more than $388,-000,000" were organized for the sole purpose of manufacturing and operating these new vehicles.

Just where all this money went is anybody's guess, but in any case, cars were scooting here and there on the city streets, scaring horses, maiming dogs which came rushing out to bark at them, startling pedestrians with their horns and blocking traffic by breaking down in the most inexpedient places. They also had a knack of getting in the way of bicycles which heretofore had enjoyed plain sailing.

Outside the cities the more adventurous motorists were crawling along the atrocious roads in a cloud of dust or a sea of mud, striving to reach the next town and shatter some record of endurance rather than speed. They were enraging the country population with their smell, their inability or unwillingness to share the right of way with horse-drawn traffic, and their heedless slaughter of small animals which happened to stray onto the public highways where they had every right to be.

All Americans, and especially those living close to the soil, have a well-developed notion that this is a free country. They don't mean to be unreasonable about it, and they will take quite an amount of pushing around. But the fact is that they can be pushed just so far and no farther. For a while they put up with what they considered the intrusion of the man behind the goggles and the woman in the veil. They kept hoping that conditions would become better; but instead they became worse. And that was when the rural population decided that something had to be done.

5 Get A Horse!

The national reaction to the appearance of the horseless carriage on the streets of America was amusement and good-natured raillery. It was greeted somewhat as a man hails an acquaintance wearing a new or a different hat, or an unusual style of shoes. The general tendency on the part of almost everybody was to poke fun at it. Especially if it happened to be a home-made job that was balky or unusually noisy.

Not until the discovery that it was to be largely a plaything of the well to do did the raillery turn to derision. Then gradually the derision became distrust and scoffing. There was a general impression that the darn thing was no good and never would be. But when it began to run well enough to become somewhat of a nuisance, the public was disappointed and the people who were depending on the horse for their transportation were downright displeased.

The city dweller—especially if he thought he would never be able to have a horseless carriage himself—confined his displeasure to grumbling and growling, and to tapping with his finger on that part of the newspaper which reported that another pedestrian had been maimed or slaughtered. But in the country districts where there was nobody to hear the grumbling and the newspaper came only once a week, the hostility took a more tangible form and resorted to reprisal.

Word went around that tacks and glass scattered in the road would keep the motorists away. There can be no doubt that the motorists were annoyed and at times very angry over this treatment—but they still kept coming. Tales are told of farmers burying old rakes in the highways, teeth upward and concealed

43

under a layer of dust. And on the route of one of the early Glidden Tours an embattled farmer buried the blade of a crosscut
saw at a narrow place in the road in such a way that every motorcar running over it suddenly found all four tires punctured and
simultaneously deflated.

Some four cars had passed over this ruinous device before
the cause of the trouble was discovered and the saw removed
and carried away. A sentry was posted at the place to prevent a
recurrence of the vandalism until the rest of the Gliddenites had
passed; but the perpetrator was never apprehended.

It was a common practice to bury empty bottles under the
dust in the road, especially on Sundays, and short strips of barbed
wire were very popular with mischievous urchins as well as very
hard to spy from the seat of a horseless carriage driven in a
cloud of dust. And if, at about dusk, the little fellows stretched
a line of barbed wire all the way across the road, anchoring it
securely from tree to tree, they were usually let off with an ad-
monition, a bit of parental clucking, and the observation that
"boys will be boys."

But this campaign of vandalism, though exceedingly pro-
voking to the motorist, was not effective in keeping the horseless
carriages off the roads. They kept right on coming. Perhaps not
the same ones on the same road; but more horseless carriages
were being built and sold, and they were running better and
faster and farther. And as the army of motorists multiplied, the
irritability of the nonmotoring public increased until the authorities began to take notice. Then came the beginning of restrictive
legislation.

Quite logically the earliest regulations were aimed at slow-
ing down the speed. And in a spirit of what they insisted was
fairness, the country communities sought to bring the speed of
the motorcar down to that of the horse. This meant a speed of
5 miles an hour in built-up sections and 10 miles an hour on
the open road.

Strange as it may seem, 10 miles an hour was at this time regarded by many motorists as a fair rate of speed on an average
country road. My old two-cylinder, canopy-top Rambler couldn't

make more than 15 miles an hour on a level highway, and hardly any of the electrics had a top speed of more than 10. But as the horsepower was increased, the motorcars went faster and soon developed a lucrative rural occupation known as the speed trap. In one form or another this occupation has been continued until the present time.

Most of this early restrictive legislation was the product of the cities, towns, and villages. It was not until 1901 that the states began to take a hand in motor vehicle legislation, with New York and Connecticut leading off. New York went about it in a backhanded way with an amendment to the Highway Law. In addition to a speed regulation of from 8 to 15 miles an hour, this amendment contained a requirement that a motorist on approaching a restive horse must, if the driver raised his hand, pull to the side of the road and stop the motor vehicle. At a further signal the motorist was required to shut off his engine and wait until the refractory animal had been led or otherwise encouraged to pass.

Often the horse preferred to do this on his hind feet, prancing and snorting as he went along. The driver of the horse was also given to snorting, and he loved to take his time. Then when the horse and his driver were out of danger, the motorist had the pleasure of getting out and cranking his car by hand. And very often at this point it was the motor that was balky.

Soon after this amendment went into effect the driver of a splendid equipage on a country road in upstate New York encountered a motorist and raised his hand. The motorist drew over to the side of the road and brought his machine to a stop, but the spirited team was still restive and the driver motioned with his hand for the motorist to stop his engine. When the motorist refused, the driver of the team handed the reins to his wife and clambered ponderously to the ground. He did not threaten to have the law on the motorist. Instead, he picked up in each hand a stone about the size of his fist and stepped over to the side of the motorcar.

"Do you intend to shut off that motor?" he demanded. "Or must I knock your brains out with one of these stones?"

The motorist complied, and the horseman managed to drive his horses past. On reaching the next town, which happened to be the county seat of Wayne County, the motorist went to a justice of the peace to swear out a warrant for the arrest of his would-be assailant. But when he had given a description of the man and the fashionable equipage, he was told that if he went on with his case he would be tangling with a judge of the state Supreme Court.

The motorist decided not to press his case, but the cat was out of the bag, the judge's political enemies spread the news, and a full-page picture of the episode appeared in the *Police Gazette*, to the delight of the patrons of barbershops all over the land.

Members of the state legislature, having officially discovered the motor vehicle, were not long in working out a method of imposing a tax on it by requiring registration. Motorists did not particularly object to being registered. It gave them a feeling of importance, and many of them smiled as they read the printed instructions (which had come with the applications for registration):

"Every owner of an automobile or motor vehicle shall file in the office of the Secretary of State a statement of his name and address, with a brief description of the character of such vehicle and shall pay a registration fee of $1.00. Every such automobile or motor vehicle shall have the separate initials of the owner's name placed on the back thereof in a conspicuous place. The letters of such initials shall be at least three inches in height."

Registration in New York State for the year 1901 was 954 motor vehicles, or one for each 8,000 of population. The following year saw an increase of 128. However, the initials proved to be an unsatisfactory form of identification, since there were numerous duplications and the printed letters were not always easy to read. The suggestion was made that the motor vehicles should be named as in the registrations of vessels so that duplication might be avoided. But this method failed of acceptance and the state began registering the vehicles according to number. For each car registered, the state issued a numbered metal disc. The disc could be carried in the pocket of the motorist, but he was required at his own expense to display the figures in Arabic numerals on the back of the vehicle where they would be plain and visible.

This brought out some fancy numerals of every color of the rainbow, and quite a few numbers from people who had not bothered to get a disc. Artistically inclined motorists painted their numbers on the body of the car, surrounded by landscapes, sunsets, or other ornamental designs. There were complaints about this, and the following year the state began to furnish the number plates and raised the registration fee to $2.

At the same time the legislature wiped from the statute books the American version of the British Red Flag Law. This had been passed in 1890 for the purpose of regulating the operation of the slow-moving steam traction engines. But instead of a red flag, our version required that a "mature person" should be sent at least one-eighth of a mile ahead to warn the drivers of horse-drawn vehicles of the approach of the machine which moved from one farm to another drawing a train of threshing apparatus. Operators of steam-driven motorcars had paid little attention to the law, although hostile magistrates had held that the law applied to any vehicle driven by steam.

The city motorist was also beset by numerous woes. From the very beginning the urban population had seemed to be unable to keep out from under the wheels of the car. Being accustomed to the slower moving speed of horse-drawn traffic, the city folk had conditioned themselves by long practice to estimate a reasonably safe margin in crossing the streets. These estimates, it turned out, were of little value in gauging the speed of an approaching motorcar. There were no traffic lights to guide the pedestrian, no clatter of hoofs to warn him, no horse's head high in the air that could be seen some distance away. Even if he could see the car coming, he thought he could make it—and all too often the mangled pedestrian would wake up in a hospital, or perhaps he would not wake up at all.

With the small number of cars on the streets it seems strange that pedestrian casualties should have been numerous enough to arouse public sentiment to such a hostile pitch that well-meaning little one-lungers, incapable of a top speed of more than 20 miles an hour, were vilified in the papers and berated from the pulpits as "devil wagons."

The city motorist, as soon as he reached home with his new car, was faced with a storage problem—where could he keep his horseless vehicle? With livery stables in almost every block, there had been no difficulty about stabling a horse. But the liveryman had quickly recognized the power-driven vehicle as the enemy of the horse and had organized against it. The motorist applying for space in a livery stable was about as likely to get it as an inebriate asking for a drink at the W.C.T.U.

The city fathers determined long before the state had thought of such a thing to keep the motorist and his devil wagon in hand. In no two towns were the regulations alike, and a bewildered motorist away from home had no way of knowing whether he was breaking the law or not.

One of the most famous restrictions of the period was originated in Urbana, Ohio, where an ordinance limited speed to 4 miles an hour and required a bell or gong to be sounded within 50 feet of a crossing and to be kept sounding until after the crossing had been passed. Perhaps Bedlam would have been a better name for the pretty little town if this ordinance had ever been enforced.

In every locality the lawmakers seemed to be outdoing themselves. On the prairies of South Dakota, which must have been a stronghold of the horse, the question of speed was quite definitely settled for the motorcar; the city of Mitchell passed an ordinance forbidding any motor vehicle to enter the city limits. This kind of legislation in a city of 10,000 supporting two newspapers and a large university will give some idea of the hostility toward the motorcar at the turn of the century.

Missouri was hostile but not averse to making a little money out of the motorcar. Registration was required in each county, with a registration fee of $2. It was worth more to drive in St. Louis where the registration fee was $10. Crossing the state from east to west would cost the motorist about $30 in registration fees. From north to south the cost would run up over $50. Most of the tourists thought it wasn't worth the price and went around. At the time there was nothing to cope with such a situation as that. What could an individual motorist do? He was up against one of the toughest organizations in the world.

In the early days the registration plate of one state was not recognized in another except for the purpose of identifying the visitor and dragging him to the registry office so that he could be gypped for a local registration plate. Michigan, the exception, welcomed all comers, and her generosity paid off in the end. New York was early in accepting the registration plates of another state, but insisted that turnabout was fair play, although never rigid about the enforcement. There were occasional spats with New Jersey and Connecticut when New York would get the feeling that her generosity was being abused.

Another first for New York State was the use of bicycle cops to make the motorists behave. Without some form of proof it was almost impossible to convict an alleged speeder for exceeding the limit. The bicycle ran so quietly that the motorist seldom knew he was being pursued until he was in the hands of the law. The force started with only two mounted officers, but when these two began to bring the speeders in, the force was enlarged. And a very famous case went down in the books where three officers were required to make the arrest of a motorist speeding through a restricted area.

Policeman Stover spied the offender at 57th Street, leaped on his bicycle, and started in pursuit. But the motorist was too fast for him, and after chasing him as far as 72d Street the cop became winded and motioned to another officer to take up the chase. Officer Van Keuren thereupon took over and pursued the villain to 92d Street where he gave up the chase, and officer Vanderpoel went after the fugitive and captured his man at 96th Street when the motorist was delayed by a traffic jam. The fine was five dollars.

Among the curiosities in restrictive legislation at this time was an ordinance limiting street parking in a small California town to fifteen minutes, not because of a shortage of parking

space, but because the dripping of gasoline from the cars was
supposed to be damaging to the asphalt pavement. Another bit of
hostile legislation was a Federal law, probably sponsored by insurance interests, forbidding the carrying of gasoline on a ferry-
boat. Draining out the gasoline on the dock and pushing the car
up the gangplank was an unmitigated nuisance which was finally
ended by a bitterly contested bill forced through Congress by
Senator Tom Platt of Amen Corner fame.

The necessity for banding together for mutual protection and
various other purposes had long been felt by motorists. An organization called the American Motor League had been formed
in Chicago in 1895 by the motorists attracted there for the big
race. But it was premature, the nucleus too small, the members
too widely scattered, and it failed.

But the idea was sound, and the need for organization was
great and growing; and in June, 1899, George F. Chamberlain
and Whitney Lyon, two enthusiastic and farseeing motorists,
caused to be published in the New York papers an invitation to
automobile owners interested in forming a club to attend a meeting at the Waldorf-Astoria for a conference on the subject.

Some thirty-odd motorists appeared in response to the invitation, which must have been a fairly high proportion of the car
owners in the city, though many automobile factories were now
coming into production and the number of owners was rapidly
increasing. Mr. Lyon, an influential banker, opened the meeting
with some humorous remarks about the need for forming a club
so that members could band together and furnish a suitable depot
or repository in which to store their horseless carriages. He also
touched upon the fact that some concerted action was necessary
to secure for members the right to drive their cars in Central
Park from which they had been excluded by ukase of the Com-
missioner. At his suggestion, Mr. Chamberlain was made temporary chairman. And in the manner of a temporary chairman who
never expects to be called upon, he produced and read a prepared
statement of the objects of the proposed organization, which in
brief form were as follows:

1. To provide a center for the benefit of members.
2. A depot for storage and care of motor carriages.
3. A means of exchanging motor experiences.
4. Hospitality to visiting motorists.
5. Organization and sponsorship of races and other sporting events.
6. Establishment of a library on motor vehicles.
7. To provide a starting point for runs and tours.
8. To promote improvement of roads.
9. To exchange courtesies with other clubs here and abroad.
10. Preparation and reading of papers on motoring interests.
11. To promote friendly relations with horse owners and public.
12. To provide a suitable clubhouse centrally located.

The meeting was most enthusiastic and cooperative. Committees were appointed, the name Automobile Club of America adopted, and the necessary steps taken which led to incorporation. General Avery D. Andrews was elected as the first president, and by fall applications for membership were pouring in.

Without waiting for a charter, however, the club took up the cudgels in the fight to do away with the exclusion of motor vehicles from Central Park. Whitney Lyon and W. E. Busby, two prominent club members, drove Busby's motor carriage to the park entrance and, on being stopped at the gate, demanded admission. Busby, after some altercation, was placed under arrest and, accompanied by Mr. Lyon and his attorney, was taken to the headquarters of the park police and from there to the magistrate's court in Yorkville. Challenged by an organization composed of wealthy and important people wielding tremendous influence in the city, the park authorities quickly backed down—and soon pleasure cars of all kinds were seen rolling along the winding drives of the park.

Nor was this matter of attempted park exclusion a local tempest in a teapot. The same regulation was attempted in Boston, Baltimore, Philadelphia, St. Louis, Chicago, and other cities, including San Francisco, which had always prided itself on being the most liberal of cities. In every case the motorists resisted with almost fanatical zeal and were uniformly successful.

Only a few weeks after the New York club was chartered it put on the first automobile parade ever seen in America. This occurred on November 7, 1899. Thirty-four horseless vehicles were in line, led by a brass band on foot. Starting from the old Waldorf-Astoria, where the club had opened and still had its headquarters, the parade proceeded north on Fifth Avenue, along Central Park, across to Riverside Drive, and thence on to the Claremont Inn overlooking the river. All along the route the streets were jammed to suffocation, the huge crowds turning out just to see a few little horseless carriages go by.

The run was considered a great success, though not all the cars were able to climb the hill on 110th Street leading to Morningside Park and were forced to go around by a water-level route to reach the place of destination.

Almost overnight the club had become one of the most desirable in the city and was besieged by persons wanting to join. From the first it was a very active organization socially and otherwise; for in addition to its balls, parties, and picnics it sponsored club runs, one short endurance contest, and even a hill-climbing event. While ostensibly given for the pleasure and amusement of the entrants, these contests were so conducted as to put the vehicles to a severe test that would bring out the strong points and expose the weak. The club was steadily working for better motoring, both in structural improvement in the cars and the betterment of the conditions under which they were used. And in spite of the affluence and high social position of many of the members, it became a great ambassador of good will toward a not too friendly public.

The wide influence of this club was almost immediately evidenced by the formation of similar clubs in all the larger cities of the country. The Cleveland Automobile Club was organized in January, 1900. The San Francisco Automobile Club followed in March. Clubs were formed in Paterson, New Jersey, and Philadelphia in April. Rochester, Buffalo, and Syracuse were not far behind. Chicago started with forty members in August.

Boston, Long Island, and Rhode Island were heard from soon afterward. Then the colleges began to form clubs and Columbia and Princeton were added to the list. Indeed, before the end of the year 1900 more than twenty-six automobile clubs had been organized, and the following year as many more.

By this time the attitude of the public was improving. Motor-cars were no longer stoned when they drove through the meaner parts of a town or city. The roads, however, were little better than when the Indians surrendered them to the white man.

As I recall those roads today, it seems strange to me that there should have been such a wide interest at the time in the development of the motor vehicle that must have at least passable roads on which to run. I suppose we were so accustomed to bad roads that we did not realize how terrible they were. Or it is just possible that the manufacturers were farsighted enough to know that if they could build and sell a sufficient number of cars, the owners themselves would eventually furnish the pressure for improving the roads. At any rate, there were numerous manufacturers who cleaned out a corner of the factory so as to have things in readiness, and began to keep a weather eye on all that had to do with the development of the automobile.

6 *The Years of Guesswork*

The period between 1895 and 1905 was a time of great uncertainty in motordom. The manufacture of cars had been begun—but the industry had no idea where it was going. Taking 1895 as a starting point, since that was the first year when a group of cars was brought together in this country, public opinion was about evenly divided between those who thought there would, and those who thought there would not, be an automobile industry.

A few cars had been made before that time, but they were crackpot products made just for fun by somebody who wanted to take a ride and had no idea of going into the business. By 1895 Duryea had a small factory running, and two or three companies were trying without much success to make and sell electrics.

Experimental steam cars had been made, though none was able to appear for the Chicago race. The Selden patent was granted in 1895, though nobody paid any attention to it since the patentee had never built a car.

Ten new makes of cars appeared in 1896, of which only the Ford and Oldsmobile remain in existence today.

In 1897 twelve new name plates appeared, but not a survivor remains.

In 1898 sixteen newcomers arrived, but all have disappeared.

In 1899 twenty-one new arrivals came. Sunk without a trace.

In 1900 nineteen appeared. None is with us now.

In 1901 production had risen to roughly 7,000, with 67 new

companies starting in business. Production in 1902 touched 9,000, with 55 new name plates coming on the market. The following year production advanced to 11,000, while 78 new factories opened their doors—figures which had the statisticians sharpening their pencils and scratching their ears.

The early records, however, are pretty sketchy. Factories were opening and closing all the time. Some of them went no further than a few experimental models. Some ran for a year. Others went sailing along for five years or fifteen or even twenty, succumbing finally to bad business, bad management, the depression, or inability to meet the competition of the gigantic combinations which by that time had come into the picture.

Nowhere in history can the story of so miraculous a growth of an industry be found. The exhaustive compilation made by Floyd Clymer contains the names of some 2,200 automobiles made in America alone, largely during the decade from 1895 to 1905, and the research is still going on. Of this number Clymer notes that 125 were powered by steam, and doubtless there were almost as many that were electrically driven.

Cars of the vintage of 1900 and 1901 were little bobtailed things running on bicycle wheels. The average horsepower could not have been much more than six or eight. With few exceptions they were tiller-steered, and many of them still used belt or other friction drive. Hardly any of them, Packard, Pierce, Winton, or Peerless, had more than two cylinders, and most of them had no means of illumination except kerosene lamps. Hardly any of them included tops as part of the regular equipment, and one maker advertised that fenders were extra. Another maker failed to equip his cars with rubber tires. They could be had for $25 extra—but they were solid rubber. Winton, one of the early casualties among the better-known cars, was advertising, "Write us direct—WE HAVE NO AGENTS."

Not much money was required in the old days to start an automobile factory. All that was needed was an experimental car. And at that point the guesswork started for both the manufacturer and the motorist.

With all the competition, the manufacturer must have the

right car to offer. And the motorist must know the right car to buy, for with factories constantly opening and closing he never knew whether he would be able to get parts if anything should break—and something always did. The guessing of the manufacturer was on a little more lavish scale. Would the popular choice be the gasoline car which was somewhat in preponderance? Or would it be the electric or the steamer?

Surely the electric car was more silent than the others and more simple to handle; the drawback was that it required frequent recharging, though this was offset by the fact that it required no dangerous or inflammable fuel. The electric was also regarded as the genteel car, the car of luxury, elegant appointments, and handsome fittings impossible with the steam and gasoline cars which were notoriously messy with most of their working parts accessible only when the operator was lying flat on his back underneath. Of course the gasoline and steam cars were faster and more powerful, but who wanted to sacrifice luxury just to go a little faster or farther?

And again there was the choice to be made between steam and gasoline. Perhaps there would be a market for all three. Who could know about that? In some states the registration of steam cars was far ahead of those driven by gasoline, and at one time or another 125 factories were producing steamers while only 69 were producing electrics. Even among the best informed men in the industry there was a wide divergence of opinion. Thomas A. Edison was not the only one who had made his guess that the electric would eventually triumph. As keen a financial wizard as Col. Albert A. Pope, an industrialist who had amassed millions building the famous Columbia bicycles, had also done some tall guessing.

From the first, Colonel Pope had recognized the motorcar as the deadly enemy of the bicycle, and he had chosen the electric as the car most likely to succeed. Since he was well entrenched with a group of Wall Street millionaires in the Electric Vehicle Company which was involved in the building and operation of trolley lines and electrically driven taxicabs, his guesswork may have been complicated by some wishful thinking, for his first defensive move was the building and marketing of the Waverly Electric, which shows that Wall Street cannot always be right.

It was not long before the Colonel, being a prudent operator, made a second guess and began establishing a line of gasoline cars in case the cat should jump that way. The only angle not covered by the Pope interests was the steam car. But there is little doubt that the Colonel was watching developments with care, for there were many who believed that the steam car would eventually predominate. Indeed, the *Scientific American,* in its coverage of the first Madison Square Garden Automobile Show, had mentioned the increasing attention being paid to steam as the most striking feature of the exhibition.

Many of our early gasoline cars were made by inventors who had experimented with steam and abandoned it largely because of the excessive weight of the steam plant. Ford and Olds are examples, though most of the initial experimenters were interested in making cars only for their own use. Even the Stanley twins who became leaders in the steam-car field had built their first vehicle as a hobby. They had seen at a county fair a poorly made steamer and were fascinated by it. All the way home they kept talking about it and were soon convinced that they could build a better car themselves. This was in the tradition of the disgruntled Colonel Packard who had stalked out of the Alexander Winton presence to build a better car for himself.

To get a steam engine the Stanleys went to an engine maker; and for a suitable boiler they consulted a boilermaker. But not until the two parts were delivered to the Stanleys at their shop in Newton, Massachusetts, did they realize that they had a 750-pound power plant to mount on a light buggy frame they had prepared as a running gear. This boxlike frame had been built in a carriage factory catering to the needs of the horse and was, as a matter of course, equipped with a patent leather dashboard to which a whipsocket was attached.

The bicycle wheels on which all this weight was mounted were never intended to carry anything heavier than a man; but the twins were willing to take a chance. So they put a match to the pilot, fired up, and watched the pressure on the steam gauge.

When there was no explosion they decided, after due consideration, to give the machine a test. But at this point another problem
came up—neither of the twins had ever driven a self-propelled
vehicle. However, the control of the steamer is simple. Open
the throttle and its goes; close the throttle and it stops—that is,
if you remember to put on the brake.

A discussion ensued to decide who should do the driving and
resulted in the discovery that there was one thing in which the
twins were not identical—F. E. Stanley had more intestinal
fortitude than F. O. Stanley. F. E. was willing to take over the
tiller, and F. O. did nothing to discourage him. They realized
that this first ride might also be their last, so they decided to take
it together. They climbed gingerly into the vehicle and firmly
settled their derby hats on their identical heads. The month was
September, the year 1897. The day was a blank to be filled in
by the stonecutter.

With a trembling hand F. E. gripped the tiller. As he slowly
opened the throttle, the car began to move, whistling like a
teakettle and leaving a little white cloud of vapor behind. As
they emerged from the alley somewhat more rapidly than they
had intended, a horse hitched to a produce wagon standing in
the street was so taken by surprise that, without waiting to hear
his master's voice, he gave a sudden leap which tore him loose
from the wagon and ran 4 miles before being stopped. The horse
reached Newtonville Square far ahead of the Stanley Steamer,
a feat that was not duplicated by either horse or automobile for
several years to come, for the Stanley turned out to be a remark-
ably speedy car.

Funny as the little steamer looks today, it created a great
sensation on that initial run; for the faster it went the more
shrill the whistling sound became. People stopped abruptly on
the street to stare at the machine and at the identical twins with
identical beards and derby hats, sitting bolt upright on the seat.
So identical were they, in fact, that onlookers could be excused if
they thought they were seeing double.

Of course the twins were gratified to know that their invention would run, though they alone realized how poorly it had

run and how clumsy it was to handle. But they felt sure that if they could cut down the weight of the engine and boiler to the neighborhood of 250 pounds they would get a satisfactory ride. However, they did even better than that, for they succeeded in getting a power plant which weighed only 125 pounds. Mounted on a light chassis, this ran to perfection—though they must have sat somewhat uneasily on the seat the first time they tried it out. It was easy to handle and was quiet-running except for the whistling sound which gave them a long fight before it was conquered.

Their first opportunity to find out how fast their vehicle would go came at a race meet in Cambridge, Massachusetts, where their little steamer swept the field, doing a mile in two minutes and eleven seconds—on a dirt track, three laps to the mile. A new world's record! The machine also ran away with the hill-climbing contest, being the only car to reach the top of a 30 per cent grade.

After the contests were over, the twins were besieged by people asking where the car was made and what could be done about getting one like it. In less than two weeks, without any effort on the part of the twins, they had stacked on their desk 200 orders for similar cars. So there really was a craze developing for a car that would go—and go fast.

The Stanleys realized that they were neither machinists nor manufacturing men, but still the stack of orders was something a real Yankee could not resist. So they cautiously bought an abandoned bicycle factory and started the manufacture of a run of 100 cars similar to the model used in the Cambridge races. In ordering the bodies from a nearby carriage factory, they forgot to cancel the whipsocket—and the new owners must have blushed whenever anybody invited them to get a horse.

News of the race was widely published, and in due time John Brisbane Walker, owner of *Cosmopolitan* magazine, called at the factory for the apparent purpose of selling advertising space to the new company. The twins shook their heads; they did not believe in advertising. Walker stayed around and displayed a considerable interest in the car. They took him for a ride in it and told him all about the stack of orders. On his second call he made an offer to buy the business. He had been doing some looking around and had come to the conclusion that with all its speed and the simplicity of its construction the steamer might easily dominate the industry and prove to be the most popular car. It looked to him like a good guess and he was ready to back it up with real money.

The twins went into a huddle. Their investment up to this point was only $20,000. They were not anxious to sell; still, if he was willing to pay enough money they might as well let it go. They slept on the offer and named a price of $250,000. Walker accepted, made a down payment, and went off to get the rest of the money.

With Amzi Barber of New York, who became a partner in the venture, Walker formed the Locomobile Company. However, after only a few months there was a disagreement and a split between them. Barber continued with the Locomobile, but Walker started a new concern under the name of the Mobile Company of America. Both companies built steam cars of almost identical construction and rushed them into the market where they competed with each other.

It was in 1899 that the Stanley Company was sold to the New Yorkers. Up to this time steam cars had more than kept pace with the gasoline machines. Even in 1902 more than half the cars registered in New York State were steamers; but at this time the gasoline car began to come into its own. It was, however, an expanding market. Steam and electric cars were selling well, and the uninitiated were guessing that gasoline cars were selling more only because there were more of them on the market.

Only the big money and people at the top had a different idea; and when, after only some three years in business, both the Walker and Barber interests offered to sell the Stanley factory and all patent rights back to the twins, all they could get was $30,000 for a business they had previously bought for a quarter of a million.

The Stanleys still believed in the steam car and for several years turned out from 500 to 1,000 cars a year. The White Steamer, eventually the Stanley's principal competitor in everything but price, took over the luxury field; but both were destined to go down before the tremendous popularity of the gasoline machine. Largely for publicity purposes the Stanleys went in for racing. With a line of cigar-shaped racers called "Wogglebugs," they began to dominate the track and hill-climbing events.

There was a battle royal on the Readville track near Boston on Memorial Day in 1903 when the Stanley tangled with a steamer built by a Harvard student still in college, a youth named George Cannon. The Cannon entry required a two-man crew riding tandem—steersman in front and engineer behind. Both cars clipped the world's record for the mile, but the Stanley was two seconds ahead. However, the record was short-lived, for later in the day at the Empire City track Barney Oldfield clipped a second and a fifth from the newly established mark, driving one of the 80-horsepower Fords built for the races with Alexander Winton.

On the beach at Daytona, Florida, in 1906, the Stanley made a mile in 28.2 seconds, a record which stood for four years before it was beaten by Barney Oldfield with a 200-horsepower Benz; even with all that power, the little 6- or 8-horsepower Wogglebug was shaded by only 0.87 of a second.

If speed and simplicity had been the only requirements, the steam cars would easily have commanded the popular market; but they lacked the rough-and-ready character of the gasoline car, and they could not seem to live down the reputation for being dangerous. With the flash boiler which converted the water into steam practically drop by drop, they were as safe from explosion as the gasoline motor, though the man in the street would never believe it after hearing the sizzling of the pilot light while the car was standing idle. Then, too, the necessity of waiting ten to twenty-five minutes to get up steam caused even greater sales resistance than the danger of explosion.

For a number of years the steamers hung on with loyal motorists who preferred them to the finest of gasoline cars. But it was a losing fight, and after the death of F. E. Stanley in 1917 the company passed to Chicago interests. However, in spite of new money and new blood, the business languished, for by this time the guesswork was over and both the steamer and the electric were on the way out.

As a business venture the steam car is extinct, and in spite of its good qualities and many admirers it has shown little evidence of coming back. Had the same care and effort been spent on the development of steam as on the improvement of the gasoline car, we might not be puzzling our brains today over the hidden workings of the automatic transmission or worrying about the depletion of our underground oil reserves.

7 *The First Auto Show*

By the turn of the century members of the Automobile Club of America who had attended the Grand Salon in Paris, at which the new European automobiles were shown to the public, had returned home with a very definite idea that the time had come for America to have an automobile show. They recalled how the annual Cycle Show, which was gradually dying on its tires, had been rejuvenated by the presence of a few motorcars the year before. There had been not a little comment about the crowds around the few cars on exhibition while the bicycle displays were deserted.

The virus of greatness was already at work in the brain of the A.C.A. Even the title of the club suggested the possibility of having national scope, and when in 1900 it announced an "all-automobile" exhibition for the fall of that year it had every intention of making it the Grand Salon for the entire nation.

However, the A.C.A. was not the only institution awake to the possibilities of a successful show devoted exclusively to the automobile. A representative of one of the most progressive of American newspapers, the Chicago *Inter-Ocean*, had also attended that first dual display of cars and cycles. He, too, had been struck with the idea that a show devoted entirely to motorcars would almost certainly attract large crowds to Chicago. And with the show held under the sponsorship of the *Inter-Ocean* there would be reams of publicity for his newspaper—and he undoubtedly recalled the immense amount of copy obtained for the *Times-Herald* by the historic Chicago road race of 1895, even though the race had been almost completely snowed under by a blizzard of snow and sleet.

The announcements of the Chicago Automobile Show, issued in July, 1900, read as if Mr. P. T. Barnum might have had
a hand in their preparation. The gala affair was to be held in
God's Great Outdoors at the Washington Park race track, and
was to begin in the true Greatest-Show-On-Earth tradition with
a parade of some five hundred vehicles—count 'em!

After that there was to be a contest for "general practical
utility." In other words, the cars must prove that they could carry
passengers. (*a*) Owner-driver; (*b*) chauffeur-driver; (*c*) delivery type with 1,000 pounds of load.

Next came a twisting-turning contest in which the skill of
the operator would be called upon to demonstrate that a motorcar
could be driven as easily and as safely as a horse and carriage.

And since there was a track handy there must, of course, be
races—all kinds of races—long, short, steam-car, electric, hydro-
carbon, obstacle, and, to cap the climax, a backward race. This
description probably referring to the cars, not the drivers.

Also in the true Barnum tradition, the ladies were to be well
looked after. One entire day out of the six days of the exhibition
was to be devoted to the fair sex. The fast ones could participate
in the races; the artful ones in dodging dummies; the climbers
in ascending grades. There were other classifications for practically every feminine capacity except back-seat driving for which
the fair ones had not yet developed their latent possibilities.

Full lines were entered by some twenty exhibitors, with gasoline machines in a slight majority. While not quite so numerous,
the electrics were far more elegant and luxurious, and they were
shown in a wide variety of models, mostly for two passengers.
Steamers were not so popular in the West, for only four exhibitors were showing their models.

Only one thing went wrong with this first Chicago show,
and that was the weather which, to the secret delight of all the
Chicago papers except the *Inter-Ocean*, went on a terrific binge.
The rain came down in torrents, and when it was not actually
coming down it was threatening to come down. The skies were
dark and gloomy, and the dampness took the starch out of practically all the events except the mud racing which was dominated

by some little three-wheelers made by a French concern. Winton's big racing car was there, and one day when the rain stopped long enough, the thundering machine ran an exhibition mile in a vain attempt to break the world's record.

Let us be kind and say that the Chicago show was only a meager success, so meager, indeed, as to arouse some apprehension on the part of the New York club which was planning the big all-automobile show for the first week of November. The slim attendance at Chicago might be an augury that public interest was not as great as the club members had imagined. And then there was the weather to consider—what would happen if they should have a rainy week? Of course the show could go on, since it was to be an indoor affair; but what was the value of a show if nobody came to see it?

However, they needn't have worried. The weather was fine, the place was continuously thronged with people, the manufacturers were well represented with their exhibits, and the show was a great success.

Though the automobile was steadily gaining in public favor, there was still plenty of latent hostility—or perhaps it was envy. It is easy enough to develop dislike or even hatred for a thing if you think you can never have it. Well aware of this fact, the committee thought it advisable to provide something more in the way of entertainment than merely allowing the visitors to walk through the aisles and peer at the automobiles on display. They did not go so far as to furnish the variety of entertainment put on at the Chicago show, where the motorists themselves were allowed to participate in the events; but they had constructed in the grand auditorium an oval track on which cars in motion were actually demonstrated, though that was not the word in use at the time.

A somewhat spectacular feature was provided on the roof of the Garden by John Brisbane Walker, one of the new owners of the Mobile Company of America, who had delayed so long in applying for space in the main hall that there was no room available for his exhibit unless he was willing to place it on the roof. Being resourceful and extravagant, Mr. Walker put on a roof-top stunt that was the hit of the show. He constructed a steep runway up the side of the tower and then on into the blue, on which his drivers gave demonstrations of the hill-climbing ability of the little Mobile steamer which he was then manufacturing in Tarrytown, New York, in a factory later occupied by Chevrolet.

Twenty times a day his daredevil drivers would run the little car to the top of the crooked incline, hold it there a few moments as if to catch its breath, and allow it to descend slowly —backwards—stopping at intervals to show the efficiency of the brakes, which were (for the occasion) equipped with double-action facilities not part of the regular equipment.

Again the trend to gasoline was to be noted, for nineteen of the exhibitors were showing cars powered by internal combustion. Seven were pinning their faith on steam. Six were building nothing but electrics, and two were following the principles of safety first by equipping their electric cars with gasoline motors to bring them home in case of emergency.

Many familiar names are to be found among the exhibitors of these two early shows. The entire hyphenated Pope family was there—Waverly, Hartford, Toledo, and the rest; Locomobile steamer, National, Riker, Stanley, Orient Buckboard, Winton, Duryea, Haynes-Apperson, Knox, its cylinders bristling like porcupines with cooling fins, and many others. But of all the automobiles exhibited at both shows the Packard, a newcomer with the paint hardly dry on its first car, is today the sole survivor. All, all are gone. Over the hill to the junkyard, and thence into the hands of collectors and old-timers who are doing such a worth-while job of saving for us with their restorations many irreplaceable specimens of the craftsmanship of the automotive pioneers.

Visitors came to New York for the show from all over the country. Some were there out of curiosity, just to have a look. Others came to compare and perhaps to buy. Technicians were there, and all sorts of scientific men, to examine and learn, to predict, and to be interviewed by the press. Thomas A. Edison never missed an automobile show as long as he could get around, and he never hesitated to give an interview to the press in which he usually predicted that the horse was doomed.

In an interview at the time of the Chicago race in 1895, after making his usual prediction about the horse, the Wizard (as he was called by reporters) remarked gloomily that the animal shows a greater economy of force than man, with 70 per cent of its energy available for work. Then he remarked in almost the same breath that the horseless vehicle was the "coming wonder."

Asked if these wonder vehicles would be run by electricity, he replied, "I don't think so. As it looks at present it would seem more likely that they will be run by a gasoline or naphtha of some kind."

This was very good prophecy, much better than he made five years later when he was quoted by *The New York Times* as saying, in connection with an electric car he was planning:

"Next year I will wager I can take a car of my own design fitted with my [electric] motor and battery and go to Chicago and return in less time, and with more pleasure, than any other machine in existence. There will be no breakdown, no explosion of gas or gasoline, and the trip will be made at an even twenty-five miles an hour."

It was indeed a time of wild prophecy when the Providence *Journal* could predict "a telephone in every household just as it has other modern facilities"; and Col. John Jacob Astor could prophesy that with the development of the automobile "keeping horses in large cities will doubtless be prohibited by the Board of Health, as the stabling of cows, pigs, and sheep now is." The Colonel was also looking forward to second-story sidewalks of glass—in less than twenty years—leaving the street level to vehicles, an improvement which, alas, has not yet come through.

And since prophecy was the order of the day, the ebullient H. G. Wells was heard from on various subjects. His prediction of a motorcar capable of a day's journey of 300 miles or more "not obnoxious to sensitive nostrils" has come through rather handsomely, though his gloomy prophecy of the future of the airplane was wide of the mark. "I do not think it at all probable that aeronautics will ever come into play as a serious modification of transport and communication." And his refusal to see the submarine "doing anything but suffocate its crew and founder at sea" comes as somewhat of a surprise from a man who made a sizable fortune writing of such things as *The War of the Worlds* and *The Time Machine.*

At the time of this show the automobile industry in this country was a toddler less than five years old. During the year 1900 some fifty new manufacturers started to make cars, and production for the year was around four thousand.

Only a small proportion of the car builders in the country were represented at this first of the automobile shows. Not many of the builders were sufficiently financed, and capital was still looking at the industry with a fishy eye as if they expected it to hit the slide at any moment and go the way of the bicycle. And for a small factory that was getting along on a hand-to-mouth basis the expense of shipping models to the show was not to be lightly undertaken. Nor had the show at this time demonstrated that it had any particular value in the production of sales.

If the factory owner managed to finance a visit to the show for himself, his designer, and the head of his sales department, he felt that he was doing all that could be expected of him. However, the factory owners, large and small, were there in droves. They scrutinized one another's products with care and were able to observe that very few cars were sold over the counter, so to speak.

They could plainly see that cars cost too much to be bought out of hand. Customers did not carry that much money with them, and besides they wanted to try a car and be sure it would run. They wanted to get the feel of it and be reassured that they would be able to drive it after a reasonable amount of instruction and practice. Then, too, the public was not at that time accustomed to spending a thousand or possibly two thousand dollars for a plaything—or for anything else short of a house and lot.

After all, the automobile show wasn't anything like a bazaar —a place where you could take your choice and pay your money straight out of your pocket or your wallet. People came and looked, and they asked an endless number of questions; then

A.M.A.

That woman driver! During the 1905 Glidden Tour, a venturesome woman contestant had her White Steamer plunge off a 9-foot bridge with three passengers aboard, but no one was injured. She was Mrs. John N. Cuneo, Richmond Hill, Long Island, the only woman entered in the tour.

A.C. Buffalo

A Stevens-Duryea, in background with rear wheels turning, managed to churn through this creek, which stalled a large percentage of entrants in the 1911 Glidden Tour, and finish the route with a perfect score. At the wheel was former State Senator Wheatley of Americus, Georgia.

Traffic was heavy, indeed, for contestants along the route of the 1911 Glidden Tour, as they jockeyed for the best of the muddy, deep-rutted Florida roads. The tour that year wound through all the South Atlantic states, where roads at that time were among the poorest in the nation.

Hooper

Water holes, heavy sand, and a tight time schedule accounted for many of the penalizations in the 1911 running of the Glidden Tour. Above, an "American," entered by the Atlanta *Journal*, splashes through a water hole. Winner of that contest was a team of three Maxwell cars.

This crude assembly line was the forerunner of mass-production techniques that made it possible to build cars of increased quality at lower costs. Roughly a hundred million passenger cars and twenty-five million trucks and buses have rolled off assembly lines since 1900.

An early impact of the automobile was on women's fashions. As seen in this photograph, posed for by the smiling ladies about 1905, the fine linen duster, chiffon veil, and large hat were *de rigueur* in the period. Milady, on an outing, was stylishly protected from head to toe.

A Sunday afternoon outing of motoring enthusiasts customarily looked something like this at the start, as the vehicles chugged and puffed about the meeting place, their drivers eager to head for the open road and a day of adventure and exploration with their motor-borne cohorts.

In the early days a fellow certainly was thankful for the assistance of a crew of willing, sturdy friends along the road when a flat tire or dead engine befell him. Reciprocal aid was one of the primary interests of the early automobile club members.

Along early tortuous, undeveloped mountain passes, getting by another car sometimes posed a serious problem, involving hours lost en route. Here the solution seems to have been to jack the cars one around the other, with the usual cussing and fuming about the mess they're in.

Water for a car on the King's Highway, California, 1906. The motorist in desert regions often had to take his water where he could find it, and more than one took advantage of this water tank, used by the road crew of Santa Cruz for an ox-drawn sprinkler wagon to control dust.

Blacksmith shops got in line with progress, and became repair stations at which the early broken-down auto might be puzzled over and made to run again. Hard to believe that here was a forerunner to the efficient super-service station which is commonplace on today's modern highways.

Great-uncle Harry must have wept when he contemplated this 1910 wreck of a couple of prized early automobiles. Even then, it seems, traffic accidents were taking a costly toll in life and property, and safety interests were beginning to awaken to the need for remedial measures.

they accepted a catalogue and moved on to the next exhibit where they repeated the operation. People from New York or New England did not care to buy a car from Detroit or Kenosha and have it shipped to them by freight. That was unthinkable—they wouldn't have known how to unload it, or set it up, or even how to start the engine. They wanted to deal with somebody who would deliver the car at their door, with the tank full and ready to go; somebody who would teach them to drive it and who would be within reach when the car broke down or was stuck in the mud.

The result of the early shows was not so much in the direct selling of cars as in arousing the interest of prospects and inducing the manufacturer to send out an agent with a car. Manufacturers like Winton who had been advertising "Write us direct —WE HAVE NO AGENTS," and the others who had been selling their cars without tops, without lights, and even without mudguards soon realized that if they wanted to stay in business they would have to offer their cars fully equipped and ready to go.

Many agency deals were initiated and some closed during the show. And some factory representatives who had come there only to look were converted into exhibitors for the following year.

This first show was strictly a motorist's affair, initiated by club members and promoted and managed by motorists largely for glory though somewhat in the hope of increasing the ranks of the motorists and combating the hostility of horse owners, bicyclists, and the underprivileged masses. Automobiles were still being stoned by hoodlums whenever they thought they could get away with it; and the scattering of tacks and broken glass in the streets was widely regarded as a crude form of humor.

There is no doubt that the A.C.A., which had promoted the show, was well satisfied with the outcome, for the club put on another show the following year, and this time the exhibitors came in such large numbers as to tax the capacity of Madison Square Garden. After a week of unprecedented crowds the manufacturers were so completely sold on the idea that they formed a national association for the purpose of cooperating with the

A.C.A. in automobile-show promotion. This partnership lasted for two shows before being disrupted by the organization of the Association of Licensed Automobile Manufacturers, which was a by-product of the Ford-Selden litigation.

The Seldenites, refusing to show their cars in cooperation with the Fordites, shook themselves loose from all nonmembers of the A.L.A.M. as well as from A.C.A. sponsorship and ran their show exclusively for manufacturers operating under the Selden Patent. Mr. Ford and the independent manufacturers took up the gage and put on a show of their own at Grand Central Palace, stealing a march on the licensed group by dating their show ahead of the exhibition at the Garden.

This curious bit of snobbery continued until the final decision had been rendered in the patent case and peace was restored. Thereupon the industry returned to the single standard, with one show a year managed by the manufacturers and open to all makers of cars and accessories, gadgets, and all sorts of related products and appurtenances.

8 *The Coming of AAA*

The early motorist was constantly on the defensive. Everything he did was regarded with the fishy eye of prejudice. If he went over 8 or 10 miles an hour, he was fined for speeding; if his car broke down or he stopped to repair a tire, he was bawled out for obstructing traffic; if he squawked his horn or rang his bell on Sunday, he was desecrating the Sabbath; if he did not give due notice of his approach, he was charged with negligence. As he ventured out on the highway he had the feeling that every man's hand was against him; and not only that— he realized that in the eyes of the law he was nowhere regarded as the equal of the horse.

Starting off alone, the motorist was apprehensive, nervous, worried. What if his vibrator should stick or his driving chain come off? It had happened before. What if he should get stuck in a mudhole? It had happened. What if his machine should scare a horse into running away and injuring a lot of innocent people? What if his car should get out of hand and run into a ditch or start to climb a tree? What if he should have a smashup with another vehicle? Did he have money enough in his pocket to meet such emergencies?

However, going out for a run in company with a number of congenial club members was a very different matter. Here was fellowship, security, solidarity. If you should have a breakdown, friendly assistance was at hand. Should you be unfortunate enough to get stuck in the mud, somebody was right there to pull you out. And traveling with a group of cars, one was less likely to receive insolent treatment from grooms and hangers-on

71

when stopping at a tavern for refreshment or at a hardware or paint store for gasoline.

As soon as the motorists were able to drive their cars out of town, the country innkeepers began advertising in the motoring magazines that they were equipped to supply automobilists with meals, and with gasoline "at regular rates"; and one offered the extra inducement of water free of charge.

Then, too, on these club runs there was always sure to be somebody at the head of the line who knew the way. Knowing the way was important, for road signs were few and far between, and such as there were led only from one town to the next. The old horse and buggy signboards were almost invariably weather-beaten and in need of repainting. If a signpost rotted and fell, or a board was knocked off by a boy with a rock, the local population was likely to take the attitude that by this time everybody knew the way, so why bother to make repairs.

Many of these old signboards had been standing since the days of the stagecoaches, and some had never been repainted since the coming of the railroad had sounded the death knell of travel by stage. In western New York where I lived as a boy I cannot recall seeing a readable signboard on a country road that was not there solely for purposes of advertising. Often these advertising signs were painted on a fence or boulder, or perhaps on the broadside of a barn. Indeed, some of the old black-and-yellow liver-pill signs are still visible on upstate barns.

The Salvation Army was a consistent advertiser, though it was after your soul and not your business, and it never mentioned mileage. The only signs that gave any indication of distance were those which told you how far it was to some specific store.

The countryfolk, with their intimate familiarity with local landmarks, paid little or no attention to their signboards and probably never missed them if they collapsed and were carried away. The city motorist, however, accustomed to a street sign on every corner, began to feel lost when he had passed beyond the city limits; and soon pressure began to be put on the newly formed clubs to do something about the country road signs. An attempt was made to develop some cooperation on the part of the localities where signs were most needed; but this resulted only in cynical smiles by town officials and county boards of supervisors who were not at all anxious to encourage the city motorists to make use of their roads. Some of them went so far as to intimate that the sooner the motorists were lost the better they would like it.

Annoyed and disgusted but not discouraged, the clubs began in a small way to put up an occasional signpost where guidance was most needed. This was greatly appreciated by the venturesome motorist, but was of local and limited assistance. For a tourist who wanted to go some distance an occasional guidepost was not enough. To post the road even for a single day's journey would have run into quite a little money and into numerous complications as well, for it would have come up against state boundaries; and if it could have surmounted these, it would have invaded the territory of other automobile clubs which in the East were never very far away. The New York club thought of a better idea. Why not post a single through route at the expense of the clubs along the way?

The original plan was to post the route from New York to Boston, sharing the expense with the Bridgeport, the Rhode Island, and the Boston clubs. The idea proved to be so popular that further routes were posted from New York to Philadelphia on the south, and to Albany on the north, and thence across to Buffalo.

The project was greatly appreciated, but it had its limitations, for it could be carried on only in areas where the distances were not too great and clubs along the way were reasonably numerous. And there was almost always some jurisdictional friction in reaching from one state into another. The immediate result, however, was the rapid development and popularity of touring by individuals as well as the extension of club runs and reliability contests. But even after he had his way marked out for him, the motorist was still bedeviled by two great hazards—bad roads and inclement weather.

The early motorcar was no more prepared for bad weather conditions than a bicycle or a baby carriage. At the first drop of rain the motorist scurried to get under cover—a barn, a shed, a tree, anything that would keep off the rain. And after the rain was over he would have to wait for an hour or two for the roads to dry off.

With the coming of cold weather, the motorcar went into winter storage along with the croquet set, the bicycle, the lawn-mower, and the fishing tackle, and there it stayed until the frost came out of the ground in the spring. But the car was by no means forgotten. There was the Automobile Show to keep it in mind, and the recounting with other club members of past experiences or making plans for the future.

Over in Brooklyn, where a tree grows and spring comes early, there would occasionally be a mild midwinter day which would bring a longing for the open road. Such a day came near the end of January, 1901, and with a touch of the madness of spring members of the Long Island Automobile Club attempted a run to Bay Shore. Only five hardy souls turned out, but the adventurers departed in high spirits. Then suddenly the wind shifted, and what had been a balmy zephyr from the south changed to a howling gale from the north punctuated by stinging flakes of snow, and by the time the little open cars had reached Jamaica the tourists were ready to give up.

To quote the newspapers, "Difficulty was experienced with the water jackets. Several of the rigs froze up and had great difficulty in reaching home." When they did, the machines went back into storage for the rest of the winter.

The A.C.A., while attempting nothing so hardy as cold-weather touring, was nevertheless determined to keep working for the betterment of motoring. It accordingly issued an invitation to some of the more active clubs to meet in New York for a discussion of the very important subject of improving the roads of the country. The meeting was timed for midwinter when the outlanders love to visit the metropolis while the theatrical and entertainment season is at its height. They met and they talked, and they saw some mighty good shows and other forms of entertainment—but with the roads buried under two feet of snow there was not much to be said on the subject at that time.

Hardly any of the states had a highway department. Country roads, regarded as comparatively unimportant, were left by the states to the counties; and by the counties to the towns; and by the towns to the farmers who were permitted to pay their road taxes by giving a couple of days of labor per year dumping gravel in the worst of the mudholes.

This was done under the direction of a "pathmaster" who worked out his own road taxes by telling the teamsters where to empty their wagons, meanwhile discussing with them the best means of discouraging "automobilism," a new word just coming into use which was uttered with almost as much distaste as the word "cannibalism" when spoken by a missionary.

The good-roads meeting was fun, but it came to naught. What could a club or several clubs do for a road condition that was nationwide? Some of the car manufacturers were trying to meet the situation by making their cars powerful enough to negotiate any kind of roads. A Winton motor carriage had been driven from Cleveland to New York—in ten days; and there had been other remarkable feats of motoring, though they were largely stunt accomplishments financed by factories and carried out by skilled mechanicians and professional test drivers.

As soon as the frost was out of the ground, the various automobile clubs began to bestir themselves with cars that had been up on sawhorses all winter. Some of them put on club runs to an out-of-town tavern or perhaps to a nearby city just for the fun of riding along in a caravan of cars and eating in an unaccustomed place. Others promoted reliability runs, endurance contests, nonstop affairs, anything to add a little variety to just taking a ride.

The A.C.A., which was a live and energetic club, ambitious to be regarded as a leader in motordom, promoted a 50-mile road race on the roads of Long Island, then regarded as the best in the country. It was won by a 5-horsepower electric— not much of a speed contest, but everybody had a wonderful time. The club, however, turned from racing to reliability and put on a club run to Bridgeport, and a little later another to Philadelphia—an all-day run at that time. The Philadelphia run happened to strike some fine weather and was so successful that the club decided to pull out the stops and put on a reliability run all the way across the Empire State from New York to Buffalo and return, by way of Albany, to give the members an opportunity of enjoying a really worth-while club run as well as visiting the Pan-American Exposition which was being held in Buffalo that year. The tour was described as a 1,000-mile run, though this gave the jaunt a more impressive than accurate description, for the distance was only a little over 800 miles.

Through what appeared to be a most fortunate bit of planning, the motor caravan was scheduled to arrive in Buffalo during the visit of President McKinley who was coming to see the Exposition and deliver an address of welcome to the citizens of all Pan-America.

According to the contest rules, the course was divided into six controls of about 65 miles each, this being considered an average day's run. Under the management of the New York club the event took on a very fashionable flavor. The list of entries looked like a page from the Social Register. Eighty automobiles lined up for the start, but the motor caravan was not yet out of the city when the first accident occurred. The car of Col. John Jacob Astor crashed into a bicycle, with disastrous results to the smaller machine. Although bystanders asserted quite positively that the Colonel was not to blame, he generously gave the wheelman $50 to buy a new bicycle. Then to relieve the tension, the Colonel pulled out and started to pass other contestants to regain his former position in line. He was just beginning to make some headway when one of the Astor passengers lost his hat and the Colonel had to stop while he retrieved it.

From the opening day of the tour the weather was foul. Rain came down in torrents, washing away portions of the road and melting what was left into a quagmire. But the contestants were for the most part good sports. They went grinding along in low gear for miles at a stretch, splashing through puddles and bumping over pitchholes.

There was not a closed car in the entire group (and probably not in the world). Several of the machines had stripped off their tops before starting, so as to be relieved of the additional weight.

Once they were on the course, no racing was allowed; if a car arrived ahead of its scheduled time, it was penalized. Reliability was the watchword. Penalties were provided for any kind of failure, even tire trouble.

Some of the cars came to grief before reaching the first control, and there was hardly a day when others did not fall by the wayside. And the rains came down. How they did come down! And the longer the rains continued the more bottomless the roads became. The first day the tourists were slithering and splashing; the next day they took to floundering and wallowing; and after that their progress was a combination of all these things and a lot more besides. Somehow they reached Albany and crawled through the Mohawk Valley.

Natives in rubber boots and raincoats lined the streets to watch them go through the towns mud-stained and sodden. The countryfolk shook their heads and asked each other how anybody could get any fun out of that kind of trip. They wouldn't mind going to the Pan-American, but the railroad was good enough for them.

Each night when the roll was called, a few more of the contestants would fail to answer. How the sponsors even managed to keep the line moving as far as they did is a mystery. But they finally reached Rochester with only a single control remaining. By this time the ranks had been thinned to fifty-one mud-stained, bedraggled, battered, patched-up, almost worthless vehicles.

It was here that news of the death of President McKinley came to them and so depressed their already drooping spirits that the touring committee decided to abandon the contest and make the awards according to the records as far as Rochester. Thus ended the first long reliability and endurance tour ever attempted in this country.

The first year of the new century was leaving its mark on motoring. It had seen the production of 7,000 motor vehicles, nearly 1,000 of which had been registered in New York State. The speedometer had come into use. Shaft drive had begun its campaign to supersede the chain. Thomas B. Jeffery had built and ridden in the first Rambler, wearing, like Henry Ford in his first car, a derby hat. The first White Steamer was sold to a customer. More than sixty new automobile name plates had come on the market. The public had pretty well settled on the word "automobile," though they were still a little shaky about where to place the accent. And the suggestion about getting a horse was becoming a little stale, especially to motorists.

Among the more general news was the discovery of oil in Texas, the death of Queen Victoria, the formation of the United States Steel Corporation, and the feat of Marconi in sending the letter S across the Atlantic by wireless, all three dots of the Morse code being received in good order.

For some time there had been rumors that an amalgamation of the automobile clubs in the country was being seriously considered, and in June the following item appeared in *Horseless Age:*

> As was long ago foreseen, the Automobile Club of America is considering an alliance for common defence and advantage with other representative clubs of the U.S. It is generally conceded that such an alliance would add greatly to the effectiveness of the good roads campaign and enable the organization to guard more securely the rights of automobilists upon the highway.

That this feeler had been more or less official was indicated later in the year when overtures were made by a circular letter issued by President A. R. Shattuck of the Automobile Club of America to some thirty of the clubs.

That there was some lack of understanding among the automobile clubs at this time is apparent from the reports in the papers in October, 1901, of a "secret meeting" held by certain members of the A.C.A. to discuss the question of federation. The New York club, it was said, was to be the "parent organization with power to govern all future sporting events, giving a share of responsibility, however, to that particular club under the auspices of which a race or other event is held."

At this time the Automobile Club of America, the pioneer club, was less than three years old. There were now thirty-six recognized clubs in the country. Nine of them were in New York State, six in Massachusetts, five in Ohio, four in New Jersey, three in Pennsylvania, and one each in nine of the other states.

Though the many advantages of an amalgamation of the clubs were obvious, there still was a certain reluctance on the part of a number of the clubs to surrender any of their powers or privileges to one of the companion clubs, pioneer or otherwise. In urging the amalgamation, *Horseless Age* refers to the opposition as "local pride and jealousy."

There was undoubtedly more than this to it, for there is a strong inhibition on the part of people dwelling outside New York against being controlled or managed by those dwelling *in* New York. And this is especially noticeable among the residents of our large cities outside the Empire State. But whatever the cause may have been, the opposition showed no signs of backing down, and the plans for the amalgamation were at an impasse.

This was the situation in December, 1901, when Frank C. Webb, treasurer of the Long Island Automobile Club, made a speech before 125 members of his club in Brooklyn in favor of a federation of the clubs in a new nationwide organization which should be dominated by no single club, but in the government of which all the clubs should have a fair share.

Mr. Webb's proposal was received with such great enthusiasm not only by the members of his own club but by the membership of a number of the other clubs which had been opposing the "parental" advances of the New York club, that the A.C.A. lost no time in passing a resolution definitely withdrawing its proposal to head an amalgamation, and hastily climbed on the band wagon. Exactly ten days later a formal call was issued, inviting two representatives from each club to attend a meeting in Chicago for the purpose of organizing a federation of the country's automobile clubs along the lines proposed by Mr. Webb.

That Chicago was chosen as the meeting place was undoubtedly due to the efforts of Frank C. Donald, president of the Chicago Automobile Club, and Samuel A. Miles, manager of the Chicago Automobile Show which was to open the first week in March. The date for the organization meeting was fixed for Monday of the show week.

The objects of the proposed federation, as set forth in the call, were as follows:

> Enactment of liberal laws regulating the use of automobiles on the public highways.
>
> Protection of the legal rights of the users of motor vehicles.
>
> Improvement of public highways.
>
> Development and introduction of the automobile.
>
> Equitable regulation of automobile racing and trials of endurance and efficiency.
>
> A medium for counsel and interchange of information, ideas and suggestions tending to the development and advancement of the art.

This time the proposal for a national organization came not from a single club but from five of the most active and influential clubs in the country, being signed by the following:

> The Automobile Club of America
> The Philadelphia Automobile Club
> The Long Island Automobile Club
> The Rhode Island Automobile Club
> The Chicago Automobile Club

Arrangements had been made for the meeting of delegates to open at the Coliseum in Chicago on Monday, March 3, 1902, at 11 A.M. But at that hour only a single delegate had arrived— Mr. F. C. Donald of the Chicago Club. Surrounded by leering newspapermen, Mr. Donald explained that trains en route to

Chicago had been delayed by unprecedented flood conditions, and that the meeting would not be called to order until a reasonable number of delegates had been given a sufficient opportunity to appear.

He gave the correspondents a partial list of the delegates expected and the names of the participating clubs, some of which had signified their intention of joining the project but had failed to furnish the names of their delegates. Before long, however, trains began to reach the city and tardy delegates came hurrying into the big convention hall. It was only a short time after midday when Mr. Donald felt that he had enough delegates to warrant calling the meeting to order.

There are some discrepancies in versions written in later years as to the attendance at this original meeting, but it is known from contemporary accounts that eight clubs were represented as follows:

> Chicago Automobile Club—President F. C. Donald and Vice-President E. F. Brown.
> Automobile Club of America—Governors A. C. Bostwick and W. E. Scarritt.
> Automobile Club of New Jersey—Secretary W. J. Stewart and W. F. Harris.
> Long Island Automobile Club—Treasurer F. G. Webb and Edwin Melvin.
> Rhode Island Automobile Club—Secretary H. H. Rice and W. J. Titcomb.
> Philadelphia Automobile Club—Secretary F. C. Lewin.
> Automobile Club of Utica—President Charles S. Mott.
> Grand Rapids Automobile Club—Walter Austin and C. B. Judd.

By acclamation, Mr. Donald of the Chicago Club, one of the prime movers in the amalgamation, was elected temporary chairman. Delegates presented their credentials and were accredited, and the convention was ready for business. Mr. Webb of Long Island, who has long been credited with being the father of the AAA, was recognized and offered a very practical agenda which was promptly adopted. Two committees were thereupon appointed, one to report upon the plan and scope of the new association, the other to formulate a proposed constitution and bylaws.

Messrs. Webb, Scarritt, Austin, Brown, and Lewin were named as the Plan and Scope Committee; and on the Constitution and Bylaw Committee were the names of Messrs. Bostwick, Stewart, Titcomb, Mott, and Judd. Since these two committees were not scheduled to report until the following day, Mr. Scarritt proposed that the plan and scope of the new association should be discussed before the committee dealing with those subjects should begin its sessions.

The idea was immediately adopted, and an animated though thoroughly polite and friendly discussion explored both subjects with enthusiasm. It had been expected that some friction might be generated by the New York club, but fortunately such was not the case. The best of feeling prevailed, and the sense of the meeting seemed to follow quite generally the original suggestions made by Mr. Webb. The Constitutional Committee profited largely by this discussion, for it came into the meeting the following day with a constitution and bylaws so clear and uncomplicated, so just and equitable, that they were adopted after only forty-five minutes of discussion.

Next on the agenda was the election of officers for the ensuing year. If the lid was coming off—this would have been the time. But the spirit of friendly cooperation which had prevailed up to this time continued to the end, and the slate prepared by the nominating committee went through without a contest. The first officers of the new organization were elected as follows:

President—Winthrop E. Scarritt, Automobile Club of America.

First Vice-president—F. C. Donald, Chicago Automobile Club.

Second Vice-president—W. W. Grant, Long Island Automobile Club.

Third Vice-president—W. G. Morris, Automobile Club of Philadelphia.

Treasurer—Jefferson Seligman, Automobile Club of America.

Secretary—S. M. Butler, Automobile Club of America.

Directors—F. G. Webb and A. R. Pardington, Long Island

Automobile Club; A. R. Shattuck, Automobile Club of
America; W. J. Stewart, Automobile Club of New Jersey;
F. C. Lewin, Automobile Club of Philadelphia; Dr. J. A.
Chase, Rhode Island Automobile Club.

The election of Mr. Scarritt of the New York club as president was not only a pleasing bit of diplomacy but a very handsome gesture of friendly cooperation which buried the hatchet
and augured well for the new Association which had adopted as
its name—American Automobile Association.

It is revealing to observe that the first official act of the
AAA was to sponsor national legislation providing for a bureau
of highways with appropriations to carry on a constructive program. This was the opening gun in a fight which has lasted
fifty years and which may, like the brook, go on forever. The new
president was a little more specific in his own first official act,
which was to offer a resolution that a national highway should
be built from New York to San Francisco. The resolution said
nothing about the cost or who was to do the building—but it was
carried with a whoop and a cheer, and the convention adjourned
sine die.

In the minutes of the Chicago meeting the following brief
summary is found:

> Those who laid the foundation of the American Auto-
> mobile Association at Chicago, March 4, 1902, recog-
> nized that in the growth of a great pastime and industry
> —wherein healthful recreation and the benefits of
> commerce were blended—there was need of a national
> organization which would assist in the general progress
> of the motor-driven vehicle by safeguarding the interests
> of the users and at the same time aiding the maker in
> perfecting a better car.

The first regular meeting of the Board of the AAA was held
April 1, 1903, at the clubhouse of the Automobile Club of
America in New York City, which had very kindly extended the
use of its quarters to the new Association until it should find
itself and until it had a better understanding of its needs; and

the two organizations were a long time in discovering that no one house was large enough for two families.

President Scarritt opened his administration with a full roster of business which he had classified under six departments: Racing, Highways, Membership, Technical, Legislative, Auditing.

The interest of the Association in good roads was given a fine send-off by a gift of $10,000 from one of the member clubs with which to promote the Brownlow-Latimer good-roads bill, the first legislation of its kind ever to be offered in Congress.

As to racing, an application for sponsorship was already pending for a race meet at Brighton Beach promoted by speculators. The application was denied by the Association on the ground that its sanction would be granted only to duly organized clubs. This rule was later revoked because of the insistent demand of the entire motoring fraternity for AAA sponsorship, not only of racing but of all kinds of contests, tours, endurance runs, and every other sort of motoring activity.

There was plenty of activity ahead for the legislative department, for the rapidly increasing number of cars on the roads had stimulated the passage of unfair and unreasonable restrictions based largely on public hostility to the automobile. Cries for help were coming from almost every state in the Union, and right in their own front yard a member of the Board of Aldermen of the City of New York was making his bid for the Hall of Fame by attempting to jam through the Common Council an ordinance forbidding the carrying of gasoline by any motor vehicle within the city limits. After lively opposition from motorists, led by the Association, the bill was defeated.

The membership committee also had its problems, since the new Association was somewhat hampered by its inability to speak for more than a portion of organized motordom; for there were still a considerable number of clubs in the country which had not yet joined the organization. Most important among these were the several clubs in Massachusetts, not one of which had attended the organization meeting in Chicago or had shown any interest in becoming a member. Sooner or later something would have to be done about this, but the time was not yet.

Fortunately the AAA was starting its career with an unusually able president and board of directors. It tried no high-pressure tactics to bring in the stand-off clubs, but went quietly about the business for which it had been formed, gaining steadily in prestige and looking forward to the time when it could serve and represent the great body of organized motorists of the entire nation.

9 *Speed and More Speed*

From the time that automobiles would run, drivers wanted to race them. Not always for the same reason, however. Some only wanted to win races, and some wanted the impression to get around that their cars were speedy. Winton and Ford were not the only builders who realized the promotional value of speed. With the exception of makers of the wagon-wheel type of vehicle which was intended to retain all the joys of the buggy ride except the smell, every manufacturer gave due consideration to speed in designing his car. Ford and Winton would not have squandered their money on those early racing monsters if the public had not been clamoring for speed.

During the period when the AAA was confining its sponsoring services to the affiliated clubs, the sporting fraternity as well as the owners and proprietors of horse-racing tracks had a spree of unregulated races in which the sky was the limit. To match the big professional racing cars with the stock models built for the trade would have been ridiculous, and the promoters themselves shook down the racing cars into two classes, the professionals and the stock cars. It was a step in the right direction, the only difficulty being that every manufacturer had his own definition of a stock car. These were matters that could not be handled effectively by the individual car builders. Their standards were as diverse as their dispositions, and though the methods of some may have been meticulous, there were others who were slipshod and just possibly dishonest.

Finally the trackmen and manufacturers themselves came begging the AAA for sponsorship. Here was an organization built on honor and devoted to the general welfare of all motoring interests, and when it agreed to provide a sound formula for the accurate and honest testing of cars in runs, races, or any kind of contest, all hands were ready to listen.

"If your car comes through OK," the Association offered, "we'll say so. If not, that's your hard luck and you'd better go back and try again."

The affiliated clubs, of course, had long since subscribed to the rules and regulations threshed out and prescribed by AAA, and when the outsiders agreed, the Racing Committee of three members was reorganized into the Contest Board with fourteen members, for it was quite evident that a large increase in business was ahead. Naturally in the beginning, the Contest Board stepped on a lot of toes and made some of the manufacturers very uncomfortable and even angry because it failed to support their unwarranted boasts and claims. But the rulings were so fair and so unbiased that the defeated contestants had no comeback except to comply.

Automobile racing soon found itself on an even keel and it has come through the years as the one major sport the conduct of which has never been involved in a scandal.

The growth and popularity of spectator racing came along with great rapidity. Everything in the country that looked like a race track was covered with speeding cars. This included not only the well-built racing plants near the big cities, but also the scraped-together dirt tracks of the county fairgrounds. Nor were AAA sanction and sponsorship confined to racing alone. It reached out to reliability and endurance contests, hill-climbing contests, time trials, and beach records—indeed to every kind of sporting event connected with motoring in which jurisdictional questions were not involved.

But all this did not happen in a moment. The Association was some two years in arriving at the decision to extend its sponsoring function outside its own membership; and the race-track people as well as some of the manufacturers were cautious about taking advantage of the opportunity they had been begging for. Then, too, the Contest Board, also feeling its way, was carefully selective in its early sponsorship of events promoted by outsiders.

In the meantime the Contest Board was busy with various events among its own member clubs and was steadily growing in the wisdom that comes only from experience. By this time the Board had become very skillful in developing techniques suited to the various types of contest. This for hill-climbing events, that for a nonstop contest, and something else for a reliability tour. In the earlier days of the Board the reliability tours were mostly one- or two-day affairs; but as cars were improved and their power increased, the need for longer and more difficult tests was recognized by motorists and manufacturers alike, for it was becoming obvious to both that performance on the road in comparison with other cars was the best possible testing laboratory for the automobile.

With the difficulties and eventual disintegration of the A.C.A.'s Pan-American tour still in mind, the Touring Committee sent out feelers for a proposed reliability run from New York to St. Louis, with an opportunity to visit the Louisiana Purchase Exhibition as an inducement. The prospective tour was routed by way of Albany, Buffalo, and Chicago, with appropriate stopovers along the way. Club members, realizing that their current cars were far superior to those used on the Buffalo tour, were ambitious to try them out, and their response to the feeler was so prompt and so enthusiastic that the contest was definitely scheduled.

This time the officials in charge did not wait for the "fine September weather" which had made such a shambles of the A.C.A. tour. Instead, they decided to take a chance on the hot weather of July and August rather than risk an early visitation of the fall rains. Entries coming from Boston and cities along the way would join the main touring party en route; and a supplementary contingent of motorists from Philadelphia, Baltimore, and other cities of the East and South would follow a more southerly route, with their journey so timed that the two groups could come together at East St. Louis for a triumphal entry of the combined contingents into the Exposition city.

On the 28th of July, 1904, the New York contingent gathered at Fifth Avenue and 59th Street ready to take off for St.

Louis, some 1,218 miles away, more or less, depending upon detours, inability to keep from getting lost, and various other hazards of the highway.

With the exception of electrics, which were not suited to long-distance driving, cars of all types were parked around the neighborhood. Some of the vehicles had a full complement of passengers and others the minimum of two. Packed in with the passengers in some of the cars were spare tires, extra springs, accessories, luggage, raincoats and blankets, and even umbrellas.

Only one woman was among the starters, Mrs. Laura Lillibridge, who was seated high up in the tulip body of a White Steamer. Mrs. Susan Malpas, who had been expected at the starting line with three woman companions, telephoned at the last minute that she could not be ready in time but would endeavor to catch up with the tour at Syracuse. Other women were planning—if all went well—to join their husbands on the tour as it went along.

The confetti car had gone on ahead; indeed, it had left soon after daybreak to mark the route by scattering confetti along the highway at reasonable intervals and especially at turns and junction points. Although the AAA Touring Committee in charge of the expedition, headed by Augustus Post and Charles J. Glidden, was composed of a dozen members, not all of them were in the line-up. The secretary, A. L. Tucker, and his assistant, Mr. Downs, who were to handle the checking in and out, the reservations, and other details of the tour, gave the starting signal to Mr. Post at exactly nine o'clock and the big White Steamer went rolling up the Avenue with a plume of white vapor coming from the exhaust.

Twenty-three cars had been expected to start, but only eighteen were there and ready to go when Mr. Post took off. In the line-up were a Pope-Hartford, several White Steamers, a 70-horsepower Peerless carrying six passengers, followed by a two-passenger Haynes-Apperson. A waterless Knox failed to start when its turn came, but promised to catch up later. A little two-passenger two-cycle Elmore, which had just returned from a pathfinding trip to St. Louis, popped and backfired when

cranked, but finally got under way, followed by a big Darracq carrying five passengers and thundering like a distant artillery barrage. Another air cooler, a Franklin tonneau, went
next with its long driving chain flapping up and down as it passed
over the crosswalks. Next in line was an Oldsmobile tonneau
model carrying two passengers and looking very neat and efficient. An experimental Yale with solid-rubber tires drew away
from the curb, accompanied by a college yell from a group of
youths on the sidewalk. It was followed by a heavily laden Pope-
Toledo carrying three passengers and a pile of luggage. A little
Buckmobile with the number 60 was the last to take off. And
after Mr. Tucker and Mr. Downs had closed their books and
had taken an electric taxicab to the railroad station to go by train
to Poughkeepsie, the first control, a single-cylinder Cadillac
came chugging up and stopped to ask if anybody knew where
the tourists were assembling. The little car was immediately
surrounded by remnants of the crowd who were lingering nearby.

The occupants were not at all dismayed when told that the
tourists had already gone. They laughed and blamed their tardi-
ness on the driver's watch. After thanking the crowd, they said
they would catch up with the rest of the party, and thereupon
they departed amid laughter and cheers. They caught up at
Poughkeepsie and went through to St. Louis with a perfect
score.

At that time it was possible to get to Poughkeepsie by train
faster than by motor, and although it was after three o'clock
when Mr. Tucker and his assistant reached the Nelson House,
the first of the tourists had not yet arrived. Soon, however, they
began straggling in. One had killed a dog. Another had lost
a fan belt. Several had been stopped by tire trouble. And just
as the tourists were coming out from dinner the little one-lung
Cadillac drew up in front with a cheerful blast from its bulb horn.
It was never late for another meal throughout the entire journey.

The end of the second day of the tour found the travelers
at Albany where they were joined by several Albany cars and
a number from various points throughout New England. In all
the large cities through which they passed they found others

waiting to join them, and the entourage was growing like a snow-ball as it went along. Of course there were incidental breakdowns, some of a simple nature that could be repaired by the driver or patched up by a local blacksmith. Then, too, some of the cars entered by manufacturers were manned by expert mechanics who were willing to help but were often miles ahead of the un-fortunate victim. Many of the tourists carried a few spare parts and were very generous about loaning them.

Tire troubles were almost universal, some of the machines having several in a single day, nail punctures, blowouts, blisters, and frequent instances of rim cutting. Whenever the tourists were caught in the rain there would be an epidemic of electrical troubles from wiring shorted by the moisture. On the third day one car was a complete wreck when it overturned in a ditch, caught fire, and was burned beyond recognition. There was hardly a day without broken springs while the cars were cross-ing New York State; and though they were not bogged down in the mud of the Mohawk Valley like the cars on the Pan-American tour, they found enough pitchholes to wrench their frames and axles. One tourist was heard to remark that they needed no confetti to show them the way, since they could follow the route by the trail of broken spring leaves.

Because of the great length of the journey, the management had decided not to enforce the strict regulations of a reliability tour, but to allow the entrants to travel on a go-as-you-please basis. There was no penalty for punctures, repairs, or delays, nor was there any rigid enforcement to prevent checking in ahead of your turn; but there was a gentleman's agreement not to do any racing, and probably none of the gentlemen indulged in it, though there were some drivers who made a superhuman effort every day to be first into the night control. So long as the roads were reasonably damp, little objection was made to disagree-able conduct of the speedsters, but after a particularly dusty day between Rochester and Buffalo an indignation meeting was held to protest against the conduct of certain unnamed drivers.

Feeling that his secretarial position gave him no power to reprimand a high officer of the AAA, and that it would not be politic to rebuke a man of the importance of the worst offender, Mr. Tucker made an urgent appeal for all the tourists to forego racing, and allowed the meeting to adjourn.

The tendency to indulge in racing on an endurance or reliability run was not new to the AAA. Racing had indeed become enough of a nuisance to require special attention after coming to a head on the 100-mile endurance run of the Long Island Automobile Club earlier in the year. Mr. Pardington of the AAA committee in charge had disqualified all the offending speeders.

Naturally no question of disqualification would arise on a go-as-you-please tour, and the culprits who had been doing the speeding continued their daily contests to be first into the night control.

A day of rest was allowed in Buffalo so that the tourists could visit Niagara Falls, as if many of them had not spent a honeymoon there. Most of the cars went into dry dock to have springs repaired, axles straightened, engines overhauled, or steering connections adjusted. Some of the tourists went to parties and some went to church.

The tourists had been entertained by local automobile clubs in all the cities they visited. In Albany they were given the pleasure of visiting a brewery. At Syracuse they inspected the Franklin plant, and in Rochester they were taken through an optical works. In every place where they stopped they were greeted by the mayor, and Mr. Tucker was usually entrusted with a letter sending flowery greetings to the mayor of St. Louis.

An interesting occurrence in Buffalo was a suit brought against the driver of the 70-horsepower Peerless for frightening a valuable horse while in Rochester, and late that same night the big Peerless was towed in with a broken steering knuckle.

Despite the indignation meeting at Buffalo, the racers were up and off with the chickens. Indeed, one of them ran into a flock a farmer was calling to breakfast. Though several were killed, the motorist went speeding on, and the farmer hung the dead fowls on the fence as a warning. When, an hour or two later, Mr. Charles J. Glidden came along, he was unfortunate

"Turn left at the red oak. . . ." This party of tourists in their 1910 Pierce-Arrow is engaged in an exchange of touring information typical of the days before adequate road maps and route marking. The farmer at right sets the folks straight, while his wife chats with the ladies.

A spin in the country often involved fording streams that flowed over those early-day roads. While a submerged roadbed had been no problem to the horse and buggy, the "horseless carriage" owner soon demanded, and got, roads which would not jeopardize his expensive automobile.

"Get a horse!" was the cry. Situations like this, where the early car proved not quite up to the task of fording an inundated road, prompted more than one occupant of horse-drawn vehicles to taunt the pioneer automobilists. This took place on what is now the Lincoln Highway.

Albert Mecham

This photograph, vintage 1904, shows an old-time Packard creeping down the slope to a waiting ferry. Ferries were often the only way to cross large bodies of water for many years before bridgebuilding boomed under the impetus of road development and public transportation needs.

Take to the shoulder! With roads like these, it took the average car owner months to make a transcontinental tour. As late as 1912, west of Chicago, the motorist got his roads, gasoline, water, and oil "where he found them," so usually stocked up well in advance of starting.

Travel in our Western deserts was a real venture for many years before modern roads came upon the scene. Here the driver of a 1911 Franklin takes advantage of a plank road built on the powder sand south of Blythe Junction, California, by a community truck company in 1913.

Inland A.A.

It was a matter of delicate balance. Here the gentleman in a duster waits while his chauffeur centers the car aboard the cable ferry ready to take off while the current is running right to push the boat across the river. Scene is the Snake River, southeastern Washington, in 1920.

Colorful touches on the early American motoring scene were the covered bridges, widely used in the East and particularly in New England. Now only a few remain, preserved as interesting relics of a less frenetic age. Covering was provided to protect the bridge from rain and snow.

The manner in which original road reports were made available to early auto club members is reenacted by a senior employee of the Automobile Club of Buffalo. This type of exchange of touring data among members led to the development of modern clubs' touring counsel and materials.

A pioneer AAA transcontinental Pathfinder was the late A. L. Westgard, whose road information, gathered in several cross-country trips before World War I, proved invaluable in planning America's highways. He is pictured during a stop for refreshment on the route of his 1912 tour.

Before motor clubs took over the task, signposting and route marking of the nation's roads was inadequate, at best. One of the first functions of automobile clubs became identification of the highways within their areas and distribution of trip logs, maps, and other touring materials.

Charles M. Hiller

Road sign maintenance followed naturally in the path of erecting signs by the clubs. This Model T road sign maintenance patrol car was among the California State Automobile Association fleet of the early 1920s. The CSAA's record of signing and maintenance dates back to about 1914.

enough to run over a hen that happened to be crossing the road; whereupon the irate farmer stepped out with a shotgun and demanded payment for all the deceased fowls. Mr. Glidden offered to pay for the one he had killed and finally settled for one dollar, though he neglected to take the hen.

As the tourists went on, they found the attitude of the country-folk along the way far less cordial than in the East. They came out in crowds to watch the tourists pass, and whenever a car stopped for any reason whatsoever they advised the driver to enlist the services of a horse, a remark that never failed to bring a gale of laughter. In the cities, however, the attitude was quite different. At Cleveland the crowds were large and friendly, cheering with enthusiasm at each arrival and surrounding the cars while they asked numerous questions about the cars and the roads, and invariably somebody would ask how they liked Cleveland.

On reaching the rendezvous at the Hotel Boody in Toledo, each member of the party was halted by a fierce-looking United States Marshal and served with an awesome-looking summons of the United States Circuit Court charging the defendant with running over and killing a valuable dog. At this point the prisoner would usually stop to protest his innocence—but on reading further would discover that the legal-looking document was in reality an invitation to a gala dinner given by the local automobile club.

During the run from Toledo to South Bend, the longest day's journey of the tour, 176 miles, many casualties occurred. Several cars went into a ditch, smashing fenders, wrenching axles and frames, and bending steering connections; and the big Peerless, after being late at practically every control, was finally struck by a passenger train at one of the innumerable grade crossings. Fortunately nobody was killed.

By ten o'clock that night only about half the machines which had left Toledo that morning were checked in, eighteen being hung up at various points along the way. All except the defunct Peerless came stringing in the next morning; and since the tourists were to have a day of rest at the luxurious Hotel Oliver, the

entire party had assembled by the time that a car bringing envoys from Chicago arrived to escort them on a triumphal entry
into the Windy City.

It was the custom of the day for visiting tours to be met outside the city by members of the home club and accompanied into
town with a great din from the auto horns and other noisemakers.
The envoys explained that a large delegation was to meet the
visitors at Hammond, and that an even larger group would await
them at Jackson Park where the grand parade was to form.

There was a rather heated discussion about the order in
which the cars of the tourists should enter Chicago. Tom Fetch,
a famous test pilot for Packard, had joined the party at South
Bend and was awarded number 13, since nobody else had cared
to carry it—and he had no sooner fastened it on his car than his
bad luck began.

The Touring Committee had decided that the cars of the
tourists should enter the city in the numerical order of the
numbers assigned to them on their entry blanks. Because of
the failure of some cars to start and defections due to accidents
along the route, this would have placed Fetch fifth in the line.
There had been some discussion about whether this would be
fair to members who had been with the party from the start. But
Mr. Tucker was firm. He ruled that the numerical order had
been established and would be carried out.

Tired, road-weary, and overstrained, the tourists had many
mishaps on the run into Chicago. Three cars went into a ditch
and were upset, though with miraculously small damage to the
occupants. All three were righted and were found able to proceed. Several runaways were caused, one of them being a team
which bolted without a driver. The owner was picked up by one
of the tourists who overtook and passed the runaway team, which
was then headed off by the farmer and, with the cooperation of
the motorist, was caught in a narrow stretch of the road.

At Jackson Park an attempt was made by Col. Albert A.
Pope, one of the contestants, to reopen the discussion of the order
of procession by insisting that the cars should enter Chicago in
the order of their arrival at Jackson Park, his car having been

the first to get there. He was so insistent on the point that an emergency meeting of the Touring Committee was hastily called. All the manufacturers in the tour lined up with Pope, and it looked for a time as if the tour might fall to pieces before going as far as Chicago. But Mr. Post and Mr. Glidden so vigorously supported Secretary Tucker's ruling that the insurgents grudgingly yielded.

With 150 gaily decorated Chicago cars trailing behind, the tourists paraded up Michigan Avenue to the Coliseum to such an ovation as only Chicago can give.

The visitors were sumptuously entertained over the weekend while their cars were being repaired, rebuilt, refurbished, or perhaps only washed and lubricated for the jaunt across the state of Illinois to East St. Louis for the previously arranged conjunction with a second division of AAA tourists coming in over the National Highway from Philadelphia. But the grand spectacle of massed motorcars of the two divisions miscarried; for by some error in calculation the second division arrived a day ahead of time, and there being no suitable accommodations for them at East St. Louis they paid their toll at the Eads Bridge and entered the city with very little of either pomp or circumstance, looking only like a lot of muddy cars and tired occupants.

In the meantime the division of Main Line tourists was being augmented by numerous entries from cities as far away as Cedar Rapids, Minneapolis, and even Denver. And after leaving Chicago their ranks were increased daily by motorists stimulated by the enthusiastic press reports of the grand motorcar invasion from the East.

On leaving Chicago, Colonel Pope violated the rules of the contest by disregarding entirely the control at Springfield and spending the night some 40 miles beyond the city to insure his being first into St. Louis. He sent a substitute back in an attempt to register his car at the control, but the registry was refused. He was, however, beaten into the city by another of the contestants who had slipped ahead unbeknown to Colonel Pope, and was there to greet the Colonel on his arrival.

But with characteristic resourcefulness the Colonel obtained a special permit to drive his car into the fairgrounds where, decorated with boastful signs, it was exhibited as the first car of the great motor entourage to reach St. Louis. After this spectacular sally the car was returned to the official garage so that it might participate in the grand parade of the tourists which was held a day later.

The progress of the tourists down through Pontiac and Springfield was not without its exciting features. A night mechanic in repairing a car lighted a match for a better view and set fire to the gasoline dripping from a leaky carburetor. The car, an Oldsmobile tonneau which had come all the way from New York, was of course destroyed, and the tourists upon hearing the alarm rushed out in their night clothes to push their cars out of danger. Naturally the newspapermen were anxious to get the story on the wire, and when it was found that the local operator had gone home for the night, Mr. Glidden, a former operator, peeled off his nightcap, put on an eye shade and took over the key.

For their entertainment while in Pontiac the members of the tour were taken to the Chautauqua Assembly Grounds to attend a revival meeting conducted by a high-powered evangelist of the Billy Sunday type. However, on a checkup at the starting line the next morning it was noted that none of the tourists was remaining behind to hit the sawdust trail. So no better and certainly no worse for the experience, the tourists moved on to Springfield.

From Pontiac to Springfield the expedition lost all appearance of being a concerted run. The confetti car, though starting early enough, broke down a short distance out of town, to the great annoyance of Mr. Frank X. Mudd who had been in charge of the road signs and confetti since leaving South Bend. He had, on the way into Chicago, equipped a car with an automatic confetti spreader designed to drop an ounce of paper fragments every 300 yards through a tube located near the tail pipe of the muffler. It was a good idea but Mr. Mudd had forgotten to provide any confetti. With great resourcefulness he substituted a supply of corn and beans which, being scattered along the roads ahead of the tourists, attracted hundreds of farmyard fowls. The swift passage of a car would of course scatter the fowls, but after it had passed, all that had managed to escape slaughter would come back to the feast in time for the next car. It was reported, however, that the feathers provided a fairly good substitute for the confetti.

Another day the confetti car sent out by Mudd was a low-powered roadster which was unable to keep ahead of the tourists; but after they had passed, it dutifully followed, scattering the confetti at the proper intervals. When one of the official cars bringing up the rear asked the confetti man why he was dropping the confetti behind the tourists, he replied sheepishly that he thought some of them might want to come back.

When the confetti car broke down between Pontiac and Springfield, the tourists, not at all dismayed, went rolling along, getting their bearings from the sun. This was quite satisfactory until the sun went under the clouds, to be seen no more that day, leaving the tourists to travel by dead reckoning aided by the uncertain calculations of countryfolk, few of whom had ever driven to Springfield. Signboards, if any, were merely reminders of Lydia Pinkham, Radway's Ready Relief, Dr. Miles Nervine, or Piso's Cure for Consumption. Everybody was lost nearly all the time, yet all but one of the cars reached Springfield, though no two had come by the same route. The missing car was a single-cylinder Rambler which seems to have been living up to its name plate. In the summary of the tour this car is marked as "dropped out."

Supplementing the confetti work of Mr. Mudd, the St. Louis Automobile Club sent out its own confetti car to meet the tourists and guide them into the city. The driver's first mistake was in taking the wrong road which he tagged very effectively. In getting over to the right road he ran into a pitchhole and bent an axle. Being a persistent fellow, he kept on going until he had reached the proper road—and then he ran out of gasoline far away from a supply. While he sat there waiting for gas, the tourists came along and one of them gave him enough fuel to get back to town.

For a few days after the termination of the long grind, the cars of the tourists were seen around the streets of St. Louis proudly exhibiting their mud stains and damages honorably received in the battle against bad roads and the elements. Thoroughly sick of touring—for the time being—many of the vehicles which had come the whole distance were shipped home by train. The more seasoned tourists like Augustus Post, Glidden, Percy Megargle, and a few others tuned up their cars, filled the tanks and started on the homeward trek as casually as if they were going for a drive in the park.

By the end of the week all visible signs of the tremendous task of putting through the tour had vanished from sight, and many who on their arrival had waved aside the whole business of touring as they muttered "Never again!" went rolling out of town by the dawn's early light in answer to the call of the road, hoping for a safe and leisurely journey home.

In summarizing the tour for *Horseless Age,* Harry B. Haines, after detailing the difficulties of the heavy cars in negotiating the bad roads, has this to say for the light car: "It is easy to be seen that the ideal touring car is in the 2,000 pound class and should have a motor developing not less than one actual horsepower for every hundred pounds of weight carried. A car so designed can average twenty miles an hour uphill and down."

If Mr. Haines had but known it, Henry Ford was just then perfecting such a car as he described, only it would do far better than 20 miles an hour uphill and down.

10 *The Glidden Tour*

The most persistent American tourist both before and after the St. Louis tour was undoubtedly Charles J. Glidden, a Boston millionaire who had made his fortune in the telephone business. Ever since motorcars had been on the road, Mr. Glidden had been riding in one. He had probably been over more miles of our American roads than any other motorist, and had motored through Europe from the shores of the Mediterranean to the land of the midnight sun. He was familiar with the utmost joys of touring, and he wanted American motorists to know what they were missing by doing most of their motoring in and around the old home town.

By the time he had reached Buffalo on the St. Louis jaunt, he was convinced that what this country needed to popularize touring and at the same time to arouse public attention to the need for improvement of our roads was a series of reliability tours, passing first through one part of the country and then through another until all the populous areas had been aroused and had become interested. After a discussion with his friend, William H. Hotchkiss, president of the Buffalo Automobile Club, he announced his intention of making a formal deed of gift to the AAA of a magnificent trophy to be open to annual competition on a reliability tour by members of the AAA and affiliated clubs. It was Mr. Glidden's obvious intention to exclude manufacturers who had been making a nuisance of themselves on the St. Louis tour; but the manufacturers refused to be excluded and horned in by the simple expedient of joining the AAA.

This could not have been very pleasing to Mr. Glidden who had undoubtedly intended his tour to be more or less of a society

99

event, entered largely for the pleasure of touring, and certainly not for business reasons. But it was, after all, the mad scramble of the manufacturers which gave to the Glidden Tours the immense popularity they achieved.

It was the second of November, 1904, when the AAA formally accepted the deed of gift of the Glidden Trophy. In addition to other qualifications, there was to be an entry fee of $100, half of which would be returned at the start of the contest. The owner must drive or be a passenger in his own car; the contest was to be run under rules made by the Touring Committee of AAA.

Mr. E. P. Ingersoll, speaking for *Horseless Age,* scoffed at the conditions. He doubted that many bona fide owners would be willing to pay so large an entrance fee for the privilege of submitting themselves to the rigors of a 1,000-mile endurance run for no greater reward than a slip of paper which would be of no particular value to a private owner, and opined that if there were any considerable number of starters one could be reasonably sure that the majority of them would be manufacturers' representatives in disguise.

Regardless of Mr. Ingersoll's gloomy predictions, the sponsor and donor went ahead with their plans, fixed the date of the run as the following July 11–22, and opened a special office where the details of the pilgrimage could be worked out and managed. New England was selected for the initial tour starting at New York, going as far as Bretton Woods, and ending at New York, with overnight stops at the following places:

Hartford, July 11; Boston, July 12; Portsmouth, July 13; Bretton Woods, July 14. Here the tourists were to sojourn until July 19 when they would start the return trip by driving to Concord; then on to Worcester, July 20; Pittsfield, July 21; they would then return to New York City, July 22.

Each tourist was furnished with a little booklet giving many details of the tour, routes to be followed, a list of hotels, and the names of local appointees in charge of arrangements at the various stops. Mr. Glidden's heart had been softened to the extent of dispensing with observers, which had long been the bane of conducted tours. But the owner of each car was put on the honor system to make a faithful report of all stops, their cause, duration, and such other details as might be pertinent.

As the cars checked out in the morning, usually between six and ten, they were to be given a limit within which they must be registered for the night stop. Speed laws were to be strictly observed, and no credit would be allowed for speed in reaching the destination.

On the morning of July 11, 1905, the entrants lined up at the rendezvous near the Hotel Plaza for the start of the initial Glidden Tour. They were sent off according to number, with Hartford, 122 miles away, as the first control.

From the list of entries it could be seen that this was a top-flight tour. There were White Steamers galore, one of them occupied by Walter White, president of the White Company. Of several Pierce Arrows, entry No. 14 was driven by Percy P. Pierce of the George N. Pierce Company, along with a chauffeur and five passengers. Smart-looking Packards and Peerlesses could be seen here and there, and of the various species of the Pope cars three were driven by members of the Pope family. Mr. R. E. Olds was at the wheel of one of his own Reos. J. D. Maxwell, president of the Maxwell-Briscoe Company, was there with a car bearing his own name, and Benjamin Briscoe was in another of the same. There were several Cadillacs in the party, and a Rambler with a canopy top. Two waterless Knox cars were noted, the occupants smiling with satisfaction as one of them jokingly advised the White Steamer drivers not to forget about taking along plenty of water. And the foreign flavor was there with a Darracq, a Panhard, and Mr. Glidden's own Napier.

A number of ladies were observed in the party, only one of whom, Mrs. John Newton Cuneo of Richmond Hill, was occupying the driver's seat. She had not gone far, however, before she had the misfortune to crash the rail of a bridge and drop into a small stream some 10 feet below, just as she was entering Greenwich. Luckily she was unhurt and was soon fished out. Her car was righted and, though somewhat battered, continued on its way, followed by cheers of the onlookers who even then were making remarks about "those woman drivers."

At Hartford, home of the Popes, the tourists were lavishly entertained. The ladies of the party were received and feted by a special committee of society matrons while the men were being banqueted in the grand ballroom of the best hotel by Colonel Pope and a large gathering of local club members. The Colonel and Mr. Glidden gave a fine imitation of the lion and the lamb while corks popped and compliments ran wild. It must have been painful for some of the tourists to get out of bed the next morning —but soon after six o'clock the caravan began moving.

The roads were fairly good and the run into Boston not too difficult. All the tourists had checked in at the Hotel Lenox before the afternoon was well started. Even the two baggage trucks had come rumbling in with the luggage before it was time to dress for dinner. However, the tour took a serious turn at Boston, for all the contestants were required to deliver the report cards for the first two days, made out on honor and giving almost as many intimate details of their private affairs as are now required by an income tax report.

In addition to Mrs. Cuneo's crash, only two accidents marred the day. The Napier broke a jackshaft and had to be towed into Worcester where a replacement was readily made. And in a skidding accident in Springfield a 200-pound passenger thrown from a Cadillac had landed in a sitting posture in the gutter with only slight injury, mostly to his dignity. The car did not fare so well, having smashed a running board (a wooden step formerly used on automobiles) by crashing against an iron lamppost.

At Boston the tourists rested, rambled about the city, and, being subjected to no serious municipal reception or entertainment, dined quietly by themselves. The next morning they took their time about starting the shortest day's run of the tour, the 63 miles to Portsmouth, accompanied by a large escort of cars occupied by members of the local automobile clubs who turned back after lunching at the great sprawling Hotel Wentworth.

On leaving Portsmouth the tourists encountered the peculiar type of hospitality which was at that time extended by the people of New Hampshire to visitors who had the audacity to come in their motorcars. The Granite State was among the last in the

Union to issues licenses to automobiles, and though it did not carry its hostility so far as some of the counties in West Virginia which were still enforcing laws forbidding to motorcars the use of the public roads, it gave the Gliddenites to understand that they were there only by sufferance and must watch their step.

The first evidence of this attitude was observed at Dover where tricky police traps had been arranged. Officers disguised as workmen were posted along a measured route equipped with ropes which could be readily swung across to stop any unwary traveler who happened to exceed the 8-mile speed limit. Fortunately the tourists had been warned of the trap by friendly motorists in Conway and crept across the measured portion at a snail's pace which caused several of the cars to stall, thus delaying the cars behind, since the stalled motors had to be cranked by hand and did not always start readily.

Sandy roads and steep hills had been anticipated for the run to Bretton Woods, but the tourists received a pleasant surprise. A rainstorm in the night had packed the sand, and the worst of the hills proved to be easily taken on second. Though a team of horses had thoughtfully been provided to help the cars up one of the steepest of the grades, only a single tourist needed help. The supply of gasoline in his tank was too low to get to the carburetor by gravity feed—and, alas, the penalty for being towed went down on his report card.

A rather serious accident marred the day's run. A Cadillac which was "comparing speed" (so stated in report) with a White Steamer attempted to pass in a cloud of dust so dense that the driver failed to see a narrow bridge ahead until too late to stop. His effort to cross on two wheels failed and the capsized car pinned the occupants underneath. They were rescued by friendly onlookers who had gathered nearby to watch the tourists go past. All that saved them from being crushed was the high "tulip body" of the touring car which, as the report explains, "saved them from any more serious injuries than several gashes in the forehead, contusions of the body, and wrenched arm muscles."

The car, it seems, did not fare so well, receiving a sprained axle, a fractured front wheel, a crumpled steering pillar, and some abrasions and contusions of the fenders. Fortunately there were no internal injuries—the motor was not involved—and after repairs had been made to the car and occupants they went on their way, reaching Bretton Woods only a day behind the others.

After a pleasant week end at Bretton Woods the caravan started the return voyage with a run to Concord. At the start the skies were bright and promising, but after the tourists had been on the road for some two hours they were caught unawares by a severe electrical storm which came suddenly over the mountain and doused them before they could find suitable shelter. Mr. Morrell, one of the tourists, driving a Locomobile without a top, was caught in the open and he and his party were thoroughly drenched in a matter of moments. As they felt their way slowly along, they caught sight of a farmyard and turned in, hoping to get the party under some sort of cover. Hardly able to see where he was going, Mr. Morrell drove his car as close as possible to the house before stopping.

Glancing up on the veranda he saw a man asleep in a chair and was about to call to him to ask if they might come in, when a bolt from the sky struck the gable of the house, ran down the roof of the porch and, after jumping over the car, grounded with a blinding flash and a terrific concussion which threw the sleeper out of his chair.

The luckless fellow, rudely awakened, saw the car directly in front of him and, thinking that the explosion must have come from the car, fled indoors in terror. Without waiting for an invitation, the tourists leaped from the car and sought the protection of the porch. Eventually a woman came to the door and invited them in; but saturated as they were they preferred to remain on the porch until the storm had moderated sufficiently for them to go on.

Some of the other tourists also had narrow escapes. R. E. Olds was almost struck by a falling tree splintered by lightning not 20 feet away from him. And Mr. J. Sheridan's car was nearly wrecked when a bolt of lightning striking the road ahead threw all the party out of their seats. Only his presence of mind in clinging to the steering wheel saved them from going down a steep bank. One of the two baggage trucks which had left the Mount Washington Hotel hours ahead of the tourists stalled on a hill and completely blocked traffic until pushed over the top by a force of drenched but determined tourists.

Only two of the earliest cars to start reached Concord ahead of the downpour. The rest came straggling in during the afternoon, and even the passengers in the cars equipped with tops had not escaped a wetting, so fierce and blustering was the wind and so heavy the downpour. Others caught with the top down came in so saturated that they squished when they walked, and left puddles whenever they stopped for a moment. Their clothes were still wet the next morning when they started for Worcester, and they were all glad to see the last of New Hampshire.

Apparently the people of New Hampshire were equally glad to see them go. The Manchester *Union,* one of the influential papers of the state, regarded their visit as an "unmitigated nuisance" and an "outrage that ought to be stopped once and for all . . . If these people think of coming here another year we hope the law against speeding and scorching will be promptly and vigorously enforced. Let a few of them stay in jail two or three days and they and all the rest of us will be the better for it." Such was the hostility to the motorcar in 1905.

Even in Massachusetts the tourists found themselves fair game for the local constables who laid a trap for them in Leicester at the foot of a hill where speed was necessary to get up momentum to take them up the next grade. Eight of them were arrested and haled into court where they were fined $15 apiece. After court had adjourned the tourists decorated their cars with crape, and hired a band to lead them through the little town where the arrests had been made.

To the mournful strains of the "Dead March of Saul" the parade moved through the main street at 2 miles an hour, making a stop in front of the inn and another at the post of constable Quinn who had made the arrests. Just how this was going to help the development of the motorcar in America does not appear; but it made them all feel better and they enjoyed one of the finest days of driving on the entire tour as they traveled across the state largely over excellent macadam through Springfield, Westfield, and Lee to Lenox where they put up at the beautiful Aspinwall Hotel in the woods far above the town, and were stared at with disapproval by some of the most exclusive matriarchs in the whole of New England.

They completed the tour the next day, driving back to New York City over the roads of Connecticut which they found far inferior to those of Massachusetts, so rough in fact that one of the passengers was thrown clear of the car by a pitchhole and quite seriously hurt. After a rendezvous at Yonkers the caravan paraded back to the point of departure for a final check-in.

Only two of the original starters failed to finish—Mrs. Cuneo whose car eventually developed weaknesses from the damage received in the accident at Greenwich, and Mr. Hutchinson whose large foreign-made machine was disabled in an attempt to climb Mount Washington.

Quite a little time passed before the award of the trophy. The tour had ended as planned on July 22, but there was a vast amount of actuarial work to be done before the standings could be arrived at. Certificates of completion were issued to all who had finished the tour without disqualification. Seven of the contestants had perfect scores, though the names were not given out to the press; but when the contestants were given the opportunity to express their preference by voting, Percy Pierce was far ahead of them all with seventeen firsts. Augustus Post was second with seven votes, and Col. Albert L. Pope along with five others received three each.

Thereupon the committee awarded the trophy for the first Glidden Tour to Percy Pierce of the Buffalo Automobile Club.

For the 1906 Glidden Tour the committee in charge provided an international flavor by including a portion of Canada in the route. The tour was to start at Buffalo July 12 and make its daily runs as follows:

	Miles	Hours	Minutes
Buffalo to Auburn	135	7	52
Auburn to Utica	76	4	20
Utica to Saratoga Spa	95	5	34
Saratoga to Elizabethtown	94	5	54
Elizabethtown to Lake Champlain	37	2	29
Lake Champlain to Montreal	72	6	8
Montreal to Three Rivers	96	6	53
Three Rivers to Quebec	97	6	56
Quebec to Jackman, Maine	109	8	13
Jackman to Waterville	93	6	34
Waterville to Rangely Lakes	105	7	16
Rangely Lakes to Bretton Woods	124	8	37
Total Mileage	1,134		

Again the official observer was to be by-passed for the honor system. While the word "racing" had been avoided in the reports of the preceding tour, there had been a consistent amount of hurrying from one control to another so as to have time for minor repairs and replacements. However, it was thought that with short and frequent controls, even the hurry could be kept well in hand. But the new arrangement had exactly the opposite effect. Since all work on cars, even filling the tanks and lubricating, was required to be done after checking out of one station and before checking in at the next, the contestants made the distance in between with all possible speed, stopping just short of the in-station and working industriously until the exact moment for checking in.

Contestants found the ride eastward across the Empire State rather prosaic, with practically all the cars making a perfect score. The roads, though far from perfect, were wide and reasonably level, and as far as Saratoga could be covered at good speed. Soon after leaving the Spa, when the route began to follow the single-track wagon roads of the Adirondack foothills, the picture changed completely. Water bars and old well-developed pitchholes slowed down the speed, and with the infrequent turnouts the passing of a slow-going car ahead became a very hazardous adventure. The cars began to take a terrific beating; and since getting into controls ahead of time had become almost impossible, the perfect scores began to diminish. The tour that Mr. Glidden had hoped to make into a comfortable pleasure trip became more like a nightmare.

In spite of all the contestants could do, the penalties began to pile up, and to make matters worse they ran into an area of army maneuvers where the moving of heavy artillery and other equipment had broken down most of the small bridges on the regular route. To the Army, crushing a bridge presented simply an interesting problem that might take the engineers a day or two or even a week to solve. But to the Gliddenites it meant a detour over little used back roads many of which were mere trails that had never before been crossed by a rubber tire. Even the pilot and confetti cars frequently bogged down, ditched or disabled; and between the broken springs and twisted axles on the one hand and the disarranged schedules of the controls on the other, the morale of the caravan was at very low ebb.

Another matter which added considerably to the unrest of the tourists was the inadequacy of the hotel accommodations. This had begun to be felt at Auburn, the first night out, where the principal hotel in town had not been large enough to accommodate the 350 persons in the party, and it was found necessary to disperse them among second-rate hotels and even rooming houses. Naturally there had been wailing and gnashing of teeth, and muttering about favoritism. The burden of all this had fallen on Mr. Tucker, manager of the tour, who had nothing whatever to do with the making of advance reservations.

However, a good dinner at the Osborne House and a moonlight sail on Owasco Lake had done much to calm the ruffled feelings, and the commodious rooms and perfect appointments of the hotels in Saratoga had stilled the complaints. Here the tourists had spent a delightful week end, and after that came Elizabethtown.

Only a few of the cars arrived on schedule time, but under all the circumstances the schedules were adjusted fairly and equitably. However, there was no way to adjust the hotel accommodations. There simply was not enough room for the tourists, even with four or five cots in every room, and a number of them elected to sit on the porch all night where they greeted the late arrivals as they came limping in at all hours. Two of the more resourceful members of the tour went over to the county jail where an amiable sheriff booked them as vagrants for the night.

Spirits rebounded the next day when, after completing their repairs, they found fine roads all the way over to the Lake Champlain Hotel where they were again in the commodious surroundings of a de luxe summer caravansary. Once more the tour was riding on the crest of the wave. In Canada the roads were decidedly inferior but the hotel accommodations were excellent— with the exception of Three Rivers, where most of the tourists slept in the stuffy berths of a dilapidated steamboat on which, for a purse of fifty dollars, they bribed the captain to take them for an evening cruise several miles up the river.

At Jackman, Maine, the entire party slept in tents and some of the members carried out the illusion of roughing it by cooking their own meals. They spent the evening gathered around a large campfire, and since they were quite definitely camping out, nobody made any complaints about the hardness of the cots or the scarcity of blankets, though there was loud wailing over the excessive charges for sleeping outdoors.

In spite of all the accidents and breakdowns, the bad weather and the unspeakable roads, the caravan arrived at Bretton Woods exactly according to schedule. Sixty-five of the eighty cars starting from Buffalo completed the tour, with fifteen of the contestants still holding perfect scores. All were cheered and enlivened to be once more in so spacious an hostelry and among the luxuries and conveniences of the Mount Washington. The dress suits and evening gowns came out of the luggage, those who could dress for dinner did so, and the tour ended in a large and gala party.

Among those holding perfect scores was Percy Pierce, winner of the trophy the preceding year. The Contest Committee, basing their decision on the fact that nobody had beaten him, sidestepped a difficult situation by ruling that he should continue to hold the trophy for another year. Under the circumstances Mr. Glidden very generously awarded to all other perfect score holders handsome silver medals. The Deming Trophy offered to noncontestants went to C. W. Kelsey who had entered and driven one of the small Maxwells.

By this time it had become quite obvious that the rules and regulations under which the tour had been conducted were hopelessly inadequate. They had originally been copied from those of the Gold Cup contest in Italy and were not suited to American conditions. The replacement and rebuilding, even though done on running time, had been so excessive as to amount to unfairness to careful or fortunate drivers who had brought through their mounts intact or with only trifling adjustments. There had been cases where an entire rear axle assembly had been installed without penalty, and a number of new radiators had been put in, one by experts who had bragged of doing the job in ten minutes.

The rules for 1907 required that parts for replacement must be inventoried and carried from the start. And to stop the speeding a pacemaker was to be employed, the overtaking and passing of whom would result in disqualification. Another novelty in the rules was the provision that the trophy should be awarded only to a club and not to an individual member however meritorious his score might be.

In 1907 the tour was to start at Cleveland, go west as far as Chicago, and return to New York through Indianapolis, Pittsburgh, Baltimore, and Philadelphia. The new rules put the clubs on their mettle, and entries came pouring in from the larger organizations. Eleven were received from the New York club alone, nine from Cleveland, seven from Chicago, and five from Pittsburgh. The total number of entries enrolled at the start in Cleveland was eighty-one, among which were fourteen noncontestants who were going just for the ride.

The amiable Mr. Tucker was not among those present. After the recriminations and repercussions of the preceding tour it was thought best to place the tour under the management of the chairman of the touring board, Mr. F. B. Hower who, though not so agreeable as Mr. Tucker, was much more of a big shot and, as it turned out, much more inclined to be a martinet.

On the bright and sunny morning of July 10 the large caravan of motorcars went rolling out of Cleveland for the now familiar run to Chicago. Hotel accommodations for the tour were in the hands of Thomas Cook & Son who had been instructed to treat everybody alike and play no favorites. But even the admirable booking agency could not produce desirable rooms when there were none to produce. However, nobody was asked to sleep in a tent, or on a porch, or in a hard-bottom berth on a water-logged tub of a river boat.

The general attitude of people along the route was far more friendly than when the tourists had passed on their way to St. Louis. Indeed, the only evidence of hostility occurred in Cleveland where some miscreant had scattered nails and tacks in the street which flattened the tires of ten of the tourists before they were out of the city limits, and a carpenter working on a new house was caught in the act of tossing into the street a board through which he had driven scores of nails until it resembled the bed of spikes on which the religious zealots of the Far East are said to repose. This board was picked up by one of the tourists and carried away as a souvenir.

The vandalism, however, was more than offset by the pretty young Maryland belles who tossed bouquets of flowers into the cars of the tourists as they passed, or presented them with baskets of fruit and packages of sandwiches. Between Bedford Springs and Baltimore the tourists were more amused than annoyed by the eighteen toll gates encountered, with tolls running as low as two cents and as high as twenty-five. They enjoyed bantering with the toll takers who were usually women, and though nobody complained very much, the tolls paid for the entire party amounted to $174.60.

Quite a different kind of Southern hospitality was furnished by the Baltimore Automobile Club which had arranged free passage through all the Maryland counties traversed by the tourists where ordinarily a local automobile license would have been required.

From Philadelphia to New York the run was familiar and uneventful, except that in crossing the state of New Jersey they were frequently welcomed and treated to refreshments, some of them bottled and placed in buckets of ice, for it was a hot day. Every town of any size turned out to entertain them and made them feel that they were returning like conquering heroes.

After crossing the 23d Street Ferry they rendezvoused, formed a procession, and paraded back to the clubhouse where they were enthusiastically welcomed home and incidentally checked in.

The trophy for the third time went to the Pierces of Buffalo with a score of 981 points over the runner-up, the Pittsburgh Automobile Club with 977, a close squeak but still a victory for the hand-controlled Pierce Great Arrows equipped with no foot throttle.

On a tour which took in so much mountain country it was the brakes that showed most of the failures. The experts talked about enlarging them, cooling them, strengthening them, widening them—everything but the correct answer which was right before their eyes. The Berliet entry, equipped with four-wheel brakes, had no trouble at all on the long grades; it came down without smoking or slipping. It required no roadside adjustments and could always stop easily and quickly. And still nobody saw the significance; not a single manufacturer gave the four-wheel idea so much as a second look for almost a decade.

In 1908 the Glidden Tour again took off from Buffalo, the resting place of the trophy. The entry list was not so large as the year before, but, including the entries for the trophy donated by Mr. Hower, the caravan left Buffalo with seventy-five automobiles in line. The tourists started in a southerly direction, with Cambridge Springs as the first night control. Thence the route went to Pittsburgh, Harrisburg, Philadelphia, Albany, Boston,

Poland Springs, Rangely Lakes, and Bethlehem, and ended at
Saratoga Spa.

It was a wandering zig-zag course going nowhere in particular and still touching almost everywhere. The main lines of travel
were ignored as the route swung back and forth over mountain
ranges, along valleys, up hill and down dale, encountering every
kind of highway to be found convenient to overnight accommodation for so large a party which must have numbered at least
250 persons.

Once more the rules and regulations had been overhauled
and tightened for the purpose of making perfect scores harder to
get, and with Mr. Hower again at the helm the rules were rigidly
enforced. It had been expected that the new restrictions on replacements would pile up the penalties almost without end. But
either the cars had been greatly improved or the drivers were
more careful, for in spite of the very difficult course the caravan arrived at the Grand Union at Saratoga with so many perfect
scores as to be embarrassing. In the Glidden contest twenty-three
cars had come through without a penalty, and in the Hower
contest five received a perfect mark.

The club scores, however, were something else. Only three
of the clubs came through intact: Buffalo, of course, with three
Pierce Arrows; Columbus with three Peerless cars; and Chicago
with a mixed group of two Haynes cars and an Oldsmobile. A
suggestion that the winner be decided by tossing a coin was
promptly vetoed by Mr. Hower who ruled that there must
be a runoff.

An immediate objection was made by the Oldsmobile entry
who explained that he had previous engagements which could
not be broken or changed—and Hower promptly ruled that the
Oldsmobile withdrawal disqualified the Chicago club. Thereupon an observer divulged that one of the Pierce cars had failed
to account for a three-minute stop made to remove tire chains
and should have been charged with a penalty.

The Pierces loudly denied the charge and insisted that the
observer was a spy in the employ of business enemies. Mr.
Hower, who had been riding throughout the tour in one of the

Pierce cars, ruled against the observer and insisted that the runoff must go on. The Peerless cars indignantly refused, and Mr. Hower awarded the trophy to the Pierce team.

Mr. Henry May, president of the Pierce Company, accepted the award and declared his club the winner; but the raised eyebrows were a little too much for him and he belatedly announced that inasmuch as the dispute had arisen, he would allow the trophy to revert to Mr. Glidden, to be contested for the following year.

However, Mr. Hower's arbitrary decision was overruled by the Contest Board, and in the book of records of the AAA the winner of the Glidden Trophy for 1908 is entered as a tie between the Chicago club team and that of Columbus, Ohio.

Detroit was chosen as the take-off for the 1909 Glidden Tour, and though the entry list was one of the smallest in history the send-off was one of the most magnificent of all time. Only thirty cars were in the starting line-up, fourteen entered for the Glidden Trophy and sixteen for the Hower. With the exception of Mr. Charles Clifton's Pierces entered for each trophy, the entire list was mediocre, and curiously enough not a single make of car entered in either contest has survived to this day.

It may have been the distance—2,636 miles—that scared the entries away, and it may have been the route which passed through a sparsely inhabited part of the West. Leaving Detroit, the route cut across to Chicago, then swung up to Madison and Minneapolis; there it turned south to Fort Dodge, west to Denver, where it swung back to Kansas City for a terminus. From Fort Dodge on through the treeless country the caravan was accompanied by a special train of Pullman sleeping and dining cars for the accommodation of the tourists. Breakfast and dinner were eaten on the train, and box lunches were packed every day for refreshment along the way, since towns were few and far between. This service was most satisfactory and the charge of $7.50 a day per person was extremely reasonable. And when travel by motorcar became too hot, too dusty, and too monotonous for comfort, Mr. Hower and some of his assistants would travel by train instead of staying with the tour.

Again the Pierces were successful. They won both the Glidden and the Hower trophies. The special trophy donated by the Detroit club was won by the Chalmers-Detroit.

Motorwise, the year 1910 was a busy period for the AAA Contest Board. Dates for ninety-five contests of various sorts were on the schedule, with forty-three track meets, twenty-two reliability contests, fifteen road races, and numerous hill-climbing contests. And the Glidden Tour was now having its name changed to "National Tour for the Glidden Trophy."

For the Glidden event a route had been laid out starting at Cincinnati and going into the South by way of Louisville, Memphis, Little Rock, and Dallas where it was to turn north and proceed to Chicago through Wichita, Kansas City, Omaha, Des Moines, and Davenport. The distance had been clocked by the pathfinders at 2,850 miles, and the start was moved forward to June 15 in order to escape the hot summer weather.

But even with the romance of the Old South, the prospects of crossing the Mississippi River on a string of lumber barges, and a visit among the cattle ranches of Texas, the entry list for the National Tour was disappointingly small. The number was given out as "about three dozen" but it finally shook down to nearer two dozen, with only twelve starters in the Glidden division.

Mr. Hower, the stormy petrel of former tours, had dropped out. David Beecroft and Mr. S. M. Butler, chairman of the Contest Board, were in charge of the tour, with Secretary Ferguson as general factotum. The tour was off for a bad start with a fatal accident caused by a runaway horse. Some time later matters were enlivened by legal proceedings instituted by Max Parry, entrant of the Parry car, who sought an injunction en route against the officials for alleged prejudice in assessing penalties. The application was promptly thrown out of court and the Parry entries disqualified and forever disbarred from contests sponsored by the AAA. A suit brought by Premier at the end of the tour was also thrown out of court.

It was an undistinguished tour by little-known cars over indescribable roads. The Glidden Trophy was taken by the Chalmers, and a secondary trophy, donated by the Chicago club, was captured by the Moline.

This could easily have been the last of the Glidden Tours had not a wave of highway improvement swept over that part of the Southland lying between the Middle States and Florida. The interest was inspired and nurtured very largely by the distinguished governor of Georgia, the Honorable Hoke Smith. It was to be an affair of three-car club teams, and from Georgia alone ten of these teams were entered. Florida raised four, and various other states contributed one apiece until an entry list of sixty-four had been compiled.

Eventually a line of seventy-seven cars rolled out of New York, with a police escort to the city limits. Once again it was like the old days. Huge crowds gathered to watch the caravan pass. Towns all along the line strove to outdo each other with their hospitality. The prettiest girls were all out with their most charming smiles, strewing flowers and handing out presents of fruit and refreshments. The tour went along merrily until its final day—and then disaster struck.

Riding in the car with Referee and Mrs. P. G. Walker, Mr. Butler had just left Tipton, Georgia, when suddenly the car swerved off the road and upset, instantly killing him. The tour was halted, but it was decided that it must go on, for it was only a short distance from Jacksonville at which it was scheduled to end. So the caravan went on.

But all the gaiety had suddenly departed, and even the countryside had become dark and gloomy as the tourists felt their way along a rutted wagon road through the sands of the pine barrens. They had the sensation of being walled in by the overhanging trees from which the festoons of Spanish moss brushed the faces of the tourists as they passed.

As they went on, the clouds hung low, and just as they were about to enter Jacksonville the storm broke, releasing a deluge

which sent the crowd scampering for cover and seriously inter-
fered with the gala entertainment that had been planned for
the tourists.

The Maxwell team from Tarrytown came through with a
perfect score and captured the Glidden Trophy. Penalties incurred by a single car spoiled the perfect score of five of the
teams, the Ford among them on its first appearance as a Glidden
contender. And on a drawing for the Anderson Trophy, the
Maxwell of Governor Smith was the winner. Both the Pierce
cars entered in one of the Atlanta teams incurred penalties and
the period of Pierce supremacy was over.

Another tour into the deep South was planned for 1912,
but not enough entries were received to warrant going ahead.
The general impression at the time was that the Glidden Tour
was a thing of the past. But in 1913, with the aid of James J. Hill
of the Great Northern and the thriving automobile clubs of the
Twin Cities, a final fling was had at the great reliability tour.

The course, largely dictated by Mr. Hill, was to parallel the
tracks of the Great Northern for 1,245 miles across the rolling
wheatlands and the picturesque terrain of the Northwest and
terminate at Glacier National Park, Montana.

As on a previous occasion, the hotel accommodations for the
tourists were to travel along with them by means of one of the
magnificent transcontinental trains of the Great Northern, giving
the contest all the conveniences of a tour de luxe.

Of the twenty entries, sixteen were from Minnesota, and of
the sixteen, ten were from Minneapolis. Most of the cars were
little fellows carrying only two passengers. No Pierce cars were
entered, and the Glidden Trophy went to the Metz team from
Waltham, Massachusetts. The new AAA Trophy was won by
a Locomobile, and the Anderson Trophy by a Hupmobile—all
the prize winners, alas, having long since become extinct.

Thus ended the Glidden Tours, having fulfilled with honor
and great distinction the purpose for which they had been established.

On two different occasions I was fortunate enough to sit in

my own car by the roadside and watch the Glidden tourists go by. To my youthful eyes they had an enchanted appearance, as the Crusaders of old in quest of the Holy Sepulcher must have looked to the feudal yokelry. Another time I drove over the route taken by a previous Glidden caravan. I did not make a perfect score, though I might have if my radiator hadn't sprung a leak, and if one of my brake linings hadn't burned out.

But that trail of the Glidden Tour had given me a taste of the open road, and the curiosity of the trail blazer and pathfinder. I kept thinking about it all winter after I had put my car up on the jacks and stored my tires in a cool dry place in the cellar. And though I didn't know it at the time, there were some big doings ahead for me.

11 *The Vanderbilt Cup*

In the year 1904 most of the people in America thought the motorcar industry was booming. It was, and still there were those among our traveled folk who were greatly concerned because our automotive development was so far behind that of Europe. In our earliest races our cars had been able to run away from the foreign machines, but of late they were being completely outdistanced. This worried Mr. William K. Vanderbilt, Jr., who firmly believed that racing was the best proving ground on which the manufacturers could test the quality and merit of their product. Mr. Charles J. Glidden, on the other hand, was equally confident that speed was unimportant, and that the qualities most needed by the American motorcar were reliability, endurance, and touring comfort.

Neither of these gentlemen had any ax to grind. Neither had anything to sell. Both were loyal Americans greatly interested in motoring and ambitious for the successful development of the American motorcar; both were men of considerable means and each took the same method of establishing his point by offering a magnificent trophy to be won by competition.

Mr. Vanderbilt, it will be recalled, was among our earliest racers. He had driven in a number of European road contests in the days when a racing driver could wear a derby hat in a road race without exciting comment or having his hat blown away by his speed. In 1902 he had placed third in a Belgian contest, and in a time trial he had lowered the record for both the kilometer and the mile. He had hung up some beach records at Ormond, Florida, but he took no interest in cash prizes and had never been classed as a professional. He was, in fact, strictly an amateur and was often spoken of as a gentleman racer.

Though he was a member and a former vice-president of the bluestocking A.C.A., he established the race for his trophy under the sanction and sponsorship of the AAA. This could not have been a popular choice around the clubhouse of the A.C.A. which, as a club, was very jealous of its prerogatives. Being copied after the Automobile Club of France, it had from its inception cherished a longing to be the representative club for the whole of America, which, as we have seen, was an unfulfilled ambition.

It would have been quite possible for Mr. Vanderbilt to place the sanctioning authority of his trophy with the A.C.A., had he cared to do so. But Mr. Vanderbilt, for reasons of his own, preferred the AAA.

Just how openly the A.C.A. may have opposed the Vanderbilt road race is not definitely known; but there were other opponents who did not hesitate to express their views. Under the heading of "The Mad Moribund Race," Mr. E. P. Ingersoll wrote in *Horseless Age* a powerful three-column front-page editorial excoriating road racing in general and protesting violently against the use of the public roads of Long Island for a sporting event which he characterized as a detriment to the industry as well as a public nuisance. He scoffed at the waste of money used in building the great racing monsters described as a danger on the course and useless anywhere else; and he vilified road racing as tending to set up false standards and foster the speed craze which he branded as the bane of automobiling. Taking another slant, he condemned the state law for permitting certain sections of the public domain to be used for a useless and dangerous sport, declaring such laws to be not only ill-advised but unconstitutional. And he unctuously reeled off the death toll already claimed by the high-speed motorcar.

Opposition to the big race also simmered in the daily press, and quite naturally the clergy had their say about it, though they had some difficulty about tying in the element of sinfulness, as will be seen from the pulpit utterance of the Reverend Newell

Dwight Hillis, a Brooklyn divine with a flair for publicity. Said Parson Hillis in sermonizing about the race: "Oh, the degradation of such a scene! As foolish as a bullfight; as vulgar as reddening the sands in a gladiatorial contest; as revolting as bartering Christ's garments for a few pieces of silver." It is quite evident that he did not care for road racing, but he still did not charge it with being either sinful or illegal. However, he did get his name in the papers.

In the meantime, entries had been coming in steadily—six from France with some of the most famous cars and skillful drivers; four from Germany; two 90-horsepower Fiats from Italy with daring and colorful pilots. Five American cars came through the elimination trials, three of them White Steamers which failed at the last to be ready for the start. None of the foreign entries had less than 60 horsepower. Three of the Panhards, however, almost failed to make entry into the country because of some irregularity in the customs papers. The combined influence of Mr. Vanderbilt, the AAA, and eventually the diplomatic touch of the French Ambassador were required to get them to the starting line.

Mr. Vanderbilt was well aware of the opposition he had stirred up. He was probably amused by all the to-do. He had long since obtained the consent of the Board of Supervisors to set aside certain roads for the purposes of the race, and some three months in advance of the event he and his sponsors had caused to be posted along the roads of the course a notice which read as follows:

> An automobile race over a distance of between 250 and 300 miles will be held for the William K. Vanderbilt, Jr. cup on Saturday, October 8. The start will be at Westbury at daylight.
>
> All persons are warned against using the roads between the hours of 5 A.M. and 3 P.M.
>
> Officers will be stationed along the road to prevent accidents. The Board of Supervisors of Nassau County has set aside the following roads for the use of the racers on October 8.

Jericho Turnpike, from Queens to Plain Edge;

Massapequa Road, Jericho to Plain Edge;

Plain Edge Road (Bethpage Road), Plain Edge to Hempstead;

Fulton Street, Hempstead to Jamaica.

A reduced rate of speed will be maintained while passing through Hicksville. Three minutes will be allowed to pass through the village. Six minutes will be allowed to pass through Hempstead.

All persons are cautioned against allowing domestic animals or fowl to be at large. Children unattended should be kept off the roads. Chain your dog and lock up your fowl.

To avoid danger don't crowd into the road.   .

If, as has been said, there were "loud outcries from many quarters" upon the posting of this announcement, it may be stated with certainty that they did not come from car owners, car builders, or others interested in the development of the automobile. Nor did they come from the owners of taverns, hostelries, or other places of public resort and entertainment on Long Island. Curiously enough, one of the most indignant protests came from the determination of *The New York Times* to give "all the news that's fit to print." On October first, this distinguished journal printed the following commentary: "The farmers of Nassau County are asking what the common roads are for and who has the right to surrender them for purposes which put in jeopardy all who use them in a legitimate way for intercommunications and the movement of merchandise. To notify those who need to use the roads for purposes which are designed and maintained at public expense to keep off them on a certain day between the hours of 5 A.M. and 3 P.M. that the owners of road locomotives may run at dangerous speed is calculated to start an inquiry as to who has the right to thus devote public property to private use.

"It is to be regretted that those interested in promoting the development of the automobile have a talent for doing things to antagonize public opinion so bitterly."

The *Times* was evidently not familiar with the law under which the Supervisors were acting, for only four days before the race it carried another story in which it described the farmers on Long Island as being "embattled," and told how they had announced to their "unfaithful supervisors that it is their fixed intention to use the highways of the county for their lawful occasions in exactly the same way on the day set for the automobile race as on any other day . . . They also announce their intention of carrying firearms to protect themselves in case their lives should be menaced by the precipitate scorchers. The speed maniac while he is yet accessible to reason will probably pay heed to the warning of the farmers of Nassau."

But the *Times* seems to have been more riled than the farmers, for with all the talk and all the columns of newspaper comment and the thunder of press and pulpit the only serious attempt to stop the race was made by the Citizens Protective Association of Nassau County which presented to the Supervisors a written protest signed by 188 members out of the thousands of persons residing in the area.

The Supervisors responded by calling attention to the provision of the State Highway Law under which consent for the race had been granted. They called a public meeting and, after hearing both sides, refused to revoke their consent. Upon an appeal to the County Judge, the action of the Supervisors was approved and affirmed—and the race went on.

Precautions had been taken to make the course as safe as possible for both spectators and contestants. The roads had been scraped and oiled, and the AAA Racing Committee had, at the expense of the club, erected at Westbury near the start and finish line a grandstand seating 400—in all probability *The* Four Hundred. Boxes in the stand had been reserved by the club for President Teddy Roosevelt, Governor Odell, and Mayor McClellan.

Eligibility for the race was limited to American clubs recognized by the AAA, and European clubs accepted by the Automobile Club of France. The cup was a stupendous trophy nearly 1 yard in height, and was reputed to contain 481 ounces of sterling silver which by troy weight would amount to nearly 40 pounds. I have several times examined the vessel, though I was never able to look under the base for the word "Sterling," since the trophy was always in a glass case.

More than fifty breakfast parties had been scheduled at the Waldorf-Astoria for the day of the race, which was to start at six o'clock in the morning, though the roads of the area were to be closed to traffic after five. This meant that the breakfasters would have to be on their way soon after midnight if they were to reach the grandstand in time for the start, for it was quite obvious that the dirt roads leading out on the Island would be choked with the vehicles of spectators going out for the race. It was told afterwards that never before had so much champagne been served at a Waldorf breakfast.

The race officials, who had established headquarters at a Garden City hotel, went out the day before. That and every other hostelry on the Island was filled to suffocation, some of the patrons paying fabulous sums to sleep on army cots or even on couches or billiard tables. For with all the opposition that had been aroused, there was a general impression that there might never be another Vanderbilt Cup race, and if people ever wanted to see such a spectacle they had better take advantage of the present opportunity.

Hundreds, perhaps thousands, of people who were a little too late in leaving New York became so tangled in the traffic jam that they did not get within walking distance of the course until the race was nearly over; for instead of lasting until three o'clock, as planned, the race had to be called soon after midday because of the unruly conduct and riotous behavior of the great crowd of spectators numbering some 25,000 who came swarming out on the course, endangering not only their own life and limb but that of the race drivers as well. They resisted all attempts to hold them back, and after George Heath, an American resident of Paris, driving a 90-horsepower Panhard carrying the colors of France, had crossed the finish line closely followed by Albert Clement also of the French team—the racing authorities

Fifty years ago, it was not uncommon for club members to roll up their sleeves and repair roads in their neighborhood. Shown here in 1910 are members of the Lancaster (Pennsylvania) Automobile Club, working on a stretch of what is now the Lincoln Highway (U.S. 30).

The first AAA Emergency Road Service crew went into operation in 1915, in St. Louis under the sponsorship of the Automobile Club of Missouri. Today, through contracts with more than 19,000 service stations and garages, AAA clubs give emergency road service to millions of members.

Broken glass created a real menace to motorists' tires in those early days, too. Shown above is a member of the "broken glass crew" of the Automobile Club of Southern California clearing the street. Arrest and conviction of persons throwing glass in streets was rewarded by clubs.

Besides working for better roads, motor clubs early began battling for removal of tollgates. Tolls were virtually abandoned as a method of highway financing for a time, but since World War II toll roads have spread rapidly, providing fast, high-type but expensive expressways.

Dr. H. Nelson Jackson, authoritatively credited with being the first motorist to cross the United States, posed at the wheel of his Winton on completion of his two-month trip from San Francisco to New York in July, 1903. A Packard finished the cross-country trip that same year.

The roadside repair of a broken spring was a frequent occurrence to the early motorist. Above is the author somewhere on his transcontinental trip of 1912, removing a wheel to facilitate the change which by this time was an old story to him.

Here the author is seen keeping an appointment in the Nevada desert, made months before with A. L. Westgard (whose car is in foreground), who had strongly advised against burdening a transcontinental automobile with any unnecessary luggage.

This is what usually happened in 1912 when two cars happened to meet in the rutted trails of the cow country, an occurrence that was not likely to be repeated for several days. The talk was always about the bad roads ahead and how to avoid or worry through them.

decided that in the name of common safety the race must be called.

Heath had driven a fine race over a difficult course, making the 284.4 miles in five hours and twenty-six minutes at an average speed of 52.7 miles per hour.

Five cars, three of them American and two German, were running when Clement crossed the line. But when the word went out that the race had been called, the crowd did not even wait for the racers on the track to get back to the starting point, but hustled into their cars and started for home regardless of the racers who might come crashing into them at 70 miles an hour —and in no time at all the entire course was jammed with homeward-bound traffic.

Quite naturally the American entries, Pope-Toledo and Packard which were running in third and fourth place, were indignant at having the race called without giving them a chance to place. But with all the crowding out on the course to watch for the racers, the constant crossing from side to side, and the tossing of trinkets at the cars of the racers as they sped past, only one fatal accident marred the day's sport. Carl Menzel, mechanic for the Mercedes driven by George Arents, was crushed under the car and killed when Arents lost control while making a turn at high speed. Arents, though catapulted some distance, was not seriously hurt.

Lesser casualties were numerous, however, disabling ten out of the total of eighteen entries making the start. Werner (Mercedes) blew a cylinder. Tracy (Royal Tourist) broke his driving shaft and cracked a cylinder. Teste (Panhard) had clutch trouble. Arents (Mercedes), complete wreck. Gabriel (Panhard) broke pump chain and damaged engine. Webb (Pope Toledo) bent steering knuckle by smashing into a tree. Bernin (Renault), broken gear shaft. Wallace (Fiat), broken clutch spring. Sartori (Fiat), engine trouble, started two hours late—evidently an optimist. Tarte (Panhard), stopped by continuous tire trouble. Hawley (Mercedes) broke both front springs hitting hole in road while trying to pass another car. Did not get by.

The mechanical-minded saw in this race weaknesses in cars that should be corrected; but Mr. Ingersoll saw nothing in it that could serve any useful purpose. For *Horseless Age* he wrote a stinging editorial under the title of "The Fatal Cup" in which he called the contest "the bloodiest event of the kind since the ill-fated Paris-Madrid race of a year and a half ago."

The people of the Island saw something quite different. It was round, it had an eagle on one side and a portrait of the Goddess of Liberty on the other. The official name for it was the Almighty Dollar. They had found that spectators would pay almost any price for a good parking place and as much as $25 for the use of a bed overnight with a bite of breakfast in the early morning. Seats on a front porch along the course were at a premium. Sandwiches and apples were in great demand, and even toilet accommodations could be charged for.

Not another peep was heard out of the Citizens Protective Association of Nassau County, nor was there any more talk about the "embattled farmers" using firearms for any purpose at all—not even holding up the customers.

So far as the AAA was concerned, the contest was a smash hit, it was a sellout, and almost before the laggard members of the crowd had reached home, plans were under way for the *next* Vanderbilt Cup race, with the Automobile Club of France, present holder of the cup, as an ex-officio member of the Racing Committee.

The success of the first Vanderbilt Cup race seems to have aroused the whole country into a furor over automobile racing. Tracks were hurried to completion; sections of beach were staked out for time trials; hills were scraped and put in order for climbing contests; and manufacturers were building racing cars and training racing crews to man them.

It was a time of low prices. Newspapers for 1905 carried numerous advertisements of prime beef and sirloin steaks at 12½ cents a pound. Custom-made men's suits could be had for $15, and Stein-Block ready-mades ran from $10 to $30. Finest corsets, regularly $1.00, were being offered at 79 cents in the best department stores. Savings banks were begging for deposits at 3½–4 per cent interest. All-night Turkish baths were to be had in every town of any size. Men's fine shoes cost $5 and those for boys only $1.25. Women's tailored suits were going begging at $7.97 to $18.98. You could buy a quart bottle of pure malt whisky for $1, and an alarm clock to wake you up afterwards for 55 cents. Railroad fare anywhere was 2 cents a mile, and if you wanted to go by boat, about half that much.

Preparation for the second Vanderbilt Cup began early in the spring. With the consent of the Supervisors, the course had been considerably revised. Instead of the sharp corners of the year before, the drivers now had a U-turn to negotiate, several S-turns, and a hairpin that was enough to turn any man's hair gray, especially at 50 or 60 miles an hour.

Because of the traffic tangle of the year before, efforts were made to improve facilities for getting to the course. Additional roads were targeted with arrows; the Long Island Rail Road put on special trains leaving for the Vanderbilt Cup course at three and four o'clock in the morning. A large party of Bridgeport folk, enthusiastic over the Locomobile racer built in their town to be driven by Joe Tracy, chartered the steamer *Isabel* to take them to Oyster Bay so that they might approach the course by the back door, thus avoiding all traffic from the metropolitan area. It was a sound idea and would have been a success had they possessed the foresight to engage transportation to take them halfway across the Island to the scene of the race.

This little detail having been overlooked, they had to get there any way they could; and by the time that they had enlisted the aid of enough delivery trucks and hay wagons to transport the party, they had missed the most thrilling incidents and caught only a glimpse of the winners before the contenders were flagged off the course.

There was no uncertainty about this second Vanderbilt Cup race. All the best talent of the European racing fraternity was on hand. Heath was back with his 90-horsepower Panhard. Germany, determined not to be outdone, had sent over two 120-horsepower monsters and two little fellows of only 90-horsepower each—all—all Mercedes. France had sent over a famous speed artist named Duray with the most powerful machine in the race, a 130-horsepower giant. But it was not a race to be won by brute force alone. Skill was required, and courage, and not a little luck. Hemery of France walked off with first place with his 80-horsepower Darracq at a speed of 61.44 m.p.h., with George Heath, also driving for France, second, and Joe Tracy in his American-made Locomobile third. This was the first time America had won a place in the Vanderbilt. And the Vanderbilt was showing its class by lowering the record of the best Gordon Bennett race which up to now was only 51 m.p.h.

Lancia, Nazarro, Hemery, Wagner, Chevrolet, Duray, Szisz, Cedrino, Tracy—it sounds like a tournament of the giants shaking the earth and the heavens above as they battle for supremacy.

Most colorful of them all was Lancia, a giant of a man, swaggering and boastful, profane and jovial. Beyond peradventure the best showman of them all. He had a big 110-horsepower Fiat under him and he did not hesitate to let it out to capacity. He had the throttle down to the floor boards much of the time and drew cheers from the bloodthirsty crowd every time he went roaring past the stand. At the starting gun he shot into the lead, and by the end of the fourth lap he led the field by more than a quarter of an hour. His first 100 miles were clicked off at 72 miles per hour—but this was only one-third of the way home. All sorts of things could happen to him in 200 miles—and did.

First he was delayed by tire trouble. Then he had to stop to take on fuel. It was as he was leaving the fueling station that misfortune overtook him and involved him in an accident which cost him the race.

Anxious to be on his way, he started to pull out of the control when his mechanician saw Christie coming down the stretch wide open and thundering like a freight train; he bellowed at Lancia to stop. But Lancia never wavered. He was gunning up his mount to get sufficient momentum for the speedway. And Christie, never dreaming that Lancia would fail to hear the thunder of his exhaust and give him the right of way, made no move to change his course until it was too late. No car traveling at 70 or 80 miles per hour can be suddenly swerved without almost certainly going out of control—and the Christie struck the Fiat almost full in the back.

The Christie car turned a complete somersault, hurling the mechanician through the air as if he had been shot out of a cannon. The body turned slowly as it went sailing along and landed in a plowed field with no worse injury than a broken rib. Christie, thrown free, came out of it with only an injured leg; but his car—a strange-looking contraption designed by himself with a front-wheel drive and the engine set crosswise over the front axle—was a wreck.

For many months Christie had been going around from track to track, from beach to beach, wherever there was a race, always trying his best but never winning. Heretofore this car had been crashproof; it had been in a number of accidents but, built low like a bulldozer, it was not given to skidding and had never before overturned. This time it went end over end and landed a heap of junk.

As a favorite, Lancia's stock went rapidly down. Many onlookers charged him with recklessness; others thought he had wrecked Christie's car just to be smart or, as one writer put it, to "play rough." Lancia's explanation was that his own motor was roaring so loud under his acceleration that he did not hear the warning and had no idea that Christie was anywhere near.

Somehow, Lancia brought his car to a stop. It was not completely wrecked, though both rear wheels were smashed and had to be replaced. By the time he was back on the track he had lost a full hour and was in sixth place. He finished fourth, a long distance back of Tracy.

After the race was over, the course looked like a junk yard. Wrecked cars costing thousands of dollars to build were strewn along the road. Discarded tires, castoff oil cans and empty bottles cluttered the right of way along with paper bags, cardboard boxes and other litter from the thousands of picnic lunches eaten on the side of the road.

Both sides of the course were well populated during the race, though the greatest number had gathered at the dangerous corners where the crowds became so large and so unmanageable that it was impossible to keep them off the course. Many climbed up into the trees which, after a little, began to resemble a human rookery. The crowd was greatest as well as most dense at Albertson's Corners where three telephone poles along a serpentine turn were most promising of smashups and bloodshed. Here the plain-clothes deputies were unable to control the crowds at all.

On his fourth round Foxhall Keene slammed into one of the poles, wrecking the car but tossing the occupants into the clear. The wreck had hardly been dragged aside before Joe Tracy came roaring along at high speed, took a gigantic skid, missed the same pole by a foot, straightened his mount, and went roaring on down the course at top speed.

One of the strangest accidents of the day occurred when Lytle's mechanician was thrown out and lost in the shrubbery while the car was going over a rough section of road through the woods. Lytle never even slowed down until he reached the pits where he reported the accident and took on a new mechanician. Mr. Vanderbilt quickly collected a doctor and took him to the woods to look after the injured man.

Another strange accident happened to one of the German entries which lost its main gasoline tank and had to drop out. And Louis Chevrolet, with his rare gift for doing the impossible, while driving at high speed on Willis Avenue, grazed a pole which deflected him into a fence, a large section of which he carried with him into a field where his axle was broken by striking a projecting boulder. Lytle, while trying to dodge a dog, missed a turn and drove into the crowd, miraculously avoiding all the people but eventually striking the dog.

With the second successful running of the Vanderbilt Cup the contest had become the most popular and most fashionable of our sporting events. It quickly took a place in public esteem akin to that of the World Series at the present time, only the Vanderbilt had a bluestocking flavor that baseball, being of the people, never could have. The big cup race smacked of the smart set, the Four Hundred, the polo field—and it wore the Vanderbilt trade-mark.

Broadway, always alert for the latest fad, quickly caught the idea, turned it into a musical called "The Vanderbilt Cup Race." With Elsie Janis as the star, it packed the theater for two opulent years while road companies were gathering in the shekels from the sticks. And by the time the musical had run its course, the Vanderbilt Cup was a fixture.

For the 1906 contest a much more sizable grandstand had been built and the course had been greatly improved by the addition of several new and more difficult curves, along with the inclusion of two fairly steep hills. And by this time the most noted aces both in this country and abroad were vying for places on the starting line of the Vanderbilt, and the early morning of October 5 saw seventeen of them drawn up in their places and ready to go.

Profiting by the experience of other years, spectators were starting early. They began leaving New York by midafternoon. They took any kind of transportation that promised to land them at or near the course. By six o'clock traffic had begun thickening on the main roads and soon it was headlight to taillight all the way. A newspaper observer with an interest in statistics estimated that nearly $50,000,000 worth of motorcars were gathered within a 10-mile circle around the grandstand, and that a quarter of a million people were lining the course to watch the spectacle and the speed and the carnage.

Promptly at six o'clock Le Blon, a Frenchman with a black spade beard, led off with an American-made Thomas Flyer. The others followed at the usual intervals, but hardly was the last car out of sight when word came that a man had been killed at Krug's Corner where the Hotchkiss driven by Elliot Shepard, W. K. Vanderbilt's cousin, had gone out of control and charged into the surging crowd. At almost the same moment at another part of the course, Tracy's Locomobile had gone into a skid as he was rounding a turn and plowed into the unrestrained crowd, tossing two onlookers like an angry bull and breaking a boy's leg.

Tracy did not even stop. He wrenched his mount back onto the road and sped on to the grandstand where he begged officials to keep spectators off the road—which with a quarter of a million frenzied onlookers was obviously impossible. There were a number of other accidents but no more fatalities. Two had been killed in the elimination trials and an innocent bystander was mowed down in the big traffic jam on the highway.

It was, however, a sorry day for American cars and drivers. Of the five American entries, not one placed, though all were still running when the race was called. Tracy had run the fastest lap of the day. That was all.

Again the French were first, with Wagner on the Darracq. Lancia came in second, and Duray third, closely followed by Clement and Jenatzy.

The sponsors, and indeed all the contest officials, were dismayed at the size and conduct of the crowd. More than 20,000 spectators were jammed around Krug's Corner alone, and over 7,000 at the U-turn. All were thrilled and excited, and eager for sensational developments. They probably did not hope that anybody would be killed, or terribly maimed or mangled—but if such a terrible thing should happen they did not want to miss it. They wanted to be in a position to see, and they did not hesitate to smash down barriers and fences in order to get into an advantageous if extremely hazardous position.

It was rumored that the race would be moved farther down the Island and held on a privately owned course where admission could be charged for every spectator, and the conduct of onlookers could be strictly regulated and controlled. However, the plan failed, and in 1907 the most popular sporting event in the world was allowed to languish because of the inability to secure proper policing of the crowds.

Strong pressure had been put on Governor Charles Evans Hughes to furnish military protection for the course; but being an individual without the slightest interest in sports of any kind, the governor had refused, citing an array of authorities to sustain his position. And the AAA having publicly announced that no future road race would be held over the public highways of the Island without military protection, the month of October, 1907, was very dull for the inhabitants of Long Island and all others having occasion to go there.

In the meantime Mr. Vanderbilt had been busying himself with the promotion and construction of a concrete motor speedway on the Island in which the New York Central and other moneyed interests were reputed to have some participation. By the spring of 1908 more than 10 miles of the Motor Parkway had been completed, and since it was the first concrete road in the country, people used to drive out just to see it. For one dollar a visitor could take his car on the Parkway and stay as long as he wished. It was well protected with strong wire fencing so that there would be no cheating.

I paid my dollar and drove through the gate. It was like a motorist's heaven. Roadway smooth as a ballroom floor. No speed limit. No grade crossings. No motor cops. No dust, no mud, no pitchholes, no bumps. In a dream I drove as far as it was finished, and went back and forth several times. This would be something to tell my children, if I ever had any.

The news went around and more motorists drove out to visit the Parkway. Rumors began to be heard that this was to be the new course for the Vanderbilt Cup race. Whether that was originally intended or not I would not know, but the records show early AAA cooperation with the project; and demands for a renewal of the famous race became so urgent and so insistent that the donor and the sponsor decided to give it another trial.

As laid out, the new course covered a 10-mile section of the Motor Parkway which, with portions of the Jericho Turnpike and other public roads, made a circuit of 23.46 miles. The required distance for the race was eleven laps. As had been predicted, it turned out to be a fast course and the race was won by George Robertson, an American driver in an American car at a speed of 64.3 miles per hour, the fastest time yet made in the Vanderbilt. Robertson drove the same 120-horsepower Locomobile driven by Tracy in the preceding Vanderbilt classic.

Herbert Lytle in an Isotta-Fraschini came in second, some two minutes behind Robertson.

Out of a field of sixteen entries with six foreign cars and ten of American make, two Locomobiles and a Waterless Knox finished in the first division along with the Isotta and a Mercedes. It was an immensely popular victory and gave to the automotive industry of America an impelling forward thrust as it went careening on to the colossal success it has since achieved.

The management had made arrangements to have the course well patrolled, as they thought, by a regiment of Irish Volunteers assisted by a large force of Pinkertons. This was believed to be sufficient to keep the crowds in order, and probably would have been except for an unfortunate time lag. Nobody seems to have explained to the constabulary that the spectators would be arriving all night; and by the time the patrol had arrived between five and six in the morning, the huge crowd, estimated to number over a quarter of a million, was already out of hand, especially on the part of the course which was being run over the county highways. To a large extent, the vandals had spared the barriers along the Motor Parkway, but they were just getting their courage up to the point of tearing down a mile or two of the Parkway fencing when the Pinkertons moved in and put a stop to the fun.

Along the public parts of the course, however, the constabulary had all they could do to open a wide enough lane in the crowd to let the racers go through. There were many close calls, but luckily not a spectator was injured. Nor were there any more serious casualties among the drivers than happened to Foxhall Keene when his Mercedes cracked a cylinder directly in his face and squirted him with steam and hot water. He was not seriously burned—but was his face red!

Naturally there were the usual number of minor mishaps, clutches burning out, ignition trouble, flat tires, and gears that failed to stand up. Strang's 100-horsepower Renault conked out just before reaching the starting line and had to be pushed across to qualify. He managed to get it started after half an hour but withdrew after limping around for three laps.

As usual, the crowds swept out on the course as soon as the race was called, and the only collision of the day occurred when the White Steamer of a spectator in a hurry to get home was rammed by one of the racers who did not realize that the contest was over.

After the running of the third Vanderbilt, a rivalry between the AAA and the A.C.A. that had long been simmering came to a boil. The A.C.A. found it somewhat embarrassing to have the AAA operating just outside the city limits with such a world-shaking success as the Vanderbilt; so after strengthening its ties with some of the big European automobile clubs, the A.C.A. made the triumphant announcement of an international trophy to be known as the Grand Prize to be competed for annually in this country. Quite obviously the trophy was patterned after the most famous of the French races known as the Grand Prix, though it was to be managed in the Vanderbilt manner.

Long Island not being available for the new contest, it was inaugurated at Savannah, Georgia, in 1908, where it was run with some success a month after the Vanderbilt. The Grand Prize was a good-enough contest, but it lacked the excitement, the romance, the all-night entertainment, the unruly crowds, and the socialite flavor of Long Island.

In 1909 the policy of the Vanderbilt Cup management was completely changed. Contests of the giant racing contrivances having been pretty thoroughly tried out, it was decided that to be of real benefit to the everyday motorist on the road the Vanderbilt should be run as a stock-car race, strictly stock—in the AAA interpretation of the term—no others being eligible.

The entries were divided into three classes according to price. Sixteen were in the top flight, four in the medium, and six in the low-price range. Only the higher-price cars were in competition for the Vanderbilt Cup, the medium division running for what was called the Wheatley Hills Sweepstakes, and the lower price for the Massapequa.

Among the sixteen cars competing for the Vanderbilt Cup,

five were of foreign make—three Fiats, a Mercedes, and an Isotta—all strictly stock.

The course, almost entirely along the Motor Parkway, consisted of twenty-two laps around a 12.7-mile triangle. It was won by Harry Grant in an Alco built by the American Locomotive Company. Grant sent his car around the course at a merry clip, winning at 62.7 miles per hour, which was not at all bad for a stock job. The big crowds were there but they seemed overawed in the well-protected precincts of the Motor Parkway; and only along the short stretches of the course which were run over the public highways did they make any attempt to take things into their own hands.

Grant won again in 1910 with the same Alco car, and he raised his speed to 65.18 miles per hour, the record for the life of the course. It could not be said on this occasion, as had been said the year before, that the Vanderbilt Cup was losing its flavor. There was a feeling abroad that this was to be the last appearance of the famous cup race on the Island, and all who had never gone to one wanted to go, along with those who had been before and wanted to go again. Never before or since had there been such a crowd at an automobile race—and this time they did not intend to be overawed into behaving themselves. They went prepared with wrecking bars and wire cutters, determined to have one final orgy of fun, frolic, deviltry, and destruction before the famous trophy went into Cain's Warehouse, the museum, the attic, or wherever it is that 40-pound trophies go after they have served their purpose.

It was the maddest of the Vanderbilts, the most thrilling, the most destructive—the most wonderful, and the most unforgettable. I know, for I was there.

My friend John and I left the Algonquin Hotel at ten o'clock the night before and went to the Brooklyn Bridge which we thought would be less crowded than the new Queensboro Bridge or any of the ferries. Without any standing in line we crossed in a slow-moving procession of horse-drawn vehicles which, to our delight, fell away soon after we had emerged from the bridge.

When we had reached Metropolitan Avenue we found ourselves in a line of motorcars, and at every corner we were joined by still more motorcars. For a while we went along in a single line, then two abreast. After that we were three abreast, sometimes even four—and woe betide the vehicle which tried to go the other way. There were vegetable trucks and farm wagons stranded in almost every driveway.

As soon as we were off the city pavements, the dust began to be noticeable—then bothersome—and after a little, quite unpleasant. Had the traffic been able to move with any speed, the dust would have been intolerable. But from the time we reached the dirt roads we were never able to go over 8 or 10 miles an hour, stopping often where the roads narrowed, or to pull around some unfortunate motorist who was having tire trouble.

There was a fine camaraderie about the caravan of pleasure seekers. Everyone seemed to be in a jolly humor, all out to have some fun and determined to make the best of any emergencies of the road. There was bound to be some scraping of fenders, but nobody took any offense. And once on a sudden stoppage of the line, when the car behind banged into us rather forcibly, a very agreeable gentleman came forward and handed me his card, saying that if I found later that any damage had been done he would gladly take care of it.

Though it was the first day of October, the weather was extremely mild and nearly all the cars had their tops folded down, which contributed greatly to the conversational possibilities with people in other cars and the opportunities for getting acquainted. An extra girl in one of the nearby cars accepted our invitation to come over and ride with us, and we found her very charming company for several miles. She was a pretty girl and had a lovely voice. She told me she was studying for the concert stage where, as I learned afterward from letters I received from her, she met with great success.

With the long lines of cars behind, ahead, and on both sides of us, our progress along the roads was almost as well lighted as if we had been riding along a brilliantly illuminated boulevard. Occasionally we would hear singing in one car or another, and there was some playing on harmonicas and other musical instruments; practically all the time there was gay banter passing back and forth.

Our charming visitor remained with us until we were stopped at the entrance to the parking lot behind the grandstand, and fearing that her car and ours might be widely separated in the parking lot which was not too well lighted, she left us. But to our delight after we were parked we found her party was located right behind us. There was much visiting back and forth, and her brother-in-law and sister with whom she had come had a plentiful supply of drinkables in a built-in cooler installed where the folding seats were usually to be found in the big seven-passenger touring Packard. There was also a well-filled picnic hamper. We contributed the refreshments the Algonquin had packed for us—and a pleasant time was had by all.

As the night was changing slowly into morning, the weather turned colder, and we pooled our robes and all crowded into the Packard where we awaited the sound of the bugle to summon us to the grandstand. The morning mists were still hanging over the surrounding fields when we climbed the many steps into the stand. Cars were already roaring and barking and thundering and smoking as they took their positions back of the starting line tier upon tier, each row moving forward as the row in front moved out. And somewhat to my surprise I discovered that the start is the most exciting part of a road race, for it is the only time when all the cars are seen together. A road race almost never ends in a neck-and-neck sprint for the tape. The finish is a solitary affair—a car comes roaring down the stretch and is waved off by a checkered flag. It is the winner. Another car may not come along for two or three minutes. It's a rather tame ending for such a vicious fight.

With a field of thirty in the Vanderbilt alone, in addition to the light-car entries, the racers had to be sent off only fifteen seconds apart instead of the usual interval of sixty seconds; for with a course of only 12 miles, the big fellows would be coming around under full speed in less than twelve minutes. The fact was that twenty out of the thirty made it in a little over eleven minutes, and Louis Chevrolet came past in his Buick in only 10.46, practically on the heels of the last car to get away.

After they were once started, the cars began to go past in great confusion. Big cars, little cars, medium-size cars—it was a mystery to me how the checkers could keep track of them. The race was only minutes old when word came that Harold Stone's car had leaped from the Meadowbrook Bridge and killed his mechanician. Shortly afterwards I saw the victim's wife being led from the stand.

After watching the cars go by for an hour or more, my companion and I concluded that the grandstand was a poor place from which to see any of the real excitement that was going on. Accidents were reported by megaphone from time to time, but they came in as prosaically as election returns. We had come out there to see things, so we quietly left the grandstand and went some distance down the course on an exploring trip. We found the fields dotted with tents where early comers had spent the night; but by this time the crowds were tiring of looking through or over the fences and were tearing the barriers down so that they could get out on the course for a better view.

Once more the constabulary was helpless, and it was largely in trying to avoid spectators on the roadway, especially at the turns, that most of the wrecks occurred. The story of the race reads like the account of a railroad disaster: two killed in the race, two slaughtered in traffic; twenty in hospitals, some trampled, some crushed, and some with minor injuries like broken arms and legs, cracked ribs and torn ears. And after the race was over, miles of the Motor Parkway looked as if it had been traversed by Sherman's march to the sea.

Half a million people had enjoyed their fun, and the curtain had come down on the world's greatest sporting event. The real Vanderbilt Cup race was over, finished, through. Henceforth it would be a road company barnstorming in the tall timbers. To the old-timers, the passing of the Vanderbilt was like the death of a hero.

The rivalry between the Vanderbilt and the Grand Prize

continued even after the Vanderbilt had deserted Long Island, with the Grand Prize never quite able to vie with the Vanderbilt in either popularity or prestige. In 1911, at Savannah, the Vanderbilt and the Grand Prize were run over the same course, though on different days. Always the Vanderbilt attracted the best of talent, but away from the home course its color, its character, and its social flair were lacking. There was apparently no substitute for Long Island and, followed by the Grand Prize, the Vanderbilt kept moving around. One year at Savannah, the next at Milwaukee, then it went out to the West Coast. It was run at Santa Monica with great success, and the following year it thrilled San Francisco at the Panama-Pacific Exposition.

The eleventh and last Vanderbilt went back to Santa Monica in 1916. This was a Peugeot year, with Dario Resta. He won a double victory, taking both the Vanderbilt and the Grand Prize trophies, and after the season was over both cups were withdrawn from competition.

With the passing of the Grand Prize the interest of the A.C.A. in racing sponsorship faded rapidly. Rivalry with the AAA ceased. Indeed, it was the beginning of the end for the A.C.A., which eventually disbanded and was supplanted by the Automobile Club of New York. The Triple A, however, went on in its accustomed way serving the motorist and, through him, the public with the unswerving fidelity and honesty that has been its policy from the beginning. It has seen motorcar racing almost all through its career, from its faltering days when victory was more likely to go to the car that could hang together to the end rather than to the speediest. It has seen the speed of the winners rise from 12 or 15 miles per hour on a dirt track to nearly 130 miles per hour on the Indianapolis Speedway, and over 394 miles per hour on the Bonneville Course in Utah, the fastest mile ever traveled by man on the surface of the earth —all of which it has sponsored and timed to the fraction of a second.

In the famous Chicago race before the days of official timers, the race was tabulated by some as taking as long as ten hours and twenty-three minutes and by others as seven hours and fifty-three minutes, the difference being accounted for by time occupied by the driver in hunting up machine shops in which to repair his car. There were no such discrepancies in the timing or management of the Vanderbilt contests with the AAA in charge—and it was entirely under AAA sponsorship that the great Long Island cup race became famous.

Mr. Vanderbilt had set out with the idea of proving and improving the American automobile in the laboratory of speed, and during the eleven years that his cup was in competition he had seen the American car develop from a fair example of self-propelled vehicle into a swift, powerful, reliable form of road transportation that was, in addition, handsome to look at, safe and comfortable to ride in, and easy to drive. Where the Vanderbilt races left off, speedway racing took over, and together they have brought many improvements directly attributable to the laboratory of speed.

Because of automobile racing, every owner is driving a better car, a faster car, a safer car. The motorist is indebted to the race track for all the following improvements:

Knee action	Lower radiators
Streamlining	High-speed engines
Four-wheel brakes	Better shock absorbers
Balanced crankshafts	Aluminum pistons
Improved bearings	Longer lasting sparkplugs

Balloon tires were first proved on the speedway, and the rear-view mirror was devised in 1911 at Indianapolis so that Ray Harroun could see behind him at 90 miles an hour.

Many things we need to know for the safety of our cars cannot be learned even at the speeds we drive when the law is not looking. They can be learned only at speeds our passenger cars could never make and we would never dare to use—up where the stresses are terrific, where wear is swift, and the ability to hold the car on the road is a matter of life or death.

If we are to get the answers, somebody has to go that fast.

The trained racing driver does it, and the AAA Contest Board not only checks and records the results with unimpeachable accuracy, but employs every known device and practice to make the driver as safe as possible during the hazardous task he is performing for the ultimate benefit of the driver of the passenger car.

12 *Growing Pains*

The Selden-Ford Patent case came like an evil genie out of a bottle and cast a dark pall over the motoring picture. It brought hatred and ill will into the world. It divided a great industry into two armed camps. In eight years of bitter strife it piled up over thirty large volumes of testimony, and cost the country untold thousands of dollars for the maintenance of its judicial machinery. What it must have cost the litigants in attorneys' fees and other expenditures connected with the trial is just nobody's business. And all for what? So that one group of men could extract from another royalties enough for a king's ransom simply because a foresighted patent lawyer had obtained a government grant on an invention which he never carried any further than some rough drawings on a piece of paper.

That Henry Ford happened to be the one to bear the brunt of it was a mere accident. After the patent enforcement had begun, and manufacturers (in about the same spirit with which we all pay our income taxes) were joining the licensed ranks and tossing in their ante, Henry Ford was ready to submit. He thereupon put in an application to join. If he had been accepted, there would have been no patent litigation. But enemies on the inside blackballed Henry and refused to take him in.

Henry was not a man to forgive a slight; and when the Seldenites came around a little later to admit they had made a mistake, Henry slammed the door in their faces. So it was not, after all, a patent suit so much as a case of spite.

During the eight years of bitterness the position of Henry Ford in the industry changed completely. From an inexperienced inventor who had twice failed in an attempt to establish

143

himself in the automobile business, he had become the greatest
of them all. Instead of an insolvent bungler, described by his
enemies as a crackpot with fly-by-night leanings, he was on his
way to become the richest man in the world.

When the Selden papers were served on him in 1903, Henry
Ford was a nobody. His name meant nothing at all inside the
trade or out. The man of ordinary means did not even know
who he was. It was not until 1905 that he became front-page
news because of a tag he had hung on a four-cylinder roadster at
an automobile show in the Grand Central Palace in New York.
The tag quoted a price of $500.

I did not happen to go to the show that year, but I remember
the occasion very distinctly because of the number of persons who
stopped me on the street the next day or came into my office to
ask me if I really believed there was anything to that $500 car.
The reason they came to me was because I was one of the two
motorcar owners in my town at the time.

That day might well have been celebrated as the birthday of
the so-called "low-price market," for practically all these inquiries came from low-income people, factory employees, artisans, persons who worked with their hands and who never before
had dreamed of becoming motorists; for at that time the price
of the average car was around $2,137.56 according to later
statisticians. Not one of those who came to me could have swung
a deal of much over five hundred dollars. Most of them were
living from hand to mouth, as was usual with the laboring man
at that time with earnings from ten to fifteen dollars a week. The
worker who drew down twenty-five was a rare exception.

I referred them all to the local bicycle-repair shop which was
the nearest thing we had to a garage. The bicycle man told me
later that although he had not heard from his telegram asking
for the Ford agency, he had taken more than twenty orders for
the $500 Ford car during the day.

Of course the Ford Company was flooded with orders. Customers had had to wait months for their cars and many of the
orders from small outlets were carried over to the following
year. Not many people now remember the Model N by that

name, since it was so closely followed by the world-famous Model T. Just another case of a distinguished sire being completely overshadowed by a much more illustrious son. Who, for example, remembers the first name of Teddy Roosevelt's father? Practically nobody.

The Model N, though it brought Ford more orders than he could handle, also brought him something far more valuable— the backing and loyalty of the masses. People who previously had never heard of him now took his side and began rooting for him. Never before was a litigation so played up by the press. The automobile was becoming extremely popular, and the litigation made wonderful newspaper copy. And since I was practicing law at the time, my opinion was often asked about some development of the case. Curiously enough, all these inquiries seemed to be coming from the five-hundred-dollar class—and without exception they wanted Henry to win.

When the final decision came in 1911 I happened to be in New York where I had attended both the Garden and the Palace shows. The split decision—granting to Selden assurance of the patent's validity, and to Ford the judgment of the court exculpating him of infringement—came like the judgment of a Solomon, leaving neither side any lingering desire to appeal the case, especially since the patent had only two years longer to run.

I returned home on the night train, arriving soon after eight in the morning, and as I was walking toward my office, suitcase in hand, I was stopped by various persons who had something to say about the decision. Their comments were mostly felicitous and congratulatory, as if between us we had somehow managed to win the case. One or two of them asked me if I thought there would be any further appeal; and when I told them it was my opinion that both sides were glad to have the matter settled, they seemed well satisfied.

By this time some of them had already become motorists, and others were saving up to get a car now that they were reasonably sure the low-priced cars would continue to be on the market. Why they should have thought otherwise was never quite clear to me. When told that the royalty on a Ford car would have amounted to only five dollars, many people thought the expensive litigation ill-advised. However, when one stops to think that there were years when Ford production ran above two million cars, it will be seen that the total could have run into quite an interesting figure.

For all his peculiarities, Henry Ford had a strong appeal for the common man. Once Henry had made up his mind to concentrate on the low-price market, he handled his campaign with skill and understanding. The simplicity of his own beginnings may have given him a common bond with the man who worked with his sleeves rolled up. He seemed to know what would appeal to the man of small means. Instead of reducing the price of his car with one smashing cut, he preferred to reduce it a little year by year. This looked as if he were making a real effort to economize, saving a little here and a little there without lowering the quality of his product. A slam-bang reduction might look as if he had merely decided to put in cheaper material.

When the Selden interests were threatening suit against every purchaser of a Ford car, the offer by Ford to furnish an indemnity bond with every car sold was a very popular move. And the fact that, with the thousands of cars he was selling annually, only fifty purchasers ever asked for a bond was mute evidence of the motorist's confidence that Henry would take care of him.

Ford's twenty-year hold on the motorist of small means was little short of phenomenal. The Model T had been on the market for only three years when W. C. Durant came out with the Chevrolet for the avowed purpose of capturing the low-price field from Ford. The name Durant was at the time something to be reckoned with. Starting with a two-wheeled cart, he had switched to the motorcar, eventually organizing General Motors and building it into the greatest motorcar company in the world. That he had overreached himself was neither here nor there. He had once gone to the top and could do it again, and the fact that he had trained his sights on Ford might well have caused a lesser man to say his prayers and keep his powder dry. But if Ford was worried, he certainly did not show it. He made no change whatever in his decision to concentrate all his manufacturing energies on the Model T.

Durant made a magnificent success of Chevrolet. He built it into one of the wonder cars of the day—without making so much as a dent on the upward swing of the Model T. Using the Chevrolet as a lever, Durant freed General Motors from the voting trust and then continued his campaign to win the man of modest means away from Ford. On two occasions he came close to making a deal to buy out Ford. But in the end he became a victim of his dreams of glory, losing both Chevrolet and General Motors.

By this time the country had gone through World War I and was in the throes of readjustment. Pierre duPont was now president of General Motors, with Alfred P. Sloan as his right-hand man. For a while there was a question whether Chevrolet would go on at all, so firmly was Ford entrenched in the low-price market. That it did go on was a tribute to the judgment of Mr. Sloan, who was loath to surrender the low-price market to Ford, or to anybody, without a struggle.

It so happened that at just this time William S. Knudsen had left the Ford Company, and General Motors put him at the head of Chevrolet. Marvin E. Coyle who had long been with the corporation was brought in as comptroller, and together Knudsen and Coyle went to work to put Chevrolet over the top. They correctly read the cards and were not long in coming to a decision that there had been a very considerable improvement in the taste of purchasers. Now that the days of uncertainty were over and cars would run, there was a demand for the appearance of more class, and Ford was not giving it to them. Instead, all he was giving them was the same old Model T.

So Chevrolet began piling on the improvements, keeping up every year with the more expensive cars and putting special emphasis on eye appeal. They never could quite meet Ford's low price, but they were selling their cars fully equipped, while Ford's list price included nothing but the car—not even the floor mats. Chevrolet was not the only competition to the Ford.

Numerous other makers were nibbling at the low-price market from all sides. Then, too, there was the secondhand market to cope with; and dealers who had to take in used cars in order to sell new ones were inclined to slaughter the used car prices just to get rid of them. And the question of installment selling was in the offing.

At the beginning it was necessary for the purchaser to pay cash for his car. The finance companies, though quite ready to handle the paper for installment sales of sewing machines, pianos, farm equipment, and many other consumer items, for some peculiar reason of their own turned thumbs down on automobiles —perhaps because a car was regarded as an extravagance. There may have been some private financing of installment buying, but it was on a small scale until 1914 when a Ford agency in New York City began to advertise new Ford cars for sale upon a payment of $200 down and the balance in monthly payments of $50 with interest at 6 per cent. This led the way, and soon the finance companies were taking all the automobile paper they could get. About the only reference a prospective purchaser needed was the assurance that he held a job.

During the next decade the finance companies flourished like the green bay tree until in number they had passed one thousand and were well on their way to a second thousand. By this time they had taken the installment business into their own hands and were showing the unfortunate installment buyer no mercy. It was when the AAA had let in some light after a two-year investigation that government regulation came to the rescue of the man who signed on the dotted line.

There is no doubt, however, that installment buying played a large part in expanding the business of the entire industry during this period which had come through a war, a psychological depression, an inflation, and the perils of a restoration from a wartime standard to one of peace.

But through it all the Model T kept rolling off the line, still painted any color so long as it was black, and carrying the same old features with which it had been keeping production up and prices down. In the meantime the Chevrolet had kept piling on improvements and increasing its production until it was well up into six figures. And time went marching on through the eight years of Woodrow Wilson, the two years of Warren G. Harding, and well into the elective term of Calvin Coolidge. It was, in fact, halfway through the year 1927 when Ford finally came to realize that the Model T could no longer stand the pace, but it took a production loss of 350,000 in a single year to open his eyes, while Chevrolet production went thundering ahead.

When Ford decided on a change he took no half measures, but shut down his plant in mid-year for a complete retooling. He came back the following season with the Model A, a trim little four-cylinder with many up-to-date improvements; but by that time Chevrolet had gone on to a six. Ford countered with the V-8 and for a single year regained the lead, after which Chevrolet, under the management of Coyle, dominated the low-price market until World War II put an end to civilian production.

Since the war there has been no low-price market to fight for. All prices having gone soaring up to double the prewar list, with some that were in the middle bracket—$1,500 to $1,800—now approaching the $4,000 mark. And with commodity prices still going up, the end is not yet. The man of small means now buys in the secondhand market, where guarantees comparable to those on new cars are available. Only the jalopies and hot rods are now bought on the "as is" basis.

It will be a long time, however, before the Model T is forgotten. One is occasionally seen chugging along the road— and why not? For there has been sold to the motorist of small means, since its appearance in 1909, the staggering number of 15,000,000 Model T's. Placed bumper to bumper, these cars would encircle the earth, leaving a gap not much longer than the distance between Boston and New York.

Nearly every motorist who was old enough to drive a car between 1909 and 1929 has memories of the Model T. It was the Tin Lizzie of song and story. It had family traits as readily recognizable as if they had been handed down *per stirpes*. More than any other car, the Model T brought ownership within reach of the average American family.

It never was a thing of beauty, but it would take you there and bring you back. It made no pretensions of being silent or smooth riding. The planetary gears would scream like a hyena in starting, and if you happened to use the reverse as a brake the car would buck like a bronco. The mechanism was simple, and every man was his own mechanic. If the gas line clogged, you'd take up the front seat, remove the cap, and blow a mighty blast into the tank. This might leave a ring of dirt around your mouth, but it would clear the line. Starting the motor was a problem. Tickle the carburetor, hold the choke wire at exactly the right spot—a hair's breadth either way would spoil the combination. Draw a long breath and hold it—this was supposed to protect you in case of a backfire. Then give a sudden yank on the starting crank. This had to be done just so. It wasn't a pull or a push —it was rather a flip or a flirt. You had to take the engine by surprise—make a quick delivery—and then step back out of reach. Cranking was something that had to be learned by long practice, for it was a fine art like a sinker or a knuckle ball. Some people never could learn it, and had to save up $150 to buy a self-starter.

The Model T was seldom stuck in a mudhole; but I once saw a teamster rescue a lady doctor by reaching down from his perch and seizing hold of the back of the seat. One mighty tug —and she went on her way. With all the cars that have come and gone, nothing has ever taken the place of the Model T, and probably nothing ever will. It was light and strong and had a wheel base of only 100 inches which enabled it to turn in a 12-foot circle. You could find room to park it almost anywhere, and it weighed only a little over 1,000 pounds. Steering on the left was popularized by the Model T.

Innovations came almost every year, but the Model T disregarded them all. The closed body was seen in 1910 and the electric self-starter in 1911. The metal body appeared in 1912. Forced oiling arrived in 1913 and the steering-wheel horn button the following year. The windshield wiper and the stop light came in 1916, and the rumble seat soon afterward. Hydraulic brakes were seen in 1921, though they did not reach all four wheels until two years later. Balloon tires were introduced in 1922, thereby reducing tire pressures from 60 pounds to 30. By the middle twenties closed bodies and hot-water heaters were regular equipment on most of the other cars, but the drivers of the Model T had to get along with side curtains and cold feet. It was not long after this that Henry laid his greatest masterpiece gently away in moth balls. It had been through an epic career, something that never can happen again.

Motoring in America had been making gigantic strides during the two decades of the Model T. Horsepower had been steadily increasing. Speed and comfort had been developed to an unbelievable extent. But perhaps the greatest change of all was in reliability. Cars would go, and keep on going, with a minimum of care. The owner had from thirty to sixty oilholes and grease cups to fill every Sunday morning. He had to be sure of his oil level, and that there was gasoline in the tank. By this time the foot rule had been discarded and was replaced by a gauge—but the gauge was on the tank, not yet on the dashboard—and the gasoline station was as easy to find as a cigar store.

The time had passed when the motorist in need of gasoline had to hunt up a hardware or grocery store when he wanted to fill his tank. More than once I had to go to a cleaning establishment for gas, and in one town the popcorn stand was the only place where it could be bought. However, the bicycle repairman soon began to carry a supply, usually in a drum out behind his shop, from which he drew it into a 1-gallon measure of which the motorist was likely to lose count. He used to talk learnedly about seventy gas or eighty gas, though what he put in your tank was likely to be sixty. With the coming of the high-compression engine and the call for ethyl gas, the bicycle repairman had opened a garage or a filling station, or perhaps was working for one of the oil companies.

Another cause that led the motorist to the door of the bicycle shop was tire trouble. From the time of the invention of the first pneumatic tire, the task of keeping the air inside had been exacting and perpetual. Probably nine-tenths of the bicycle repairman's job had to do with tire trouble. Bicycle tires were bad enough, but at least they were easy to handle. The big tough tires of the motorcar were something else. The bicycle man had to furnish his place with adequate implements, including vulcanizing equipment.

At first, motorcar tires had to be repaired without removing the rims from the car, for they were built integral with the wheels. In those old days the fenders were not particularly in the way. They were small and flat, usually stuck on the ends of rods somewhat like a pancake turner. Since buggies had been built without fenders, they were regarded as more decorative than necessary. Some car builders did not even include them as part of the regular equipment, and charged extra for them when ordered.

Removable rims were available as far back as 1904, but they were regarded as unsafe and were several years in coming into general use. The car in which I crossed the continent in 1912, though strictly up to date in most respects, was equipped with standard clincher rims which would hold a tire, when well rusted in place, as if it had been welded to the rim. A half-hour's work with a sledge hammer was required to loosen the bead sufficiently even to insert a tire iron under it. I finally secured a tire fork called the Atlas which expedited my labors to such an extent that, with any luck, I could change the average tire in slightly less than an hour. Of course the time required to pump it up was extra.

My earliest tires seldom lasted over 1,000 miles, and it was several years before I had one that gave a mileage of 3,000; and the cost of a tire was between fifty and sixty dollars. Much later I had a set of tires which lasted throughout World War II, all of them running up a mileage of over 30,000 before replacement. Not bad, one might say.

13 *The Lincoln Highway*

It was in 1903 when Tom Fetch succeeded in coaxing his one-lung Packard, "Old Pacific," from San Francisco to New York in fifty-two days. The exploit was a promotion stunt backed by the factory and carried out by professional drivers and mechanics. At the time, there was no transcontinental highway to follow. Indeed part of the way there was no highway at all. I obtained a copy of the Packard booklet describing the jaunt and was greatly thrilled by the exploit. Though I had no car at the time, I could imagine myself taking that trip, and when I managed to get a used two-cylinder Rambler a couple of years later I immediately began to take long exploring trips, often 15 and 20 miles away from home over strange roads. Gradually I worked up to 50 miles. Then with a great surge of courage and recklessness I planned a tour of over one hundred miles—to be exact, it was to be a trip to Buffalo, a distance of 112 miles. I chose Buffalo because the Poppenberg Rambler agency was located there, and I was sure the car would be in need of repairs if I should ever get that far.

I made the entire distance in a single day. Four times we were delayed by tire trouble, and once by a broken fender support which was mended in a blacksmith shop at Leroy, a place well known as the home of Allen's Foot-Ease. The blacksmith charged me fifteen cents for welding it. A little later I limped into Batavia with the engine missing badly, or "skipping," as it was then called. The man at a bicycle shop suggested a new set of dry cells which, he said, had solved the difficulties of another car only a few days before. He installed a new set, six of them, and we drove on to Buffalo without any further trouble, except

153

that the driving chain came off once. I had a chain tool in my kit and soon had it back on again. The entire trip had taken us less than twelve hours, and we felt that it was quite an accomplishment.

The following year I bought a secondhand Packard. This was a four-cylinder car and a beauty. With it I made a tour of New England covering 1,000 miles, and had my name reported in a New York paper as registering at this hotel or that with a Packard. While on the way home we computed our mileage as we were leaving Syracuse and discovered that if we went straight home our tour would fall about 30 miles short of a thousand; so we rambled around western New York until we had built the extra mileage by a safe margin. The local bicycle repairman had jotted down our odometer reading as we were leaving home, so we had official proof.

A year or two later we made a tour to Canada and felt that we were really becoming seasoned tourists. Later on we made another jaunt through New England, going by way of the Cherry Valley Turnpike so we would have experience on the hills, and we became so roadwise that after leaving Albany we went over to Bonnyriggs Four Corners and tackled a famous hill called Jacob's Ladder. We went down with our brakes red hot, and crawled up with our radiator boiling and gurgling. But it was worth the trouble, for we felt that we were now ready for almost anything.

It was not until 1912 that I ever heard of the Lincoln Highway. Articles about the project began to appear in the newspapers and magazines, only at first it was called the "Coast-to-Coast Rock Highway." A man named Carl Fisher seemed to be the prime mover. He was identified as the man who originated the Indianapolis Speedway, and I hoped that he would be as successful with his highway as with his race track.

I had met Robert Bruce of the AAA at the Automobile Show in January and through him had become a member of the Association. When along in the spring of 1912 I had a well-developed case of transcontinental fever I wrote to Bruce and asked him if he thought a motor trip from New York to San Francisco was at the time possible for a private owner without the backing of an automobile company.

He wrote me quite an enthusiastic letter on the subject and referred me to A. L. Westgard, the pathfinder for the Association, who, he said, had traveled all over the West in a car. Westgard was quite encouraging. He wrote that he thought I would find the trip a very enjoyable adventure if I was fond of changing tires and digging a car out of sand pits and mud holes. He warned me, however, that west of Omaha I would find the roads very informal, signboards about 1,000 miles apart, water as scarce as gasoline, and no bridges across streams under 50 feet in width. He also called my attention to the fact that there was no such thing as a road map for the country west of Chicago.

In response to my inquiry as to the route of the Lincoln Highway, he said that it had not yet been decided, but would probably follow the general route of the Union Pacific Railway. He also informed me that he was leaving shortly for a long path-finding trip and added that if I was starting for the West Coast in July as I had planned, I might meet him somewhere on the road between Cheyenne and Reno.

He advised me not to load the car down with a lot of non-sense, and to ship a supply trunk ahead from one large city to another. West of Cheyenne, he said, I should carry enough food and water for the party to last three days, and that I should always have an extra five gallons of gasoline for emergencies. He gave me the name of a garageman in Cheyenne to consult about emergency equipment for the rest of the journey.

We left New York on July 13, 1912, in a six-cylinder, 40-horsepower Matheson car. The party consisted of myself and wife and an unmarried couple. We were all good friends and we stayed that way. As far as Buffalo the road was familiar to us, but from that point on we were traveling uncharted seas though we had the Blue Book to help us as far as Cleveland. The weather was hot, and though we had started off with new rubber we had experienced several flat tires in getting as far as Buffalo. Between Buffalo and Cleveland we spent most of our time finding our way around detours, of which we had been warned by a notice on the blackboard at the Buffalo Automobile Club. The country was becoming quite road-conscious and of course they had to do their repairing in the summertime. Another complication was that there was so little touring at the time that nobody had thought of marking the detours, and not even the main roads for that matter. Our general rule was to follow the telegraph and telephone poles—if any.

We eventually entered Cleveland from the southwest and put the car in the Church Garage on Euclid Avenue, a former house of worship which had been crowded out by the inroads of business. The stained glass windows were still in place and the choir loft was used for the storage of tires and other ungodly supplies. We had our tanks filled in the vestry room, the gasoline being poured in from a gallon measure. Since we had a 25-gallon tank, this operation took some watching.

The hot weather stayed with us through to Chicago, and we were so confused by the detours in getting into the city that I would not have been a bit surprised to find out that we had turned up in Milwaukee or St. Paul. We rested a day in Chicago, and I invested in two extra springs and a few other spare parts much to the disgust of the others who thought the stuff would just be in the way.

On leaving Chicago we were delighted with the black gumbo roads which were smooth and hard and absolutely stoneless. We kept raving about them for at least 50 miles before we were caught in the rain—then suddenly our beautiful black roads became the most treacherous, slippery, and dangerous highway on the face of the earth. After a terrific skid which turned us around and headed us in the wrong direction, I climbed angrily out to put on the chains—and the minute my feet touched that black mud I found myself flat on my back. I fell down again before I could even get back on my feet, and I had to stay on my knees most of the time I spent putting on the chains.

We could see a town off in the distance and though we did not even know its name we were perfectly sure it was where we were going to spend the night. When I found that the name was Ottawa I thought for a moment that we had somehow gotten

The author could not resist patronizing this popular gathering place of cowhands in a small town in Nebraska, where he ordered a shave, a haircut, and a ham sandwich with "must'ard," all of which were quickly and expertly furnished.

Bureau of Public Roads

Steam shovel at work on rough grading, Linnville, Ohio, 1914. Spurred by increasing demand from all sides, counties and states began work on adequate roads for motor travel. It was not until after passage of the Federal Aid to Highways Act in 1916, though, that the program boomed.

With the development of more and better highways for the motorist in the twenties, "touring fever" hit the nation, and more and more people hit the open road in their free time. This family carried their roof with them—a large tent which sheltered both automobile and family.

That's a Model T Ford parked at an early gas station in the Ozark Hills, near Hogan, Missouri, in 1927. Gas pumps in those days were set up so the motorist could keep an eye on fuel outlay. Many of the 15,000,000 Model Ts produced from 1909 to 1927 are still on the road.

As in those early days, the AAA today sanctions and supervises major racing events and other automotive contests. Here tightly bunched racers get off to a fast start in the classic Indianapolis "500" race.

Every day of the year, field reporters roam the nation's highways checking road conditions, improvements, new construction, and other information useful to club counselors in routing members on trips.

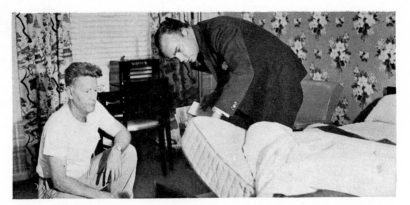

A fleet of National Touring Bureau field reporters also regularly inspects thousands of tourist accommodations and other facilities along the American highways. Because of rigid standards, only a relatively small portion of them qualify to display the "AAA Recommended" emblem.

In the National Touring Bureau Map Department, veteran map makers prepare up-to-the-minute touring materials. Here a cartographer works from a field reporter's notes and rough sketch in preparing a typical Triptik. Small drawings spot points of interest along the route.

into Canada. Then in the city park I saw a statue of Honest Abe.

I had hardly finished signing my name in the hotel register before the clerk asked me if my party had any connection with the Lincoln Highway. When I replied that we were a private party touring for pleasure, he seemed disappointed.

"Oh—I thought you might be connected with the Highway," he said. "This is a great Lincoln town, you know—one of the Lincoln-Douglas debates was held here. This place is really famous."

"Will the Lincoln Highway be routed through here?" I asked.

"Yes, sir!" he answered emphatically. "They couldn't get along without us. We're one of the anchor points."

"That's fine," I said. "I didn't know the route had been decided. I was told in New York that west of Pittsburgh the route was just a line of red ink."

He nodded his head wisely and plunged the pen into a bowl of shot. "That's what they think in New York—but out here *we know*."

"I'm glad to find that out," I said. "Where does it go from here?"

He narrowed his eyes and spoke slowly. "Davenport—Des Moines—Omaha—and Denver. That much is settled. After that it's anybody's fight."

That was good news to me, for it was the route we were planning to follow. I rather liked the idea of being in one of the first parties to go over the new highway—even before it was built. By morning the gumbo roads were dry but very rough where the ironshod wheels had cut down into the mud. Big hardened chunks the size of a brick kept flying up and banging into the fenders. One of these struck a head lamp and dented it.

When I got out to examine the damage I noticed that the trunk rack was dangling. The rough roads had broken one of the supports. While we were strapping up the trunk so that we would not lose it, I discovered that one of the spring clips was cracked and about ready to go. We drove carefully to the next town where we saw a blacksmith shop.

As we stopped in front, the smith came out in his leathern apron. He looked at our damage and said he could fix it if we would wait until he had finished shoeing a team of mules. We quickly decided to wait. The others sat in the car but I went inside to watch him shoe the mules. The mules were restless and after I had stood around for a few minutes he handed me a switcher made of a horse's tail and asked me to keep the flies away from the mule he was working on.

The acrid smell of the forge and the stench of the burning hoofs as he fitted the shoes reminded me of John Kane's blacksmith shop that I used to pass every day in going to and from school in the little western New York town where I was born. Those smells of memory—how they last. He was longer at the shoeing job than he had expected, and by the time he was through with the mules he had to go home to dinner. To a blacksmith, dinner is far more important than a little repair job, and though he was apologetic about going, he went just the same.

When he returned, he mended the trunk rack very quickly, but he shook his head when I showed one of my reserve spring clips. "No good," he muttered. "Not for these roads." He took down a pair from a nail on the wall. "These'll last you all the way to Californy."

He charged fifteen cents each for a pair of spring clips and two bits for the labor. We thanked him and went on as he rumbled something about wishing us good luck. Apart from the roads, it was a gracious countryside, flat and fertile, the fields waving with golden grain as far as the eye could reach. Once when I stopped to ask the way, I complimented a farmer on the height of his corn. He glanced up at it and smiled.

"Only ten foot," he said. "Wait till you get into Ioway. They won't cut it if it's less'n fourteen foot high. Ain't you heared their song?"

I hadn't at the time, but I heard it enough later on. As we drew up in front of the hotel in Davenport we were debating what to do with the dog which up to that point had not been well received at the hotels. I had suggested to my wife that she tuck the dog under her arm and brace right into the elevator, when a man stepped out of the group looking over our car and equipment.

"That won't be necessary," he said, reaching out to pat the dog. "I run this hotel and any dog is welcome so long as he behaves himself."

I talked with him later about the Lincoln Highway but he seemed a little skeptical about its going through Davenport. He said that every town of any size west of the Mississippi was fighting for it, and over in Indiana the town of Linton had offered to change its name to Lincoln if they would route the highway through it.

When I asked him if he knew where I could get a road map he said I would not need one and told me about the River to River Road which went straight across the state from Davenport to Omaha and was very easy to follow because of the handsome markings painted on the telephone poles. I had visions of a hard-surfaced highway, but when we began to follow the emblems the next morning, I found it to be an ordinary country road in a high state of neglect which had obviously been named and labeled to attract the attention of the Lincoln Highway authorities.

I also discovered that there was a competitive road which had banded the poles with white and was calling itself the White Pole Road. And later on we came across a road with yellow bands on the poles. These were the only road signs we saw until we were well into California.

The roughness of the River to River Road was almost our undoing. We had not gone many miles along it before everything on the car had begun to rattle, and jingle, and thump. Every little while we would stop and get out with wrenches to tighten everything that was loose—and nearly everything was. Even the spark plug connections came loose and the gas line clogged up with sediment that had been stirred from its resting place.

We finally decided to move over to another road, and just after dark while we were on an obscure and little used crossroad we ran out of gasoline—and at that time were not carrying any extra supply. Since we did not know exactly where we were, we sat and waited for over an hour before an elderly couple came along with a horse and buggy. They promised to send a garage hand out from Kellogg, 5 miles away, with a couple of gallons. Two hours passed before he came; but he excused the delay on the ground that he played in the band and could not leave until the concert was over.

Late at night we came to a town where all the roads were being resurfaced, and in the maze of detours we lost our sense of direction entirely. There was no light in any of the houses, no watchman, no policeman, nothing. Then we heard a railroad train go through and hunted up the station. The signs were there —Davenport one way, Des Moines the other. We reestablished our sense of direction and went on; but the small hours had begun to grow large before we reached the Hotel Chamberlain in Des Moines and tumbled into bed.

Westgard had told me to be on the lookout for Robert Carson in Iowa City who would be able to help me with road reports. Carson hailed me from the sidewalk as we drove into town. He had no road map but he had made a little sketch of the best route to Council Bluffs, and he also gave me a list of road mileages between towns nearly all the way to California which he had compiled from tourists and travelers. This list proved to be a lifesaver and saved us from being lured by the bright sunshine to go on later in the afternoon than we should, for the desert is a very poor place to be stuck overnight.

I had often heard of the "place where the West begins," but Carson was the only person I ever met who had the spot marked. It was, he said, at the white line in the middle of the bridge across the Missouri River between Council Bluffs and Omaha.

"When you cross that line," he said, "you'll be in the West." And it was even so.

Never until I had passed that line did anybody mention such a thing as a butte; and the first time anybody did I began to look around for a pretty girl. In the East, people will talk about a hill, a cliff, a crag, perhaps a promontory—and most of them don't even know that the word butte rhymes with fruit. Over and over again I was told to go to a butte and turn right or left. Once in Nevada we drove until nightfall in getting to a red butte which had been pointed out to us at about noonday. Don't say it—that's what one of the girls said, "It's a butte."

We were continually surprised at the number of cars we saw on the roads all the way to Chicago. They were less numerous but still plentiful between Chicago and Omaha. But after Omaha the cars thinned out and the horse-drawn vehicles began to take over. The first filling station that we saw was in a suburb of Chicago. It occupied a vacant lot where you could drive in for gasoline and oil. They had the first gasoline pump we had seen since leaving Cleveland. Motorists seemed to be wary of the pump and preferred to see their gasoline drawn from a drum and poured in from a measure. Gasoline cars equipped with a pump and trundled by hand were seen in many of the garages.

At this time motorized trucks had not come into general use though the manufacturers were working on them. This left all the heavy hauling in the cities as well as on the farms to be done by horses and mules, and all the farm implements were animal-drawn. It was after we left Omaha that we noticed practically all the horses we met were afraid of our car. By the time we had left Kearney, Nebraska, we were very definitely in the horse country and, to my surprise, the mule country. I had supposed that the mule was peculiar to Missouri and the South but we saw them on the business end of a large part of the farming implements all through Iowa and Nebraska.

If we had dropped down out of the sky it would have been very difficult for us to tell whether we were in Iowa or eastern Nebraska, so neat and prosperous-looking are the farms with the white well-painted houses and big red barns. But with all the fine farms and beautiful cultivation we found the roads outside the towns casual and neglected. Weeds and deep ruts were almost universal, and we were constantly seeing puddles the size of cow ponds, and were all too often bogged down in them until pulled out by a friendly farmer who chanced to come along. The farmers were always willing to help, almost too willing, and they refused curtly my offers to pay. We were several times pulled out by cowboys, but that was after we had passed North Platte where the big cattle ranches seemed to begin.

Gradually the character of the country changed. Farms were farther and farther apart. There was less plowland and more grass. And the time came when we discovered that there were no more farms—all cattle ranches. It was here that we met a car from California, battered and mud-stained. We stopped and talked together reporting the conditions we had come through. We both sounded rather pessimistic, but we took pictures of each other and went doggedly on hoping for the best.

It was not long after we had passed this car that we got our first good look at all outdoors. I think there must be more of it in Nebraska than almost anywhere else. You don't see much of it in the eastern part of the state, for while much of the land is as flat as a ballroom floor and very roomy, the trees and buildings interrupt any distant view. We had just splashed through the mud holes at a place called Big Springs when we ran up a longish grade and came out on the top of a tableland where for the first time we found ourselves on the plains—the western prairies of song and story.

As I looked all around and saw nothing but space—and so much of it—a feeling of loneliness came over me. Without realizing what I was doing I stopped the car and shut off the engine. For a time nobody spoke. Then one of the girls asked, "Doesn't anybody live here?"

The fact is that somebody does, only they live so far away they're not visible to the naked eye. You couldn't see a tree or a house, not anywhere. Not even a steer at that particular moment. It's a strange purifying experience to be surrounded by so much of nothing at all. Nothing good, nothing bad. Nobody to tell you what to do or not to do. No law, no Ten Commandments, no speed limits. Nothing to look forward to, nothing to look back on. No past, no present, no time. Nothing—just nothing at all. It was like being in the midst of eternity.

Nobody threw any adjectives around. We hardly said a word. And the silence of the great open spaces is so still that you can positively hear it. I listened intently for the music of the spheres, the whispering of the stars that are passing overhead in the daytime, the swishing of the planets through the immeasurable nothingness—but I couldn't hear a thing.

All of a sudden something moved, and there before our eyes was an antelope. It seemed to have materialized from thin air. But it must have come up over one of the invisible rises. It didn't seem to be scared, but it certainly was surprised to see us, and it just as certainly wasn't glad. And the next thing we knew it wasn't there any more. With a flirt of its tail it was gone. That tail was a giveaway. Otherwise it might have been an illusion. But an illusion doesn't flirt its tail. That was the real thing—it was an antelope.

Gradually we all came down to earth. So this was Nebraska. We glanced down at the rich dark loamy soil. How that beautiful soil would grow things—but what terrible roads it made. Until reaching the plains I had entertained the notion that a road was a common path or way along which people traveled to go from one place to another; but we had now reached a part of the world where every man was free to strike out for himself. If you found the ruts too deep or too dusty you simply made some new ones to suit your own ideas.

In dry weather that beautiful rich soil turned to dust which rolled along in clouds. In wet weather it became a brown liquid resembling bean soup into which the wheels of a car would sink softly down until firmly anchored. Whenever there were fences, they were set back from the roads a couple of hundred feet, except at the boundary lines, where a big ranch the size of a state adjoined a little one no bigger than a county. When we came to one of these, we found a gate across the road, which had to be opened and closed. It said so right on the gate. And some days we would open and close dozens of these gates.

It was not long after this that the distant tops of the Rocky Mountains were showing above the horizon like far-off sentinels. Some just a dark lump and others wearing a jaunty cap of snow. But once we had seen them we were never able to shake them off until we had reached our journey's end.

The drive across the vast tableland was delightful. The grass was a brilliant green from the recent rains, and the sky when we started was a deep blue. But as we went along, the clouds began to pile up ahead of us. We had been hearing at every little town rumors of bridges washed away on the Denver road, and when we came to the fork that led to Cheyenne, we stopped for a consultation. We were told that we could get to Cheyenne without any trouble, but we wanted to go to Denver since our supply trunk was waiting there. However, we did not want to become involved in any washed-out roads, and if there was any danger of further rain we thought it might be better to go to Cheyenne and take a train down to Denver.

We were still vacillating when a ranch hand came along in a high box wagon driving a pair of mules that were quite obviously afraid of our car. Here was a chance to get a bit of advice from a native who ought to know the signs, and, although he was giving us a wide berth, I motioned to him to stop and went over to talk to him. He, too, had heard of the washouts and said they must be pretty bad. But when I finally asked him if it was going to rain he gave me a dubious look.

"Young fellow," he said, "if I could tell you *that*—do you think I'd be drivin' mules for a livin'?"

We took the right-hand fork and went to Cheyenne. As we sped along over the beautiful rolling country we could see flashes of lightning in the direction of the Denver road, and we could hear some mighty peals of thunder; but we arrived in Cheyenne dry shod and put up at the Plains, a beautiful modern hotel commanding a view of a hundred miles in all directions.

Leaving the car in Cheyenne, we took the train and spent a day or two visiting Denver and Colorado Springs. We repacked the trunk and expressed it to Ogden, and returned to Cheyenne to equip for our journey across the Bad Lands.

Then I remembered that Westgard had given me the name of a man to consult about equipment, and the first three articles he ordered were an ax, a shovel, and a coffeepot. Next he insisted upon two large desert water bags and enough canned food to last the party at least three days. When he asked about firearms,

I showed him our rifle. He looked it over and said it would do. These were the necessaries. Among the comforts he suggested a blanket apiece, a block and tackle with 100 feet of rope, a small crowbar (with which to pry down the pan under the engine), and a couple of oak planks the size of our running boards. He said we could split these up for firewood if we did not need them, but we used them over and over again.

While I was at the garage, a car arrived which had been four weeks coming from Los Angeles. The driver told me it was hard work but lots of fun. But when he spoke about a broken axle, a flywheel knocked off by a high center, a smashed wheel, and a twisted steering knuckle I began to feel a little nervous. He went on to say that they had been towed a number of times and were once hauled from a ditch beside the railroad by a work-train derrick. When I asked what the fun was, he explained that they had shot several rattlesnakes, two coyotes, and a badger.

He warned me repeatedly not to take the south side of Great Salt Lake and I immediately decided to take the northern route. It would have been better if I had waited for later reports, but I had made up my mind and it never occurred to me that I could change it.

A blue sky lured us out of Cheyenne, but we had not gone more than 20 miles before the rain came pouring down, and soon we were stuck in a huge puddle. There wasn't a human habitation in miles and miles, and as I was taking off my shoes and stockings to wade to shore and see what was to be done about our predicament, a Mitchell car occupied by a handsome young couple came along and stopped just behind us. The driver showed a friendly interest and finally asked me if I had a rope.

When I showed him the block and tackle he smiled and began to take off his shoes and stockings. We found out afterward that he was in the "monumental business" and was right at home with a rope and pulley. He hauled us out of that puddle in a hurry, and then with all of us pushing we managed to get both cars around the puddle and went on our way, followed by our new friends who had introduced themselves as Mr. and Mrs. Roy Bloom of Omaha.

Laramie, where we all spent the night at the Kuster House, turned out to be a charming frontier town. The streets had the pleasant odor of saddle leather and beer, there being six saloons in a single block. Cayuses and cars were parked side by side along the streets. The town newspapers were the *Branding Iron* and the *Boomerang*. A slab of steak that you couldn't cover with a ten-gallon hat (size 7½) cost half a dollar—cooked to perfection. But, cattle town though it was, the place was very eager to get the Lincoln Highway, and Mr. Lovejoy, a friend of Westgard's, questioned me closely as to the prospects that it would come that way.

I was most optimistic about it, and he asked me if I would mind being quoted in the paper. I wrote out a brief statement for him, and he loaned me his personal copy of a hand-drawn map from Laramie to Ogden, asking me to check the mileage and mail it back to him, which I was very happy to do, giving him at the same time a brief report on the condition of the roads for other travelers.

On leaving Laramie we passed through a series of ranch gates and at one place drove directly through a large herd of cattle. Bloom warned us not to get out of the car even to take a picture, explaining that, although the cattle were not afraid of automobiles, many of them had never seen a man on foot and were likely to be frightened at such an apparition and might start a stampede.

The rain began to come down in torrents as we were eating lunch. We hurriedly put on our tire chains and all the afternoon we ground along on first and second gear with streams of water rushing down the deep ruts. One of my tire chains loosened and ripped the bolts from a rear fender. In the downpour I had to let it flop. We had no idea where we were until suddenly on a hilltop we saw an American flag and beneath it a saturated banner which read in running letters, "Boost for Elk Mountain."

We struggled up the hill, slid sidewise down the other side, and found ourselves in the front yard of a little hotel. That's all there was to boost for, but it couldn't have been a more welcome sight. Suddenly the door swung open and a plump Swiss land-lady invited us to come inside. She took us into the kitchen where we gathered around the hot stove drying our clothes while an appetizing dinner was sizzling and bubbling on the stove.

To get us out of the kitchen she whisked a large pan of hot biscuits from the oven and put them on the dining-room table with a liberal supply of butter and honey. After all these years it makes me boost for Elk Mountain just to think about it. When we woke up in the morning, Elk Mountain was covered with snow—and it was August. The rain had stopped, but the roads were still so muddy we waited for afternoon before going on to Rawlins.

Here we said good-by to the Blooms who were turning off to go to Yellowstone Park for their honeymoon. They were most agreeable companions and we missed them as we went on. Between Rawlins and Rock Springs we found frequent arroyos where the road had been washed away by the storm. Some of these washes were as deep as a cellar with almost perpendicular walls. I would not have believed they were passable had they not contained the tracks of automobile tires.

On the top of the Great Continental Divide we stopped to eat our lunch. We had approached it so gradually that we did not realize we were there until we saw the monument marking the grave of Frank Yort, the surveyor who determined the line. We thought it a rather lonely spot either to start a cemetery or to await the Judgment Day.

One by one we climbed out of the car to walk around and see what it was like to be on the top of the world. The sky seemed to be only a short distance above our heads—probably because the clouds were hanging low; but all the time we were in Wyoming I had the feeling of being up in the air. Wyoming is a rugged state. Compared with the soft gentle soil of Nebraska, the whole of Wyoming seemed like a rough tough fellow with his boots on. The roads, though winding like a cattle trail, were hard and stony. Once, when I wanted to kill a rattler in Nebraska, there wasn't a stone to be found within 20 miles, whereas in Wyoming we bumped over them constantly; and there were places where you had to keep a sharp lookout to prevent the wheels from crashing down into prairie-dog holes.

The next night was spent at Rock Springs. We were hoping to get through to Ogden on the following day, but disaster overtook us in the middle of the afternoon when we were about 20 miles beyond Granger. We had climbed up on the tableland where the heavy rains had carved some fantastic arroyos, and, in rushing through one of these where the slope made a sudden twist, the steering gear jammed and the car took a nosedive into a gully landing heavily on the left front wheel. And there we were an hour later when a big Pierce Arrow came along occupied by two newspapermen.

We had our block and tackle set up and were all ready to be pulled out. But they couldn't bother with us. They were making a fast run from Denver to Ogden and they tarried with us just long enough to take a picture—and on they went. They had promised to send help from the nearest town; but no help came. The AAA emergency service had not yet begun, and there we sat all night long.

Under the starlight strange animals came and peered at us. Some of them were bold enough to poke among the empty cans thrown out from our commissary. At daybreak Whitie started off on foot to scour the country for help. Not a sign of human occupancy was in sight. Off to the left we could see a river, and beyond it the railroad tracks. At infrequent intervals a train went by and, though it was several miles away, just seeing it made us feel a little less lonely. Whitie started in a westerly direction with Opal as a possible goal, though we did not know how far away it was.

We watched him go off into the sagebrush which in this area was almost shoulder high. He was wearing a white cap which remained visible for some time but finally vanished into a sea of dull green. While waiting I lubricated and cleaned the car. The girls took a walk up the hillside, and finally came running back to tell me they could see something moving off to the west in a cloud of dust. It turned out to be a ranch wagon drawn by a team of half-broken broncos which had never before seen a car. They had to be backed to get them near enough to attach a rope. But once the rope was fast they were perfectly willing to pull.

They had come from a big hay ranch in the valley. Whitie could not see the house from the road, but he did see a curl of smoke going straight up into the morning sky, so he went over to the edge of the table to look down. There were eight cow-punchers on the ranch and one of them, an amateur blacksmith, straightened our axle, using for a sledge the hub of an old wagon wheel with one spoke left for a handle.

With two females in the party, the cowboys wanted us to stay over so they could have a dance; but I could see that they had a lot of hay cut, and I was sure that with the unsettled weather the foreman did not want to be bothered with any social affairs. So I pleaded that our accident had thrown us off our schedule and we were afraid of losing the advance reservations we had made if there was any longer delay, and late in the after-noon we moved on.

We spent the night in Opal and the next morning made another start for Ogden. It was a hilly drive, just up and down all day long. Once more the steering gear showed signs of jam-ming and we had to take it out and overhaul it by the roadside. Not a vehicle passed while we were doing the work. When late in the afternoon we made a 12-mile coast into Evanston, we were joined by a road carrying the yellow-banded poles we had seen in Nebraska which, we were told, had come across by way of Denver and Steamboat Springs.

Soon after leaving Evanston we crossed the summit of the Wasatch Range, and after that went 38 miles down grade coast-ing much of the time until we were on the paved streets of Og-den. Here we remained for four days resting and having the car reconditioned. We had the axle trued and put in a new steering knuckle. We also had the steering gear thoroughly overhauled and a new worm installed. I haven't said much about the tire trouble though we had some almost every day. Leaky valves, nail punctures, rim cuts, tube pinches, and innumerable sand blisters.

We left Ogden with four new tires and tubes, but they were pretty well worn out when we reached San Francisco.

In Ogden we saw many cars that we had met along the way, most of them in the garage for repairs and overhauling. The majority were going south of the Lake, but I still stuck to my resolution to go around the north end. I had no reason to believe that either way would be easy driving, but the grim tales of the car from Los Angeles still lingered in my mind, and when a chauffeur in the garage told me how he had suffered from the heat on the southerly route, I immediately thought of the little town of Snowville north of the Lake that I had seen on the railroad map in the Reed Hotel in Ogden. Snowville—it sounded pretty good. But when we reached there we found it a tiny little town of only a few houses—and a log-cabin hotel with a sod roof.

However, we had a fine home-cooked dinner, and not long after we had finished eating, the carpenter who was there building a little schoolhouse came in, and since all the men were to sleep in one room we had to go to bed when he did. That was about eight o'clock. I thought myself lucky to be sleeping alone in a double bed, but when I woke up in the morning I saw a long beard spread out on the pillow next to mine. It belonged to a wayfarer who had come in during the night. Real Western hospitality.

There had been a recent cloudburst north of the Lake which left the road looking as if it had been run through a fluting iron. We should have returned to Ogden and gone around the other way, but I was too stubborn to retreat. The result was that we had to rebuild the road practically all the way to Kelton. This was done by filling in the worst of the washouts with railroad ties borrowed from the Union Pacific right of way. All day long we carried railroad ties, and when we reached Lucin late that afternoon my back was aching and my fingers were full of slivers.

Since no satisfactory quarters were available here, we took on 15 gallons of gasoline at 50 cents a gallon and went on hoping to reach Montello. With the terrible roads this proved to be impossible and when at dusk we stopped at the only ranch we had seen in miles and miles, they very kindly took us in, fed us, and gave us beds to sleep in while the children went joyfully out to spend the night in the hayloft.

Passing through the great Salt Desert country lying to the west of the Lake, we had all suffered from parched skin and cracked and blistered lips; but after we had left Montello and had come into the Humboldt River country, which has since become a great national Park and forest reserve, we noticed a difference at once. The air seemed to have lost its sting and had become fresh and winey. And running down through Wells and Deeth on the way to Elko, we passed through some of the most beautiful cattle country in the West. Snowcapped mountains on either side with hills of unbelievably brilliant green running up almost to the snow line, and brawling brooks and streams rushing down into the valley where eventually they became part of the network of forks and streams emptying into the Humboldt. Most of these streams were easily fordable, though one was so broad that I had to wade into the icy water to test the depth before we dared to make an attempt to splash through. We saw more cattle here than in crossing the full length of the states of Nebraska and Wyoming. And our souls were refreshed and our spirits strengthened for the great mountain and desert stretches yet to be conquered.

From now on we were to be constantly in the presence of peaks reaching up to eight and ten thousand feet as we grubbed along through the patches of sand and salt and alkali flats over roads which frequently followed the bed of a dry stream for many miles.

We were now in the Indian country, passing several reservations every day and often meeting Indians on the roads. Sometimes they traveled on horseback, occasionally on foot, and once we saw a whole family in a democrat wagon with the big chieftain sitting alone on the seat, and the squaw with several papooses squatting in the back.

The girls in our party were disappointed because the chief was not wearing his feathers, nor was the squaw clad in the fringed buckskins of Hiawatha. They thought the blue jeans and calico a terrible comedown from the gorgeous costumes they had seen on the Indians in Buffalo Bill's Wild West Show.

At Elko we saw squaws sitting or squatting on the sidewalk while the bucks stood around in groups saying practically nothing to each other. In another place I saw from a back window of a hotel two rows of squaws playing the famous stick game. With little sticks in their hands they were squatting on the ground beside an old timber which they were using as a table. Occasionally they would all begin to grunt and chatter, and nickels and dimes would change hands. They are very much given to gambling, though it is said that no white man has ever learned how the stick game is played.

On the run from Elko to Eureka, the wind was behind us and we were traveling in a cloud of our own dust heavily laden with alkali. My eyes and nose were suffering when one of the girls suggested my wearing a veil. I tried one and it quickly solved the problem, and for the next few days the veil was part of my regular regalia.

We spent a night at Eureka, then regarded as a ghost town. It had once been a busy mining town which had been abandoned when the narrow-gauge railroad was washed out by a flood. So far as I could see, the hotel was the only occupied building, all the others appearing to be vacant and dilapidated. A Guggenheim man who was there told me he was examining the mine tailings to see if they were worth working over by modern methods.

For some 20 miles before reaching Eureka we kept passing men on horseback. They were mostly riding alone though occasionally in pairs. They all appeared to be dressed up and were wearing gay kerchiefs and fancy shirts. We found on arriving that there was to be a dance in town that night. The hotel proprietor, Fuzzy Edwards, advised me to lock the car in a vacant shed behind the hotel to prevent any practical jokes on the part of the cowboys who, he said, were likely to do almost anything for a laugh.

The car was not molested, but when I unlocked the shed the next morning I found the place crawling with little pigs. They must have been carefully handed in through a broken window-pane about three feet from the floor. When I tried to shoo them out, they all took refuge under the car, and as fast as I drove them out on one side they would come back on another. After struggling for half an hour I went into the hotel for help, and Mr. Edwards solved my problem in a moment by releasing the mother sow and driving her over near the shed where she lay down on the ground and gave a peculiar grunt. In no time at all she was covered with little pigs squealing and fighting for their breakfast. And in the meantime I cranked up the car and backed it out on the street.

The dance, which started at about eight o'clock, was a great success. Music was furnished by a cowboy band, the leader of which explained to me that since they never had any time to practice together they had to learn the pieces separately and were just a group of soloists. The band had plenty of volume and kept very good time though I suspected once or twice that most of them were playing different tunes.

I tried to get the girls to go to the ball, but after listening to the music, they went to bed instead. Personally I think they missed the chance of a lifetime. They would have had at least ten partners apiece for every dance.

One day in the parched lands of Nevada was much like another. Uphill, downhill; alkali dust, sand dunes. We climbed some fairly high passes and had more than the usual number of tire failures. Blowouts on two consecutive days could have been serious had not Al Jolson left a tire behind when he came to Eureka looking for a ghost-town setting for a picture. Al decided that the town wasn't quite dead enough to make a good ghost. But the tire was a perfect fit.

As we were leaving, Fuzzy Edwards handed me a little printed card giving travel directions from Eureka to Ely:

    0   Eureka
    0.4 Left fork up canyon
    0.8 Left fork (sign)
    1.5 Left fork (sign)

 2.3 Right fork, follow telephone poles
 4.8 Summit
 7.3 Water (Pinto)
 9.9 Left fork, sign, follow telephone
10.0 Left fork, follow telephone
14.2 Turn right around house across flat, leave telephone
22.9 Summit. Telephone poles come in here
33.8 Coyle ranch
34.0 Take right fork, brush road, (best of three roads)
35.0 Left fork (sign)
38.1 Summit, altitude 8125
40.8 Spring, foot of grade
44.3 Ranch
46.8 Fourteen-mile ranch. At end of fence take right fork
65.8 Sign
68.0 Kimberly. Down the canyon may be seen a small settlement known as Riepetown. Head for this, pass through Riepetown, and keep on the road in the bottom of the canyon until you again meet the railroad tracks and follow
73.7 Take left fork leading toward railroad
73.8 Cross tracks and follow main road straight ahead through Lane City to
77.2 Northern Hotel, Ely.

After reading these directions we decided not to go to Ely, but to go across to Austin. We made it in a day and attended a political meeting at the hotel, where sixteen electors of the great commonwealth of Nevada had gathered to hear a political speech by a traveling electioneer who was out on the road drumming up business for Teddy Roosevelt. We had seen this emissary in Elko. The hotel-keeper there had told me privately that the fellow was an "organizer." He added that he himself was a Democrat and did not care to be organized. And a little later, when the visitor asked him if he was interested in the Bull Moose, the landlord replied that he wasn't much of a hunter but he wouldn't mind shooting one occasionally.

Knowing nothing of the West except what I had read in

Dime Novels I began to look around for a convenient table to get under. But there was no shooting. The organizer looked around the lobby with a smile and asked:

"Is there a Roughrider in the house?"

He wasn't as good as that when he faced the audience in Austin. He began by introducing the only Roughrider in town, who was supposed to give some personal recollections of Teddy at San Juan Hill; but at the critical moment his memory failed him and he began telling about his friendship with Buffalo Bill instead. At that point I tiptoed out, and I heard later that neither Teddy nor Buffalo Bill was elected that fall.

While in Austin I saw in the paper that Westgard was expected in Reno that day. But the paper was already a day old when I read it, so we were not sure when he would be on the road. Nor was I any too sure which road he would take, for I had been told of an alternate road from Reno to Elko by way of Lovelock and Winnemucca. That caused me some worry, but I thought that if I could travel fast enough I might get to Reno before he had left. However, I wasn't more than a mile out of town before I was convinced that nobody could hurry over that road. I was pretty low spirited, I guess, for the rest of them kept trying to cheer me up.

About the middle of the morning we saw a cloud of dust off in the distance. If it was a car it would be the first one we had met on the road since leaving Ogden. As it came nearer we could see that it was indeed a car. A little later one of the girls, who had either phenomenal eyesight or a good imagination, reported that she could see a red license plate. The New York numbers were red that year. Soon we could all see the red number. It was Westgard.

I pulled out of the road and stopped. He drew abreast and stopped. Before I could get out, he was over there peering into the car and shaking hands all around. "You see I'm punctual about keeping my appointments," he said.

Somebody in each car remembered to take a picture. To avoid standing in the hot sun, we divided the party between the two cars and had a grand powwow lasting more than half an hour. We exchanged road information and made an engagement to meet in San Diego the next year.

Within an hour after we had parted, one of our front tires blew out; but in spite of this we were cheerful for we were nearing the end of the desert country and were on the last lap of our journey. Later that day we were lost for the first time since leaving Iowa. We had been crossing great white flats like the salt flats of Utah where the speed trials are held. And we had crossed an arm of the Carson Sink, which had swallowed up so many of the unsuspecting forty-niners, but now was safely though roughly crossed by a road built of chunks of lava covered with coarse earth.

Beyond the Sink the roads spread out like a fan in the soft sands of a huge irrigation project. I stopped at the cabin of a forest ranger to ask directions. He gave them with numerous turnings right and left to take us over the ditches. We went on for a while but did not seem to be getting anywhere. Then I happened to see another ranger's cabin. I drew up in front— and out came the same man. There were no signs of recognition between us. I asked the same question. He gave the same answers, being too well mannered to humiliate me.

I would probably have driven away and, likely as not, would have come back again. But my wife leaned out and handed him an envelope. "Would you please write it down?" she asked pleasantly.

He did, and by following his notations closely, we were extricated from the maze and reached Fallon for our overnight stop.

During the day we had seen great veins of coal jutting out of the cliffs, with immense piles underneath all ready to be carted off. When I asked why they weren't being used, I was told that there was no convenient transportation, and further on it was hinted to me that it wasn't a very good grade of coal.

Another little matter that had been puzzling us was answered at Fallon. Ever since we had been in Nevada we had been noticing groups of little white specks far up on the mountainsides. From a distance they resembled old-time chicken coops with pointed tops; but we could not believe that the poultry business would thrive in such a location. The small objects turned out to be Indian tepees placed high enough to keep them from being washed away by the cloudbursts which, during the rainy season, are not infrequent in these mountainous districts.

From Fallon we found the run to Reno not too difficult though the road was a dusty trail with a one-way stretch across the high embankment of an abandoned railroad still ribbed where the ties had been. Not far from Reno we rescued four smartly dressed young women whose Locomobile was stranded on a badly built railroad crossing. We followed them into town and when later I saw the car in a garage and remarked to an attendant that I had pulled it off a railroad crossing he smiled.

"Four dames?" he guessed.

I nodded. "Good lookers."

"Divorcées," he explained. "They get restless around here. Try to go somewhere every day and usually get stuck. You going to be here long?"

"Not very."

"Then you ain't filed yet?"

"Not yet. Have you?"

"Sure have. I'll be outa this dam' town a week from Thursday."

"I'll be out of it tomorrow."

"You ain't gonna stay?"

"Just passing through."

He gave me an understanding look. "Lucky dog."

We went on to Carson City the next day where we left the level valley and made a 12-mile climb up the face of the mountain to King's Canyon, some eight thousand feet above. It was a single-track road with occasional turnouts, a rough and stony surface, and frightening declivities from which the dome of the courthouse below became smaller and smaller. Several of the turns were too short for our car and we had to go part way around and then back off a few feet to get a new start. Our brakes weren't too good, and the girls refused to stay in the car during these backing operations and walked around a number of the short turns which were invariably followed by a steep upgrade. I would have been glad to join them, but somebody had to stay in the car.

On the way up we met several loads of firewood drawn by teams, and the courtesy of the road required the car to keep to the outside. At one of these meetings the hub of a wagon wheel struck a 5-gallon can of 50-cent gasoline on our running board and opened a seam. Fortunately we had room in our tank and were able to save most of the precious fluid. All of us were nervous wrecks by the time we had reached the summit.

The night was spent at Glenbrook on the shore of Lake Tahoe. When we crossed into California the next morning, a change in the character of the roads was immediately apparent. We were now on highways that were full width and stone surfaced. With the Panama-Pacific Exposition coming up, the Golden State was extending itself to get its highways in condition to handle the expected crowds. Our front axle had been trued in Reno and we had put in our last spare spring, and, though we were still not over the crest of the Sierra Nevada, we were on improved roads the rest of the way to the Coast.

On September 2 we reached San Francisco where we again had access to our trunk and could get into more civilized clothes. I had almost forgotten how to tie a necktie. After a week of relaxation in the city by the Golden Gate we again put on our touring regalia and turned toward the South. By easy stages we motored from San Francisco to San Diego following the route established by the old Mission Padres and called El Camino Real, which, as far back as 1906, had been marked by the Automobile Club of Southern California with handsome road signs ornamented with large bronze mission bells.

We found the roads easy to follow and took the then unpaved mountain grades easily in our stride after the pounding we had received in climbing over the backbone of the continent. However, the roads of the thirteen states we had crossed had taken their toll of the car; still when we came to turn it in on a new one we found to our astonishment that the trip across the continent had added considerably to the turn-in value.

It was September 22 when we reached San Diego, more than two months after our start from New York, though not all the time was spent on the road. Thirty years later I again drove across the continent. It took me exactly one week, without breakdown, mechanical adjustment or tire trouble. Two of us took turns, driving an hour at a time before changing, and we reached our journey's end without the slightest boredom or fatigue. Roads were good all the way and well marked, sleeping accommodations satisfactory, and the only place where we went astray was on the Pulaski Skyway in New Jersey, in plain sight of the Empire State Building.

14 *Out of the Mud*

It was way back in 1632 when the first American road law was passed in Virginia. That same year a short stretch of road was built near Jamestown. Seven years later the Pilgrims started to carve out a road between Boston and Plymouth. By 1664 the news seems to have reached New York, and, not wishing to be left behind, they passed a law. However, it was several years before they built any road. Pennsylvania was a long time coming, but in 1692 they also passed a law. Two years later they built a turnpike between Lancaster and Philadelphia. When I passed through in 1910 the turnpike was still there, and in about the same condition as when it was built; though by that time things were looking up, for members of the Lancaster Automobile Club were out in a body using their own picks and shovels to fill some of the worst mud holes.

Europe had good roads even before Columbus discovered America. The Romans had built some highways that had become famous, and still are. Napoleon, too, was a good road builder, though his roads, like those of the Romans, were highways of war, not of peace.

In sparsely settled countries the waterways are ordinarily the earliest ways of travel, and it was so in America. When our forefathers considered the improvement of transportation facilities, they thought in terms of rivers and canals as much as highways, and nearly all our early development took place along the watercourses. The first roads of any considerable length were cut through to connect the lakes and rivers of the great Central Valley with the settlements along the Coast. The French were paddling their canoes up through the great lakes and cutting in

behind us, and we couldn't get at them to fight them off until
axmen had cut a passage through the forests of Pennsylvania.
George Washington went back and forth over that road several
times, and thought so highly of it, in spite of the stumps, that
he acquired large acreage at the western terminus, though the
title to his land, being claimed by Connecticut, Massachusetts,
Kentucky and Pennsylvania, was a little shaky.

As soon as our country had obtained its independence, it
began to talk about improving the roads. President Washington
was very much in favor of it, but even with his backing and the
cooperation of Thomas Jefferson not much was done about it
except in close proximity to cities and towns. Until the coming of
the railroads in the first half of the nineteenth century, the stagecoaches had a pretty tough time getting from one town to another.
But progress followed the railroad. Towns developed at frequent intervals and around the towns the land was cleared for
farms. The farmer required only enough of a road to get his
produce into town, and accordingly that's all he had.

The clash between state rights and national rights obstructed
the development of any great national thoroughfares for many
years. And the states, while standing off the encroachment of
Federal authority, passed the responsibility for roads down to
the local authorities, where it stagnated until the self-propelled
vehicles came on the scene.

By that time the turnpike era had pretty well worn out its
welcome, and people were getting very tired of paying tolls on
highways maintained by private enterprise. The motorist would
never have objected to a small toll for a good road. What he
objected to was paying toll for what was practically no road at all.

As late as 1904 only 7 per cent of the country's two million
miles of publicly owned roads could be classified as improved,
and at that time an improved road was one where the stumps
were largely gone and there was not much grass growing in the
middle. Pitchholes in the road were passed down from father
to son, and quagmires lasted from one generation to another.

The first serious thought of road improvement came along
in the nineties. People were traveling more and were beginning

to see the roads in other countries. It was in a way part of the cultural development of our time. A national feeling began to grow that our roads should be something more than a nuisance, and that they could possibly become a great public asset. It was important for us to discover that we were backward; after that discovery we began to do something about it.

Like everything else, the improvement started with a lot of talk. Conventions began to be held, and laws creating highway departments were passed in nearly all the Eastern and Central states. New Jersey established a highway law in 1889. New York followed in 1890, and Massachusetts in 1894. The other states were not far behind. But having a highway department was like buying an ax without a handle, and at the end of ten years New York had little to show except a few experimental miles which had been built to try out the lasting qualities of this or that construction. One of these experimental miles was near Geneva, and we used to drive over it every time we could get the chance. I know now that it was a poor piece of macadam, but we thought it grand.

It was the bicyclists of America who were instrumental in starting the movement to improve the roads. Under the leadership of Col. Albert A. Pope, they were the ones who capitalized the words Good Roads—thus turning them into a slogan. But as actual producers of good highways the cyclists did not get to first base. All they really wanted was a good cinder path; and the wheelmen were not popular at the state capitals where the rural population is usually in control. Nor did the farmers have any love for the bicyclists, who scared their horses, picked their flowers, and pilfered their fruit from the trees. The farmers were quite content to do without any improvement of the roads for themselves if that would keep out the urban invaders on their swift and shining machines; and no important road improvement was ever really under way until the motorists had become numerous and were well enough organized to act as a unit through the formation of a nationwide association.

At the time when the American Automobile Association was holding its first regular meeting in the spring of 1903, a Good

Roads bill was being introduced in Congress. It was the initial attempt to put the roads on a national basis. The motorists were solidly behind it.

Though the AAA has worked steadily for the improvement of roads, no lobby has ever been maintained in Washington or in any of the state capitals, for the organization has a much better way of promoting proper legislation. With its enormous membership throughout the country it has the ability of making contact with the legislators in their home bailiwick. Thus the pressure on individual members comes from the voters, the constituents who have placed the lawmaker in office, and as any legislator will tell you, the one thing he desires to know above all else is what his constituents want.

We did not get our present improved roads without working for them. The history of the Good Roads movement is the story of one convention after another, with many discouragements and a strong effort to keep the interest alive. It was not until 1907 that the American Automobile Association, in cooperation with the National Grange and the American Roadmakers Association, held a tripartite convention to explore the possibilities of obtaining legislative aid in getting America out of the mud. Three of these joint conventions were held, and while they succeeded in educating the farmer to some extent as to the importance of good roads in getting his crops to market, they did not immediately succeed in putting through any legislation for Federal aid in improving the highways. That was not to come until several years later.

The first resolution passed by the AAA after its organization in 1902 was in favor of a transcontinental highway from New York to San Francisco, and yet so lacking was the public interest in roads that after some ten years of effort not even the route had been decided upon. One of the principal reasons for the activity which resulted in the formation of the Lincoln Highway Association in 1912 was the hope that, by tying the project to the tail of a big California kite, a passable road to the West Coast might possibly be finished in time for the Panama-Pacific Exposition in 1915.

Of course the idea did not succeed. Too many obstacles were in the way. Not alone such obstacles as mountains and deserts; those were something that could be moved. The most troublesome barriers were the state capitals full of stubborn politicians, and a national capital which sometimes requires a tremendous lot of convincing. The project for the Lincoln Highway made a rallying point. It brought the contest into the open and showed the people of this country, and especially the motorists, that if they were going to have good roads in this country they would have to fight for them to the last ditch.

Nobody who had not seen our roads when the horseless carriage was young could ever believe how bad they were. In so far as its highways were concerned, the United States was more on a par with Siberia than with such countries as England and France. Of our 2,000,000 miles of rural highways, only 150,000 miles had been "surfaced"—a term which meant simply that something or other had been done to the road. It could have been covered with rough planks, or sawdust; or perhaps it was oyster shells or some other harmless substance for which there was no other use. Only 144 of the 2,000,000 miles were credited with being "high-type" surface—meaning water-bound macadam—and this was totally unable to withstand the impact of either horse-drawn or self-propelled traffic.

But the familiar drawback in our efforts at early road building was still the lack of a policy as to who should be the one to build them; and who should pay for them. Back in Colonial days the Federal government had taken an interest in the construction of a so-called National Highway from Maryland to Illinois. Work on it had been started in 1808 and continued by fits and starts until 1852, when it was decided that the Federal government could not legally charge tolls to pay for the maintenance of the road, and the project was passed over to the various states through which the route was to run.

Under the state and local responsibility, roads did not amount to much outside the city limits. They were dust beds in summer, snowbanks in winter, and quagmires of mud in spring and fall. In sparsely settled areas they were little more than trails. Indeed, they were so bad that eventually the railroads, always hostile to the highways, joined in a movement for limited improvement. What the railroads really wanted was improved routes leading from the farms to the loading platforms; naturally they were not interested in highways parallel with the railroad lines.

Not until 1909, when the AAA launched the *American Motorist*, did the automobile users have a national publication in which to voice their complaints and carry on the fight for the betterment of highway conditions.

Between 1890 and 1916 thousands of conventions met to discuss road improvement. These varied from small gatherings of local groups to national and even international conventions, most of which seem to have left no written record of their proceedings. Three of these were under National Grange and American Automobile Association sponsorship. Two were sponsored by the American Automobile Association alone. Four were conducted by the American Roadbuilders Association. And numerous engineering societies devoted sessions of their annual meetings to a discussion of the various methods of getting America out of the mud.

Most frequently the arguments were directed at the farmer who is pictured as standing in the mud halfway up his bootlegs stubbornly shaking his head. In the effort to overcome this rural hostility, a campaign was organized to persuade the farmer that good roads (1) would result in no great increase in taxes; (2) would reduce cost of transportation; (3) would increase the value of farm land; and (4) were necessary to the maintenance of desirable levels of rural cultural life.

This campaign met with no considerable enthusiasm on the part of the farmer though each point was developed and elucidated at great length by skilled writers and speakers. But in spite of the lethargy of the farmer, the movement for better roads slowly gathered force. There was hardly a state east of the Mississippi and north of Mason and Dixon's line where the subject was not under discussion from one angle or another. And in New York State, where a titanic battle was raging over the introduction of a full-fledged state highway system, a compro-

mise was effected in the form of a county option law—which left
some fifty out of the sixty counties still in the control of the rural
population.

Two years later, after spirited discussions in schoolhouses
and grange halls, around the cracker barrels, and over the milk-
ing machines, the legislature passed a state-aid law dividing the
cost of highway construction between the state and county, and
even letting in the town for 15 per cent. However, this also
was optional. A county had no need to go into a through highway
project unless it was so inclined. This gave the alert counties a
fine opportunity to improve their roads; and it likewise gave
the backward counties the privilege of remaining backward,
which all too many of them did—until they found themselves
still stuck in the mud while others were getting themselves established on the main-line highways.

From 1905 on, it became quite obvious that the motor vehicle owners would use their influence to bring about the construction of continuous main-line highways with a network of
coast-to-coast routes as the final objective. Highway development in the Northeastern states was by this time far outrunning
progress in other parts of the country. In 1910 the New York
legislature passed bills for the construction of a through route
between New York and Albany; and in 1911 further authoriza-
tion was passed for the completion of 1,464 miles of trunk-line
highways.

The farmers were a long time in becoming convinced that
good roads would be more to their advantage than their disadvantage; but once they were convinced, they wanted good roads
and plenty of them—and they wanted them immediately. The
case for concentrating Federal aid upon road improvement that
would be of the greatest immediate benefit to the farm population was presented with all the force that oratory could germi-
nate. Listen to the farmer's plight as described to the Senate
Committee on Agriculture.

> The farmer is unable to get to towns through the
> long, dreary months of winter because he is made a pris-

oner by the bad condition of the roads. Make the roads good and you make the farmer a better and a more intelligent citizen. . . .

For one hundred and twenty-seven years the farmer has borne the heaviest burdens of life. He has responded to every call of duty. Never before has he come to Congress and asked a single thing, and now for the first time in more than a century and a quarter he comes here and knocks at the doors of Congress and says, "Gentlemen, help us to build good roads for all the people." He believes, with Lincoln, that this is a government of the people, by the people, and for the people.

Nor was this the plea of a rural politician bent on mending his fences. It came from a metropolitan resident who had once been the president of the largest automobile club in the country, and is given to show one of the strange angles of the road discussion.

Another angle was the attempt to give preference to the routes followed by the rural mail carriers in order to facilitate the free delivery; but this failed on the ground that circuitous routes were of little aid to agriculture. Still another angle was based on the premise that the railway station should be the natural terminus for roads, "since neither freight nor passengers will ever be carried long distances over roads as cheaply as they could be over railways, and that it is an idle dream to imagine that auto trucks and automobiles will take the place of railways in the long distance movement of freight or passengers."

In 1912 a groping Congress appointed an investigating committee to report on the mooted question of Federal aid in the construction of post roads, with an appropriation of a "post road fund" of $500,000. This was the first time that Congress had loosened the Federal purse strings toward an objective for which the American Automobile Association had been struggling since the day of its formation. It did not go all the way, but it showed a weakening of the will power which had stood off an ever increasing pressure for a full decade.

The Secretary of Agriculture and the Postmaster General

were named as administrators of the fund and were directed to select and improve certain roads and to establish rural mail delivery over them. And they were further directed to promote such cooperation among the states as would insure equitable and uniform highway regulations, and to report to Congress within one year their recommendations for a general plan of national aid for the post road improvement.

It was, however, a two-way arrangement, the states or their subdivisions to contribute twice the amount expended by the Federal government. From this distance the post road provisions look like a bit of eyewash to make the bill seem a little more attractive to the more unprogressive opposition; for the post road angle was discarded after the first year. The Joint Committee, however, gathered a vast amount of valuable information which emphasized the extensive popular demand for Federal support. So by this time Good Roads had their foot in the door.

By the end of 1913 Congress took over the problem of deciding the form that Federal aid should take. This required only three years of deliberation and discussion. And after all the speeches were finished and the shadowboxing concluded, the Federal Aid Highway Act was passed and became a law in 1916, thereby opening the way for the rational development of a national highway system.

After a lapse of sixty-four years Uncle Sam was back in the road-building business under a dollar-for-dollar arrangement with the states. Within five years after the passage of this act, we had well over ten million cars on the roads. In the next decade the number was crowding twenty-five million.

That was a lot of cars; and by that time we had a lot of roads. To the restless American this combination spelled one thing—travel.

"Be there in a flash!" Through modern, two-way radio communication, it is possible today to speed an AAA Emergency Road Service truck to the scene of a breakdown or other car trouble within minutes of the time the motorist calls for help. Clubs are increasingly using this method.

Through the AAA's International Travel Department, a motorist may ship his car abroad with him. Each year the ITD arranges for shipment of thousands of cars for vacation and business travel overseas, handling necessary international driving permits and customs documents.

They learn by play. In Washington, D.C., and other principal cities of the nation, children are taught safe traffic conduct through "Safety Town" demonstrations, which dramatize city traffic problems in a manner which they can easily understand and put into daily practice.

Typical of the more than 550,000 AAA-aided and equipped School Safety Patrol members guarding their schoolmates at dangerous intersections and crosswalks these days is this young Washington, D.C., patrol boy. Safety patrol work has helped lessen the child pedestrian death rate.

For a permanent record of our trips these days, we take along the family camera. The car, with other factors in our economy such as the shorter work week, vacations with pay, and higher salaries, has done much to bring to American families a real freedom of travel.

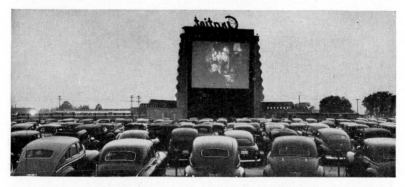

Drive-ins have become an American phenomenon. These days, in addition to the well-known drive-in theaters, we have the drive-in restaurant, bank, church, laundry, market, and—the most successful of them all—the drive-in motel. All these are by-products of a nation on wheels.

Heavy traffic at Main Street and Miami Road, in Jacksonville, Florida, is typical of the congestion which has become an increasing problem as roads and streets built during the highway boom of the twenties become glutted with the more than 52,000,000 vehicles in circulation today.

We've come a long way, but with motoring's development have come new headaches—such as where to park our millions of cars in today's congested cities.

15 *Seeing America First*

Before the motor age, travel for pleasure was largely restricted to the rich. If they had money enough they would go to Europe. Otherwise they would spend the summer at the seashore or in the mountains, or perhaps they would take the waters at some health resort. People only moderately well to do were likely to confine their travel to matters of business or to such exigencies as family weddings and funerals. Down among the white collars, and those only a notch or two above the underprivileged, travel was usually limited to a honeymoon or perhaps once in a lifetime a flying visit to the World's Fair or the centennial celebration of some historical event.

The point is that there had to be an excuse for travel. Even the very rich would usually excuse their ramblings on the ground of a need for change and relaxation. Sinbad the Sailor and his ilk seemed to be the only ones who traveled for fun and adventure.

With the arrival of the motorcar came a decided change of attitude toward travel. There no longer had to be any excuse. Every motorist began to travel just for the pleasure of riding around and seeing new places. The attraction of the elsewhere has always appealed to the human family; otherwise it would be difficult to account for our conduct, such as the vast migrations that have taken whole peoples halfway around the world. The desire for gold was not the only impulse that drew the forty-niners across the continent a hundred years ago.

Americans have never been an armchair people. If we have remained long in one place it has been because transportation was not readily available. Even when we were a horse-and-buggy

189

nation we used to cover quite a little ground. It was slow going, but in those days we had plenty of time.

It is probably just as well that the motorcar was faltering and balky when it arrived, that it developed slowly and won its way gradually. If it had arrived in the state of perfection it has now attained, it might easily have overwhelmed us and itself as well. Taking the turn of the century as the beginning of motoring, this country was at the time feeding and using some sixteen million horses. Hundreds of carriage factories and harness shops were going at full blast. Just making the horseshoe nails for so many horses was quite an industry in itself. The livery business in the country was enormous. And while the roads were usable for horse-drawn traffic which travels at a walk more than half the time, they would have made a shambles of fast-moving cars.

We don't even have to imagine what would have happened to a large city built for carriage and trolley-car traffic. All we need, to get the picture, is a glance at any large city in the country and see for ourselves the confusion and disorganization that are everywhere present even after more than fifty years in which to cope with the gradual development of the motor vehicle.

Streets have been widened, hundreds of buildings have been torn down to give room to thruways, parkways, speedways, underpasses, overpasses, parking areas—and still the cities are so clogged with traffic that the man-hours wasted in waiting for lights alone would run up into figures of astronomical proportions. Hardly a city is able to furnish parking for more than a small fraction of its registered cars.

The urge to go places seems to have been a constituent part of the ownership of a motorcar. It is perhaps a reversion against the days of the horse. Always the animal had to be coddled and spared. Every time Dobbin was trotted for half a mile he had to be walked almost as far for a breathing space. Naturally he was ambled up every hill to avoid hurting his wind. Then, too, he was walked down the slightest grade to prevent stumbling or the danger of becoming knee-sprung.

All this was forgotten when the motorist entered his new car. He went zipping along on the level as rapidly as the roads would let him go; he coasted downhill as swiftly as he dared, and rushed uphill as fast as the car could make it. His attitude was that, since he did not have to spare the horses, he might as well go somewhere.

With a car, if it would run at all, the motorist would soon exhaust the points of interest to which he could drive in an afternoon, and when Sunday came he would plan an all-day trip taking in some new territory. Travel was, in a way, like alcohol —the more you got the more you wanted. And as cars and roads improved, more and more families began taking long-distance vacation trips. Having a car, they simply could not resist the call of the open road.

The city folk with their big expensive cars were the ones who really started the craze for automobile touring. They were the first to have cars which could run 100 miles in a day, and they went rolling merrily around the country from one summer resort to another. Their wanderings were guided to a large extent by the state of the roads and the weather, and in the beginning most of their touring was done in New England because of the reputed excellence of the roads and the abundance of well-run resort hotels.

Yankee innkeepers, on the lookout for business, outlined a plan which they called The Ideal Tour. This started from New York and made a loop up through New England with noonday and night stops at roughly 50-mile intervals patterned after the arrangements of the Glidden Tours. Member hotels would send an attractive tour book for the asking, which contained an excellent map and explicit directions for following the route. The booklet gave not only the landmarks and travel instructions, but listed points of historical and scenic interest along the way.

Coming at a time when road maps were scarce and travel directions almost nonexistent, this service became very popular. I went over the Ideal Tour several times, varying the routes somewhat to satisfy my own interest and curiosity. It was almost like a club run to travel along with the same group every day, eating at the same places and staying at the same hotels. Occasionally we would stop on the road to help one another with a tire, or to lend a hand in putting a top up or down. Of course we did not travel on rainy days, but stayed around a hotel reading the papers or playing games with companions of the road, and sometimes dancing in the evening, especially where there was a hotel hostess for introductions.

We found travel by motor far less expensive than by rail. This was especially so if we happened to have four persons to divide the incidental expenses of running the car. Although motor travel in the early twenties did not have all the comforts we have today, many of the inconveniences of the old days had been removed. Cars were more reliable, roads were better, closed cars had come in and were soon to supplant the open cars. With the closed car came the passing of the linen duster. At the Poland Springs House, by the way, one was not allowed to wear duster and goggles in the hotel lobby on Sunday. By this time self-starters and electric lights had become part of regular equipment, and every car had some form of demountable rims. Service stations were becoming more numerous, and we were at the beginning of the greatest period of car building and road building of all time.

The slogan "See America First" was devised and quickly caught the popular fancy. The motorists ranged east and west as well as north and south. They spilled over into Canada and Mexico; but when they attempted to get into the National Parks they found the gates barred to the motorcar. Only horse-drawn vehicles were allowed inside. The reason usually given for this exclusion was that the only roads in the parks were bridle paths and wagon trails entirely unsuited to the use of automobiles. When queried about improving the roads, the Department of the Interior took the position that the National Parks must be kept in their pristine state of natural beauty and not be desecrated by man-made roads occupied by mechanical contraptions.

In some of the parks the visitor was not even allowed to hike, but must do his sightseeing from a horse-drawn stage provided by a government concession at so much a mile—if one can imagine seeing the sights of the two million acres occupied by the Yellowstone or the Yosemite which is almost as large—in a horse-drawn stage.

Naturally it was the American Automobile Association which organized and led the fight of the motorists for access to their own recreation facilities. As early as 1911 the Association was urging the removal of the foolish restriction which was denying the privilege of visiting our National Parks to the millions of Americans for whom they were being preserved. Every year the demand for the open gate was becoming more insistent; but the vested interests in control were stubborn fighters, and it was not until the summer of 1915 that the Secretary of the Interior, Franklin K. Lane, finally took the matter in hand, removed the barriers, and allowed motorcars access to the Parks.

This had to be started on a limited basis, of course, for time was required to adapt the roads to motor travel; but the motorists came flocking in with such enthusiasm that they completely swamped the park accommodations. The last season of exclusion, 1914, attendance at the Yellowstone was roughly 20,000, which was about all the Park could handle at the time. By 1950, however, annual attendance there had passed a million and was well on the way to a second million. And the attendance that year at all the National Park areas had reached the astonishing total of nearly thirty-three million—with practically all the visitors coming by motorcar.

As soon as the initial hostility to the motorcar had passed, the outlying communities began to discover that visiting motorists were the potential source of dollars somewhat freely spent while away from home. Only the "Tin Can Tourists" attempted to travel without funds. Their identifying mark was a tin can on the radiator cap. At one time their association claimed a membership of nearly half a million. They were about as welcome as hobos in any locality.

While driving to the Coast in 1912, we often met nomads called Wagon Tramps in the West. Usually they traveled in covered wagons, or perhaps a little house on wheels. Often they would have tied behind an extra horse for emergency use, and not infrequently a cow. I have seen them camped by the roadside with a flock of chickens around them, or a milk goat. They were not Gypsies, but wanderers. And in the sparsely settled parts of the West where grass was plentiful their animals could easily live off the country.

When asked, they usually told a fantastic tale about being on their way to some distant part of the country to visit a relative or locate a long-lost daughter. They would usually start to move very early in the morning and never travel more than 10 or 12 miles a day. Often they had a raft of children with them, dirty and unkempt, though one day I saw an entire family bathing nude in a roadside brook.

One of these Wagon Tramps, a character who called himself "Buckskin Ed," and who claimed to have been an intimate friend of Buffalo Bill, explained that he was on his way to the Great Smoky Mountains in search of a daughter who had been carried off by the Gypsies. He was squatting over a little campfire in Wyoming when we came along. His blanket, in which he was preparing to sleep in the open, was spread out on the ground not far away. On the blanket lay a long-barreled rifle, a muzzle-loader. When I asked permission to take his picture, he stood up and tidied himself by tucking his shirt more securely in his pants. When I began to focus the camera, he let down his hair—literally—by pulling out some hairpins. Then he looked as if he might, indeed, have been a contemporary of Colonel Cody. He gave me an address to which I sent a print of the picture a few weeks later. But the letter came back unopened, and marked with a large rubber stamp "UNKNOWN." I'm sorry he did not get the picture, for it was a good one.

After the automobile began to come into the hands of people without very much money to spend, auto camping became very popular. I camped all over California from one end of the state to the other, but that was before the automobile camp site for motorists had been thought of. I often slept under the stars but always on a cot since I am not fond of crawling things. I have also taken auto-camping trips through northern New England, though here I used to sleep in a sort of half-tent that fastened to the roof of the car, with an escalator arrangement by which I could retire into the car in case of a heavy rainstorm.

We pitched camp late one night in the mountains of Vermont without looking around very much to see where we were though we felt sure there were no houses within a mile or two. I was awakened in the night by a violent quaking of the earth accompanied by a blinding light which made the inside of the tent as light as day. These frightening omens were accompanied by a thunderous roar which I feared must be either a landslide —or possibly the end of the world. When in another moment I recognized the noise as the sound of a rapidly approaching train, I had the awful feeling that we must have pitched our camp directly on the tracks. I struggled desperately to get out of my blanket, but could not disentangle myself in time—and a fast freight whizzed by. It did not pass through the tent as I had feared, though it could not have missed by much more than six feet. After that we made a point of selecting our camp site by daylight.

It was in the West that official cognizance was first taken of the automobile camper when Denver, in 1919, opened a 160-acre camping site for motorists which offered not only plenty of room, but running water and sanitary plumbing. Not long afterward the Los Angeles municipal camping grounds was offering such luxuries as gas cookstoves, shower baths, and laundry tubs with hot water. At about the same time one could camp among the Big Trees of California for fifty cents a night per car, with firewood furnished as well as tables and benches.

By the following year, the National Automobile Chamber of Commerce could report: "Over a million motorists went camping last summer. About 300 cities now have municipal motor camp sites."

In bad weather automobile campers were likely to stay at hotels, or perhaps in houses along the highways where signs had been posted that could be seen from the road: "Tourists Accommodated." And while country hotels were everywhere being built or refurbished, a strange new contraption began to appear along the highways. It was the tourist cabin. In the beginning these were little more than chicken coops, but they were better than carrying your own camping equipment and were less expensive than the downtown hotel.

The early tourist cabins—particularly those near a metropolitan center—soon gained an unsavory reputation. The automobile had already been assailed by the forces of righteousness as a corrupter of morals, and the tourist cabin, it was charged, was even worse. In the case of many, particularly those offering drinks and dancing, the allegation was true.

Eventually the tourist cabins evolved into more comfortable and more legitimate accommodations. Variously known as motels, motor courts, tourist havens, auto lodges, and numerous other names, they were soon seriously challenging the hotels for the business of the vacationing motorists.

It seems as if everything connected with motoring was in for a rapid change, even the motor clubs. From the beginning these clubs had a dual purpose: to work for the improvement of motoring conditions generally, and to provide special facilities for members. In the early days the facilities for members were largely social in nature; but as the sociability waned, the clubs began substituting services, the need for which had developed from the wide extension of motoring. Most important among these was the need for touring and travel information. The old Blue Books, which had served well enough in earlier times, were abandoned, and AAA Headquarters developed a highly professional map-making department and started a type of route information second to none. Also during the early twenties the clubs began instituting the famous emergency road service for members.

The pioneer in this field was the Automobile Club of Missouri which started the rescue service of the disabled cars as far back as 1915. The practice was soon followed by other clubs throughout the country, and before long was put on a nationally reciprocal basis so that any member of AAA could get emergency service as well as travel information from any of the affiliated clubs.

As motoring became more and more extensive, the lack of

reciprocity between states in the matter of registration plates became so troublesome that the AAA started a campaign for a Federal registration law providing for a United States license plate that would have to be recognized by all the states. This never reached the point of passage, but the threat of Federal regulation as well as the growing awareness of the dollar value of the tourist business led the recalcitrant states into doing away with their border barriers.

From the first the motorist had had his troubles in finding his way any great distance beyond his own immediate neighborhood, and for some years the picture of the lost and strayed tourist puzzling over unwieldy maps and scrutinizing illegible signboards with the assistance of a match had been a popular subject for jokesmiths. Gradually the situation had been improved by the clubs, then by the communities, and eventually by the states themselves. And with the development of the major named highways, a new method of marking the through routes was developed. It consisted of painting bands of color on telephone poles, trees, and fences along the way; though this had its disadvantages since in many parts of the West there were no trees, poles, or fences for hundreds of miles.

Another disadvantage was that in some parts of the country there were so many intersecting highways that there were not enough colors or color combinations to go around. In 1925 the American Association of State Highway Officials was asked by the Secretary of Agriculture to work out a comprehensive and uniform scheme for designating interstate routes. The result was the program of highway numbering substantially as we know it today.

Among the other complex problems presented by the vast increase of car ownership was the fearful toll of accidents along the highway, resulting in injury, property loss, and death. The destructive potentialities of the automobile had, of course, been a matter of concern from the earliest days. However, all manner of transportation seems to have had its dangerous side, from the days of the floating log, the back of an elephant or camel; the dugout, the ship, the train—the horse and buggy. Indeed the fatalities from runaway horses far outnumbered the motorcar killings for a number of years, though reliable statistics are not readily available. But when the motorcar came into common use, the mounting toll of deaths and injuries caused widespread concern.

During the four years from 1913 to 1917 while the number of vehicles in use was growing from one million to five million, traffic deaths averaged some 6,800 a year. By 1922, with twelve million cars on the road, the fatalities in traffic had leaped to 12,700 per annum. And in the three years from 1922 to 1925, while car registration was rising to seventeen million, the fatalities on the road had nearly doubled, reaching the incredible average of 22,000 per annum.

While the general reaction to this rising toll was a wave of stringent legislation of a restrictive nature, the immediate result was a hodgepodge of half-baked laws and ordinances aimed at everything except the heart of the matter. In some of the backward counties of the Southern states, motorcars were forbidden the use of public roads. A California county forbade the use of cars after nine o'clock at night; and the Minnesota legislature gave learned consideration to a law limiting the speed of automobiles to 8 miles an hour within a half mile of any post office.

All this confusion brought from Herbert Hoover, then Secretary of Commerce, a call for a national conference on highway safety which resulted in the production of a Uniform Vehicle Code covering registration, rules of the road, certificate of title, traffic regulation, and other pertinent matters, which were largely adopted by the various states, thus creating a country-wide trend toward uniformity of vehicle regulation for the entire country. The death toll, however, has continued to rise, reaching in 1941 the appalling figure of 40,000 fatalities in a single year; and in the early fifties recording a grand total of a million deaths attributable to the motorcar.

Whether this was to be ascribed principally to the high speed potential of the modern car combined with the improvement of the roads, or to the innate tendency of the human being to become careless in the continued handling of dangerous objects remains to be seen. The problem has been approached from many angles, one of the soundest being the elimination of the repeater, particularly the impecunious repeater who could cause great damage and disaster without any chance of making restitution. This is being accomplished by the passage of safety-responsibility legislation providing that a driver who commits flagrant violations of the law resulting in serious damage must, either through insurance or otherwise, make restitution or be ruled off the roads.

Another far-reaching development is the education in safety of the younger generation who will be the drivers of the future. The little tots in their classrooms, coloring in pictures which illustrate safety rules; the School Safety Patrol boys and girls in their white Sam Brown belts, guarding the lives of the small fry at intersections and crossings along dangerous arteries of travel; the teen-agers who are being drilled in safe driving practices by training in dual-control cars furnished to the schools by the American Automobile Association and affiliated clubs in cooperation with car manufacturers and local dealers. These are some of the steps being taken to stem the upward curve of casualties caused by the mishandling of perhaps the greatest civilizing force in the world today—the motorcar.

16 *Is This Trip Necessary?*

The bombs fell on Pearl Harbor with an ominous thud heard round the world. We had known for some time that we were skating on thin ice, but we did not realize quite how thin it was. I was in Hollywood at the time, and as the news came trickling in cautiously to avoid divulging to the enemy how great the damage had been, the people of the Golden State were in a dither wondering if California would be next. Rumors were flying of periscopes seen off the coast; and that night we all went to bed wondering what might happen before the dawn's early light.

It was after midnight when the firing began, and for some minutes the bombardment continued to thunder while the sky was almost continuously lighted by flashes from the antiaircraft fire. Otherwise the city was in darkness, having been blacked out after a warning of unidentified airplanes overhead. We watched from our windows high over Sunset Boulevard and rightly located the cannonade as coming from the shore. When I turned on the radio I found all the California stations silent. From Salt Lake City, however, I learned that Los Angeles was fighting off an air raid. The tumult continued for what seemed like ten minutes—then stopped as abruptly as it had begun, leaving us in utter darkness.

No traffic was moving. Not so much as a whisper came up to us from the street below. All was as silent as a city of the dead. Then suddenly as the lights came blinking on, we heard the whirr of automobiles starting their engines. It was a reassuring sound; and with the feeling that life would still be going on, we went back to bed. We learned in the morning that there had

200

been no raid; that the tumult had been caused by a nervous gunner who had fired by mistake, thus setting off all the others. But it was the nearest thing to an air raid that our mainland had all through the war.

For a short time only the attack on Pearl Harbor was paralyzing. Then it aroused the nation as nothing else could have done. It was the spark which set off the great outburst of production that eventually won the war.

When the ancient Greeks coined the phrase about the "sinews of war," they were doing their warring with spears and shields, or throwing rocks into a fortified city by catapult. They had never heard of steel, without which modern warfare would have no sinews. Long before Pearl Harbor it was well known to military men that steel, not gold, would win the war. For many months civilian production had been feeling the pinch, but with the declaration of war the embargo on essential metals came with rude abruptness.

This brought the assembly lines of all passenger cars to a halt. Civilian machinery was promptly carted out of the factories and wrapped with tarpaulin for the duration, which gave the factory yards the appearance of mammoth cemeteries. The gods of war took over and soon the great production lines were humming with the manufacture of fighters and bombers, guns and munitions, tanks and landing craft—and we had indeed become the "Arsenal of Democracy."

With no new cars available there was a mad scramble for those which had been made but not yet delivered, and strong pressure was exerted to allow the manufacture of a small number —just enough to keep the motorists of the nation awheel. But Washington was at the helm, and the military mind could concentrate on nothing that was not in the line of armament. Indeed, the suggestion was made by officialdom to reduce the number of civilian passenger cars from 25 million to only 5 million. This kind of talk posed a very serious question, and when on February 10, 1942, the production of automobiles was cut short we had to find out how vital to victory our great fleet of civilian cars really was.

So the experts were put to work. The most arresting fact they soon discovered was that no less than 13 million people living in the suburbs of cities were out of reach of any kind of transit system. No railroad, no streetcar, no bus was available to them. If these people were to work at war jobs they would have to be carried a considerable part of the way by automobile. The only alternative would have been for them to move closer to their jobs in the factories and other places of employment. Obviously it was impossible to rehouse speedily so vast a number of people. The only reasonable alternative was to keep the automobiles running.

When the experts began assembling figures on this angle they were in for some more surprises. A survey in Michigan showed that of the 850,000 workers employed in industry, over 635,000 were entirely dependent on their cars to get to and from their work. In the Los Angeles area where extensive new war plants were in operation, more than 70 per cent of the workers were driving in their cars to the factory, some of them traveling as much as 30 miles a day. At another of the California plants, it was found that 92 per cent of the 50,000 workers were dependent on their cars to take them to their jobs.

At a plant in Kansas, employing some 10,500 workers, the percentage was even higher. A study made of nearly 200 war plants scattered through fourteen states showed 69 per cent of the workers driving to their jobs in their own cars. The unavoidable conclusion was that the freedom given by the automobile had made it possible for plants to be located without regard to rail or streetcar transportation, thus avoiding too much concentration in crowded areas; and it was equally obvious that if the factories were going to operate in the winning of the war, the cars of the workmen must be kept rolling.

The lesson was equally plain in the case of agriculture. The mechanized farm was geared to the automobile, and the harvesting of crops could not wait half a day or longer for a horse to go plodding into town for a broken part which could be brought in an hour or less by car. If the farmer was to continue the needed production of food he must have his automobile. There was also an educational angle. With the passing of the little red schoolhouse there was no way to get the farmer's children to school without the family automobile. The school bus could do part of it, but not all.

Out of these studies came a well-rounded picture of the meaning of the automobile in our national pattern; and after careful consideration with a vast amount of figuring and checking, the experts reached the conclusion that a large part of our automobiles should be kept in operation if our economy was to continue functioning for the greatest good of the greatest number. They also reached the conclusion that if we should lose no more than a million or two through wreck or dilapidation, we could still keep the nation at work, but they cautioned that if the nation's fleet of passenger cars were to fall substantially below the twenty-million mark, our home-front strength would be seriously impaired.

Before the war the interest of the manufacturers in the making and distribution of parts had, at best, been little more than casual. The service was always slow and often not too accurate. They would have preferred to sell the entire car and be done with it. However, with production at a halt they became painfully aware that with no cars to sell, many or most of their dealers would be going out of business if the war on two fronts should turn out to be a long and attenuating contest, which seemed quite likely. Their one hope lay in the direction of developing a considerable volume in the hitherto perfunctory business of making and selling parts. And thereupon they moved many of their best men out of sales and into parts; from selling cars to saving cars.

With no new cars coming into the market, the parts business began to thrive, and the older the automobiles became, the more heavily they leaned on the parts business. Conventions of parts men were held in Detroit and various other places. Distribution centers were established for the sole purpose of speeding up deliveries. The time came when salesmen were on the road selling nothing but parts. And what had been a very humble part of an extensive business came in for a fair share of the glory of holding together the sales organization of some of the large manufacturers.

Keeping step with the spirit of the times, the American Automobile Association launched a program of all-out conservation, advising motorists of methods by which they could save not only their gasoline and tires, but also their cars by cutting down their speed and various other changes in operation. The Association launched a nationwide tour to "Keep 'em rolling," showing the most approved methods of economizing on gas, prolonging the life of tires, and so caring for the car that it would last longer and give better service. They also helped to test and popularize the new wartime synthetic tires, toward which a public brought up on real rubber was inclined to be more than a little disdainful. Most of us have since changed our minds about synthetic rubber.

But in spite of all the economies, and the universally adopted speed limit of 35 miles an hour, gasoline had to go on the ration list when the submarines disrupted our normal tanker delivery from the southern oil fields. Even before we were in the war our rubber supplies had been so reduced that tire control was inevitable. Then, too, the rationing of food had to come. There was plenty of growling about all these things, and no doubt there was plenty of cheating; but in the long run patriotism prevailed, and the "black market," though present, was never accepted by decent people as respectable, and never amounted to a scandal.

In the three years from December 31, 1941, to December 31, 1944, car registration fell from 29½ million to 25½ million. Part of this deficit consisted of pleasure cars not really needed, but left in storage because of the rigors of regulation; however, the loss of four million cars was not crippling and we managed to get along without any serious consequences.

Motorists used all sorts of ingenuity to keep their cars running in spite of the stringencies. Some of the homemade repairs were fantastic. The pieces of timber that were used in place of bumpers were clumsy and inelegant; but the users had a certain satisfaction from knowing that some of their steel was doing its bit in the place where it was most needed. When one owner found his tires going to pieces, he filled them with his own brand of home-concocted punctureproof material which not only oozed out in places but filled the atmosphere round about with an intensely disagreeable odor. But probably he too felt that he was helping to win the war. Another crackpot made wheels out of laminated sections of specially treated wood which were not only noisy, but became very slippery when wet. And I saw a bicycle with tires made of wooden blocks hinged to the fellies so as to give them a rocking motion. The machine ran with a sound like an old-fashioned coffee grinder and occasionally threw splinters into the seat of the operator's pants.

Very early in the rationing period, car pools began to come into use, motorists sharing their cars with neighbors and taking turns in being the host from week to week. I knew of one car pool which drove the 50 miles from Glens Falls to Schenectady every day for two years, summer and winter; and while the summer driving could not have been so bad, the winter in that area is something to be reckoned with.

There was some black market in gasoline coupons taken out largely by people whose cars were in storage, and sometimes by persons who had no car to store. But one of the worst features of the stringency was the tire stealing that went on. No tire that was not under lock and key was safe from the tire snatcher. Many of these tire thieves were young boys of school age. They would not only steal a tire out of a private garage, but would let the air out of a tire on a busy street. A few moments later they would come back with a jack and wrench, remove it, and roll it away ostensibly for repairs. Of course they never came back.

In time a tire lock became as necessary as a bolt on the big front door. Cars that were parked for the whole day were often protected by a sizable chain run through the wheels and tires, and locked with a big tough padlock. I never knew a tire thief to be strung up to the nearest cottonwood tree, as in the case of horse stealing in the days of the Old West; but I once saw a miscreant caught in the act and pummeled by the owner until there was hardly a spot on his body that was not black and blue—while a crowd stood by and cheered the car owner until somebody called a policeman.

Some of the automobile clubs supported legislation providing harsh penalties for tire thieves, and others set up a special apparatus for branding tires with a special mark to make them easily identifiable.

To meet the rubber shortage, the government, grasping at straws, began to encourage the planting of guayule, a rubber-bearing plant, the juice of which was low in grade and high in price. The experiment was one of the most complete failures of a period given to outlandish and costly experimentation. However, the rubber situation was finally taken in hand and solved by the efforts of a special committee headed by Elder Statesman Bernard Baruch, which outlined a program for the making of synthetic rubber in large-enough quantities to meet the current demands. For many uses this so-called substitute has turned out to be better than the natural rubber.

New England was especially hard hit by the gasoline shortage. Most of its supply having come by sea in tank ships it lacked the facilities for handling and storing motor fuel brought in by rail. Signs reading "NO GAS TODAY" were a common sight on filling station pumps almost anywhere in New England. And it was a common practice for motorists to park their cars near a distributing station yard and wait for a tank truck to start on its round of filling stations. I have followed a tank truck many times and waited in line at or near a filling station until my turn came to get my allowance. Often this was only five gallons, and if it happened to be ten, the motorist thought he was really in luck.

We were expecting an increase in our family at the time of the most stringent shortage of fuel, and for several weeks I had safely locked in my garage and chained to a beam two sealed five-gallon cans of gasoline plainly marked "For Emergency Only!" for we were living 60 miles away from the hospital where arrangements had been made to welcome the little stranger. Neither the Big Inch nor the Little Inch was finished in time to be of any help; but when the occasion came I was ready for it. It was a boy.

By a combination of good luck and good management, the country managed to get through the emergency in spite of the submarines at sea and the shortage of tank cars on land. Even before V-J Day, controls were being somewhat eased, and only hours after the peace was concluded the welcome news was flashed to the nation that there would be no more gas rationing.

With the war over, Americans took to the highways with whoops of delight and a honking of horns. There never had been anything quite like it before. People were tired of the shortages and frustrations of wartime living. Everybody wanted to go somewhere and do something without being asked, "Is this trip necessary?" For the greater part, the cars were old and shabby-looking. Practically all of them needed new tires, new upholstery, and perhaps a new fender or two. What everybody wanted was a new car. The desks of the dealers were piled high with orders; but for a while there would be no new cars from the factories. Machinery for new models could not be obtained for many months, so the manufacturers did the next best thing—they moved the old machinery back into the factories and began making the same models they had been turning out when production was stopped by the war. These were dolled up a bit so they would not look quite the same. Grills and bumpers were different and the arrangement of the instrument board was new. Some of them were lucky enough to have new door handles—but underneath the surface was the same old model.

The market knew perfectly well what was going on, but the people bought the output hungrily. At least what they were getting was a car that had never been used. It was new and shiny and was not a collection of squeaks and rattles. Factories were retooling as fast as they could while keeping up steady production, and in spite of material shortages and an occasional strike here and there the production curve steadily mounted.

Previous to the war the peak output of passenger cars was that of 1929 when production had surpassed the 4,500,000 mark. But with all their efforts the manufacturers could do no better in 1946 than some two million cars. In 1947 they raised the output to 3,500,000, and it was not until 1949 that they went over the top with a record-breaking output of more than 5,000,000.

But the hungry market absorbed them all as fast as they came. Not only were there never any cars left over, but there were all sorts of underhand bonus arrangements and black-marketing tricks for getting cars out of turn. The used-car lots could always get new models, but the customer had to pay from one to five hundred dollars for the service. The honest dealers tried to stop this practice by backtracking from the buyer when the car came in for service; but usually the sleuthing stopped at the entrance to the used-car lot, and the black marketing continued until the supply had caught up with the demand.

The long period of privation during which no new cars were available had created a new relationship between the motorist and his car. Knowing that he must make it last, that he could not just step out and come driving home in a new one had brought a realization to the motorist of the vital importance of the car he already owned. If he lived at any distance from his work, that car was all that stood between him and his job. He developed a real affection for the faithful old bus. It was somewhat like the relationship between a boy and his dog. He knew the car was getting old and stiff in the joints, but it was doing the best it could and he loved it. He began to take better care of it. He cleaned and polished it himself. He saw to it that oil reached the wearing surfaces oftener than usual. He kept an eye on the lubrication tabs put on at the filling station during oil changes. Tires came in for special care and attention. They were inspected regularly and switched often to divide the wear. He looked more frequently at his battery and put in water before it was really needed. The knocking of the old car as it climbed a hill on that wartime gas hurt like sticking a knife between his ribs, and he would draw a long breath of relief as they reached the top.

Instead of being glad to see the old bunch of junk go when his new car was ready for delivery, the owner felt a little tug in the neighborhood of his heart. I stood watching a motorist one day when he was turning in his old car for a new one, and when he thought nobody was looking, he slipped over and patted the battered old veteran on the bonnet as if to say, "You've been a faithful old wagon, and I hope you'll get a good home." Then he hurried over to his new car, stepped in, and drove away without another look. I knew just how he felt, for I had felt that way myself.

This friendship between the man and his car has been stronger since the war than it ever was before. I have been told by men in the service stations that lubrication is nowhere near as haphazard as it was. And the wide interest in old-time cars may also be a straw in the wind, for surely there were never so many old-car collectors as at the present time. I know a man who drove all the way from Idaho to Connecticut only a few months ago just for the purpose of seeing an ancient Mercer raceabout that he had heard of. He did not stop in to see me though he came within ten miles of my home. His time was limited and he wanted to spend every moment that he could looking at the Mercer.

Another indication of this new enthusiasm for the automobile and what it means to us is the tremendous increase of membership in the clubs affiliated with the American Automobile Association. In the past few years the number of new members has gone steadily upward. Though in the middle forties it stood at 1,100,000, it has in this Golden Jubilee year of the Association risen to a membership of nearly 4,000,000, breaking all records for the half century of its service to motordom here and abroad.

Year by year the fields of activity of the Association have been extended until they now include domestic and international travel, car care and emergency road service, traffic safety, and the new field of traffic engineering, in addition to the purposes for which it was originally formed.

In the multibillion-dollar vacation travel business the Association today is a recognized authority on where to go, how to go, and what to see. Its prestige is based on the constant work of a corps of field reporters, travel counselors, road inspectors, cartographers, and hundreds of others employed by the organization to give its members—and indirectly all motorists—the last word on travel conditions at home and abroad.

Its field reporters cover each year the length and breadth of the country in seeking out acceptable touring accommodations for the motorist. Week in and week out in their assigned territories these men check the hotels, motor courts, motels, tourists homes, and restaurants along the nation's highways on the nature and condition of facilities offered to the traveler. It is their job to pass on location, appearance, cleanliness, bed linen, plumbing, and the dozens of intangibles appertaining to the comfort and reception given to the weary traveler. Out of some sixty thousand hostelries in this country the field men of the Association make regular inspections of a promising 50 per cent, with the result that only about seven thousand are found to be qualified for listing in its travel directories.

And in the meantime the road inspectors of the Association are traveling the highways of the nation checking the condition of the roads. With their firsthand information plus flash reports from key clubs along the more heavily traveled routes, the counselors in the travel department are well equipped to inform the tourist of the road conditions he is likely to encounter along his way. For the convenience of the traveler the Association distributes annually more than thirty-five million tour books, maps, and other travel material, ranking among the top twenty-five publishers of the nation.

The International Travel Department, with headquarters in New York City, also produces a wealth of material on touring abroad. It will arrange a complete foreign tour streamlined to fit the member's pocketbook and time allowance. It handles arrangements for shipping cars abroad, providing all necessary travel documents including driver's license and customs pass. Travel offices are maintained along the border in Texas to provide the required services for motorists driving into Mexico.

One of the best known and most popular services furnished to members by the Association is the emergency road service which will come to the rescue of a stranded motorist at any time of the night or day, and at any place within reasonable distance of a garage, some twenty thousand of which are under contract. All the member has to do is get to a telephone and call the nearest affiliated club. Nothing further is necessary; the club will do the rest, and in the shortest possible time one of the big red rescue trucks will come rolling up prepared to change a tire, or make a road repair if possible, and, if it happens to be a job that cannot be done on the road, the truck will tow you in. The nicest part of this service is that it comes at no extra cost, being furnished at the expense of the Association. That the service is appreciated is attested by the fact that each year the club answers millions of call for help on the road.

In addition to the School Safety Patrol with its half a million members to which reference has heretofore been made, the Association is also conducting a safety campaign for the protection of grownups with its annual Pedestrian Protection Program which now has wide participation in many states in choosing each year the "Safest City for Pedestrians" of all ages. The award takes into consideration an analysis of accident records and a number of other factors bearing on safety campaigns of the communities involved. Other safety considerations are constantly being introduced, such as the newly organized Foundation for Traffic Safety which was organized to make studies into basic causes of traffic accidents.

In the legislation and taxation fields the Association maintains an official watchdog attitude over laws affecting the rights and well-being of the motorist. For years it has fought the diversion of highway funds to other than highway purposes and was one of the prime movers in the enactment of the Dyer Antitheft Act, which makes a Federal offense of the transportation of a stolen automobile across a state line. It has also been active in extending the security-type safety responsibility law to some thirty-five of the states comprising about 80 per cent of total United States registration.

Essentially, the AAA is a grassroots organization. Its network of services both at home and abroad derives from some 750 clubs and branches working cooperatively through the national organization. The directions of both the AAA and its affiliated clubs are determined by boards of directors composed of business and professional men who serve in these councils without remuneration. The motor club has become a name on our land.

17   *Where Do We Go from Here?*

Looking back on the fifty years of motoring behind us, economists see the development of motor vehicle transportation as divisible into three roughly outlined periods.

The first is the Experimental Period of high costs and low standards of service, with a limited demand and small-scale manufacture, during which the horseless carriage was fighting for its life against ridicule and hostility.

After that came the Expansion Period in which a marked technological improvement, paced by a vast expansion of the highway system, resulted in an unprecedented production of motor vehicles, with a steadily declining cost of transportation. This period lasted roughly from the end of World War I until the mid-thirties when motor transportation seemed to have attained its Period of Maturity.

For a time the scales appeared to have been balanced. Cars had reached a high state of perfection, nearly everybody seemed to have one, and the bottlenecks were not too numerous. Then gradually the motorist became aware that highway construction was not keeping pace with car production, and standards of highway service began a rapid decline under the pressure of a phenomenal growth in traffic. With the overcrowding and congestion came an inevitable falling off in transportation efficiency, and as the quality of service went down, the cost went rocketing skyward until the man at the wheel began to wonder whether the sport was worth the candle. Economists put the problem a little more plainly by asking if motor transportation can possibly be a sound investment at the present fantastic cost of the necessary highways to keep abreast of our constantly expanding motor traffic.

To this question many experts have as yet given no adequate answer other than to malign the motor vehicle. "Has the automobile a future?" they demand. And a dean of science at a prominent technical school answers querulously that the motorcar is nothing more than a "monument to scientific frustration."

Is it possible, as the pessimists predict, that the motor vehicle can never be anything more than self-defeating? Is it true that every improvement made for the relief of traffic or parking simply creates more traffic, thus making the situation worse than before? And is it possible, or even likely, that the bottlenecks will end in one monstrous traffic jam with every road and street so choked with motor vehicles that none can move, and the only solution will be to plow them under and try some other kind of transportation? Could anybody but a well-seasoned pessimist think of such a nightmare?

It seems far more likely that when the first little Duryea wagon pulled itself a few feet along an obscure New England road it set in motion dynamic forces to confound the predictions of all the learned crapehangers. Even in its early days, when the engine was weak and uncertain and its owners were in the minority, the motor vehicle somehow exerted sufficient power to overcome the hostility and prejudice of the times and to influence the nation to lift itself out of a sea of mud and build a fifty-billion-dollar system of roadways which has no parallel anywhere in the world. This wobbling machine furnished the impetus for the foundation of giant industries and the formation of a swarm of small businesses which are key supports of the high economic level we enjoy today.

If yesterday's smoking and noisy contraptions could accomplish such miracles, what may we not expect from the sleek and powerful machines that provide transportation for so many of us today? The car and the freedom of movement it provides constitute a powerful force that has changed and is changing many of our deep-rooted institutions.

The bankruptcy courts hold the dismal records of some two

thousand makes of cars, the builders of which ignored or misjudged the wishes of the car-buying public and were consigned
to oblivion. You and I, picking and choosing the next car, influenced by experience or hearsay—or perhaps by the velvet
whim of a wife—have inadvertently caused hundreds of flour-
ishing companies to crash in ruins. And at the same time we have
brought wealth undreamed of by Midas to the small remainder
of companies which have correctly gauged—or influenced—our
needs and tastes.

Nor has the time of complete stability arrived. There are
many criticisms of the cars we drive today. They are oversized
and overornamented; one carper has compared them with Japa-
nese loveboats. But pound for shining pound, dollar for inflated
dollar, the transportation package we now get from the dealer
is by a wide margin better than anything we've ever had before.
From the standpoint of longevity alone, the current models are
wonders of durability. As recently as 1935 the average car reaching the junk pile was only a little over eight years old and had
traveled less than 60,000 miles. Today a representative vehicle
reaching the end of the trail has been in use for fourteen years
and has covered at least 120,000 miles.

Motorists may reasonably expect that the cars of tomorrow
will put less emphasis on power and speed—already far in
excess of traffic facilities—and concentrate more on lasting qualities, ease of operation, safety, and economy.

Nobody wants to be bothered with a car which requires frequent repairs. The trend has been increasingly toward the building of a part which will last for the life expectancy of the vehicle.
Contained units, self-lubricated for life, seem to be in the cards.
When automobiles were comparatively simple, nearly every
owner was to some extent his own mechanic; and it was only
when the vehicles increased in complexity that the owner was
compelled to bring his troubles to the local repairman. And further elaboration now in progress indicates that much of tomorrow's trouble will be resolved through replacement, instead of
repair, of the part that has failed.

It seems to be fairly certain that the car of the future will be much easier to operate. One by one the numerous levers, buttons, and switches required on the old-time vehicles are disappearing; the spark lever and hand throttle have long since vanished, and the clutch pedal is on the way out. Booster steering has made its appearance; and power braking may be just around the corner.

Safety provisions, always a strong selling point, have taken a new turn and moved inside the car. Borrowing the idea from aviation, there is some sentiment for the use of safety belts. Then, too, a windshield which will pop out rather than shatter upon impact is being tried out, as well as inside padding to soften the shock of collision. One car is already advertising that it has the safest front seat in the world. We are also approaching all-around bumpers to fend off cars that attack from the side. But perhaps the greatest need of the motorist is a major improvement in headlight illumination. The present lights are as bright as they can be made without completely blinding the oncoming driver, and still they are not effective enough for today's nighttime speeds, as is amply demonstrated by the sharp upward curve of accidents during the hours of darkness. A special niche in the motoring Hall of Fame awaits the genius who can solve this dilemma.

It is not the design of the car but its continuing impact on patterns of living that will hold the interest of the social historian. We have already seen how the motorcar has brought a new freedom to the American family—the freedom to travel when and where they please, and the further freedom to escape from the crowded cities and bring up their children in the open suburbs where they can enjoy the light, the air, and the spaciousness to cut the lawn and dig in the garden. We have also seen how the car has erased the loneliness and isolation of the rural communities and is breaking down the barriers of sectionalism that once so nearly wrecked our young nation.

Already there is much emphasis on better facilities in the rural areas in the East where great ribbons of concrete are being laid, usually toll-financed expressways of advanced design, along which automobiles can roll uninterruptedly and with comparative safety at speeds that would be murderous on average roads. But the question of urban traffic, how to keep it moving, and where to park and store it, is still far from a solution. The more realistic planners, accepting the idea that the automobile is here to stay, have begun developing programs intended eventually to adjust city conditions to the needs of a motor age. Some of these programs are ambitious; all are expensive. Even such comparatively simple measures as bringing expressways into and through the downtown areas and providing parking facilities for all the vehicles reasonably expected to come into the city run into hundreds of millions of dollars. In some of the more complete programs the solution of the congestion and parking problems is tied in with plans for slum clearance, housing development, park and parkway construction, and other measures that could, if carried out, bring light and air into the city.

Even as we find amusement in the mechanical difficulties and bad roads of the early motorists, our children and grandchildren will doubtless chuckle over the congestion, confusion, and the other traffic problems with which we contend today. What the eventual solution may be is still not clear, but it is all but inevitable that our way of life will eventually be adjusted to the requirements of a freewheeling people.

The motorist is constantly at war with the barrier at the boundary line impeding the freedom of movement between nations. Remove the "No Trespassing" sign and one of the principal reasons for jealousy, hatred, and misunderstanding is taken away. That was the way it worked out in our own country. To the early motorist a state line was an expensive and time-consuming annoyance. However, with comity established, the traveler goes from Maine to California without so much as a pause at most of the state boundaries. And if there is any pause, it is usually for the purpose of attaching a sticker which encourages others to come the same way.

By hundreds of thousands, American motorists go rolling into Canada with little more delay at the border than is required to make a statistical note. And swarms of Americans drive into Mexico, pausing at the line only long enough to swap dollars for pesos and obtain ready-made insurance giving protection south of the border. Also numbered by thousands are the Americans who ship their cars for touring along the European lanes of travel; or if the visit is to be short, arrangements are easily made for renting a car abroad.

World travel is no longer a prerogative of the rich. In the United States, where 75 per cent of all the world's automobiles are concentrated, car ownership is spread throughout all the income levels. This could become increasingly true in other countries as governments adopt policies designed to encourage ownership. Travel by automobile is already beginning to dent the international barriers. Under pressure from motorists and the organizations which represent them, a new world motoring agreement has been adopted that will make it possible for a motorist from an obscure American town to travel at will in any of the member countries, using his home-state registration plates and operator's license, with a minimum of delay and practically no red tape at any of the international boundaries.

This world driving agreement, worked out under the auspices of the United Nations, received comparatively little public attention at the time of its adoption, but it is in its way an important Magna Charta; for as motorists travel back and forth across international boundaries they will be smoothing the way for friendship among peoples, which is the only permanent foundation for a lasting world peace.

As of today the conclusion of any story of motoring is a pause rather than an ending. We are still in the midst of a profound but peaceful revolution brought to America by personalized transportation. The career of the horseless vehicle during the past fifty years has been little short of spectacular. As car ownership multiplies and spreads throughout the world, the car of the future may hold even greater portents in the shaping of men's affairs.

The car owner—the man behind the wheel—is the subject of proper concern to a wide variety of people; not only, as might be expected, to the proprietors of filling stations and repair shops, but also to industrialists, economists, planners, officials at all levels of government, statesmen, prophets, and historians delving deep to find the wellsprings affecting human destiny.

Quite oblivious of all these gentry, and totally unaware that his random decisions may cause the rise and fall of great industrial empires or otherwise influence the course of world events, the motorist calmly pilots his car on the daily rounds of business or his longer trips for pleasure. To him the family bus means a number of things, but above all it spells a freedom of movement undreamed of by his ancestors and known to all too few of his neighbors in other lands. Perhaps it is an unconscious realization of the deeper meaning of this freedom which puts added timbre in his voice as he drives up to a gasoline pump and calls out expansively, "Fill 'er up!"

Chronology of the Motor Car

1893   September 21, at Springfield, Massachusetts, the first successful
        gasoline-propelled motor vehicle made in the United States;
        made by J. Frank Duryea who, with his brother Charles,
        designed and built the single-cylinder horseless carriage.

1894   One-cylinder automobile, built by Apperson Brothers from de-
        signs by Elwood Haynes, driven successfully on streets of
        Kokomo, Indiana.

1895   First American automobile race held in Chicago on Thanksgiv-
        ing Day, won by Duryea over 52½-mile course at speed of
        5.05 miles per hour.
        Selden Patent granted.

1896   Henry Ford successfully operates his first gasoline car.
        Ransom Olds completes his first one-cylinder automobile.
        Charles B. King builds and drives first car seen on streets of
        Detroit.
        Barnum & Bailey Circus displays Duryea horseless carriage in
        street parade.

1897   Stanley twins establish Steam Car Company.

1898   H. H. Franklin produces first air-cooled car, with wood sills.

1899   U.S. War Department buys three automobiles, each equipped
        with provision for mule power, should it refuse to run.
        Stanley Steamer climbs Mount Washington.
        First American garage established in New York City.

1900   First National Automobile Show held in Madison Square Gar-
        den, New York City.
        The Ohio, built by Parkard, adopts steering wheel instead of
        tiller.
        Fifty-one new makes of cars announced during year.

1901   New York State begins licensing automobiles.

Oldsmobile equips cars with speedometers—first in use.

Autocar first to adopt shaft drive.

David Buick, maker of bathroom appliances, organizes automobile company.

Electric Vehicle Company, now owner of Selden Patent, threatens suits.

1902   American Automobile Association organized.

Two thousand Oldsmobiles built this year. Fifteen hundred Ramblers.

J. D. Maxwell and Charles D. King start manufacture of Silent Northern car, the first to be equipped with running boards.

Locomobile becomes first American car to mount engine in front.

Sixty-two new makes of cars announced during year.

1903   Ford Motor Company organized. Starts in business with operating capital of $28,000.

Windshield, canopy top, and shock absorbers introduced.

Tom Fetch drives Packard "Old Pacific" from San Francisco to New York in sixty-one days (elapsed time).

First Cadillac car completed and sold.

Eighty new makes of cars appear. Association of Licensed Automobile Manufacturers organized.

1904   First Vanderbilt Cup race run on Long Island. Won by Heath in Panhard.

Demountable rims appear.

Production of passenger cars, 22,130. Trucks, 700.

Prest-O-Lite Company formed to furnish acetylene gas in tanks for automobile headlights.

Henry Ford sets world's record of 91.37 miles per hour driving "999."

1905   First Glidden Tour inaugurated by American Automobile Association.

Tonneaus with side entrance appear.

Oldsmobile makes transcontinental run in forty-four days.

Report from St. Louis of first stolen car.

First car reported sold on installment plan.

American Motor Car Manufacturers Association organized to oppose Association of Licensed Automobile Manufacturers.

Tire chains, ignition locks, spare wheels appear.

1906   Buick includes storage battery as standard equipment.

The fastest thing on wheels, to date, has been John R. Cobb's Railton Racer, above, which in 1947 set the world land speed record at 394.16 miles per hour on the Utah Salt Flats. No attempt has been made since to better the mark set by Cobb.

General Motors

"Le Sabre," a futuristic custom-built sports car produced by General Motors, embodies several features which well may be stock items in the cars of tomorrow—among them, simulated tail cone and dramatically styled tail fins. The auto shown above is a full-size plaster model.

As intracity traffic has become more congested, forward-thinking city engineers are adopting the idea of expressways to facilitate movement along heavily traveled routes, such as this one in Dallas, Texas.

A portent of the future is this plan for Hartford, Connecticut, in which a garage for 900 vehicles is made an integral part of the program for building arterial expressways to speed traffic flow.

Cadillac adopts electric starter and lights as regular equipment.

All-steel body developed by Budd.

At Redlands, California, the first traffic lines were painted on the streets, starting quite a trend.

Among the seventeen new makes of cars was one called Perfex and another called Carnation.

13   Passenger car production for the year passes 461,000.

Ford production attains a rate of 1,000 cars a day.

Wire wheels offered as standard equipment.

Automatic Bendix drive for electric starters shown for first time.

Thomas B. Jeffery offers four-wheel-drive truck.

Forced-feed lubrication introduced by Packard.

914   Passenger production for the year goes above 500,000.

Cadillac introduces first American eight-cylinder, V-type motor.

Rambler changes name to Jeffery.

Spiral bevel gear developed by Packard.

Pierce incorporates headlights in fenders.

Ford announces minimum wage of $5 a day.

A Detroit ordinance prohibits gasoline pumps at curbs.

1915   Production of passenger cars reaches 895,930.

Packard brings out a twelve-cylinder model.

Briscoe introduces a "Cyclops" eye with a single headlight in center of radiator.

Cadillac adopts tilt-beam headlights.

"Jitneys" appear in various cities like a plague of locusts.

Demountable rims become universal equipment.

War in Europe creates material shortages.

1916   Passenger car production passes 1,500,000 for year.

Ford buys factory site on banks of River Rouge.

Final Vanderbilt Cup race held at Santa Monica.

Hand-operated windshield wipers are hailed with delight.

U.S. Army uses fleet of trucks on expeditionary force in Mexico.

Stop lights are seen and rear-view mirrors can now be bought.

1917   Production of passenger cars for the year passes 1,745,000, with trucks and buses going above 125,000.

Of the twenty-eight new makes of cars appearing, Nash is now the only survivor.

Radiator shutters which could be closed in cold weather were introduced, though they never became widely popular.

Front bumpers are offered for sale.

One-thousand-mile track race at Em|

First rotary engines introduced by Ad

1907 Production this year, 43,000 passenger

Ford Company makes more than a milli

Nickel plate first used instead of brass fo

Buick adopts four-cylinder engine.

Ninety-two new makes of cars appear, am

Swallow, Single Center, and Bugmobil

1908 General Motors incorporated in New Jers

$10,000.

Model-T Ford appears.

Four-wheel drive invented.

Thomas Flyer wins New York to Paris race.

Fisher Body Company organized.

Innovations: magnetic speedometer, sleeve

hand steering, silent timing chains, motor-d

1909 Production for year passes 100,000.

Selden Patent held valid and infringed upon by

Indianapolis Speedway completed by Carl Fishe

"One-man" tops appear.

Hudson Motor Car Company organized.

Cadillac joins General Motors.

1910 Cars offered completely equipped for first time.

First three-day racing meet held at Indianapolis.

First three-ton truck shown at the New York Autom

Sixth Vanderbilt Cup race held on Long Island. W

Grant driving American-made Alco.

1910 Only fifteen new makes of cars this year, one named

All now defunct.

1911 Production for year just misses 100,000 passenger car

pass the 10,000 mark.

Chevrolet Motor Company organized at Flint, Michiga

Selden Patent sustained on appeal, but held not infringed b

Cadillac comes out with electric starter and lights devel

Charles F. Kettering.

Motorcar stocks first listed on New York Stock Exchange.

1912 Production for year surpasses 356,000 passenger cars, and 22

trucks and buses.

The V-shaped windshield was introduced, and several makers were offering a coupé or roadster with rumble seats.

Many automotive companies participate in the development and production of Liberty engines for military aircraft.

Chevrolet offers an eight-cylinder model later discontinued.

1918   Production drops slightly below a million passenger cars, though trucks and buses rise to more than 227,000.

Chevrolet is acquired by General Motors.

Many car factories turning to war work.

Of the twenty-two new makes of cars started, none survives.

Gasless Sundays and heatless Mondays were proposed, though never widely adopted.

1919   Production of passenger cars for the year, 1,651,625, while trucks and buses passed quarter of a million.

Approximately 90 per cent of all passenger cars were open models with folding tops.

Ford production for year, 750,000 cars, more than one-third of total output of the industry.

General Motors Acceptance Corporation formed to handle installment sales.

Henry Ford buys out all minority stockholders and makes the Ford Motor Company a family corporation.

1920   Production of passenger cars and trucks for the year surpasses the two million mark for the first time.

Duesenberg offers the first straight eight and four-wheel brakes.

Durant loses General Motors, this time finally.

States acquire surplus war trucks for use in highway building.

Of the forty-five new makes of cars started this year, not one survives.

1921   Production nearly a million and a half passenger cars and 150,000 trucks and buses.

Hudson offers an adjustable front seat, and a coach priced at only $300 more than a touring car.

Rubber engine mountings and spring shackles appear.

Hydraulic brakes becoming more popular.

Of the fifty-eight new makes of car appearing this year, only Lincoln survives.

1922   Production this year, 2,274,185 passenger cars and 270,000 buses and trucks.

Balloon tires and air cleaners introduced.

Gasoline gauge begins to appear on instrument panel.

1923   Total production exceeds four million for the first time, more
       than half of which bear the Ford name plate.

       Four-wheel brakes and power-operated windshield wipers be-
       come standard equipment.

1924   Ford Company produces its ten-millionth car.

       Twelve new name plates this year. All gone but Chrysler.

       Double-filament headlight bulbs appear.

       Total cars in the country this year—one for every seven persons.

1925   Total production for year, 4,256,830.

       Ford production exceeds 9,000 a day.

       The 25-millionth U.S. motor vehicle made.

       Front and rear bumpers now standard equipment.

       Chain of "Drive yourself" stations established.

1926   Cannon Ball Baker drives truck from New York to San Fran-
       cisco in less than six days.

       Total production for year again above four million.

       Hudson offers all-steel body.

       Ford inaugurates five-day week.

1927   Ford discontinues Model T. Halts production six months to re-
       tool.

       General Motors stockholders receive over 134 million dollars in
       dividends.

       Lockheed internal hydraulic brakes announced.

       Sixteen new name plates are seen. None survives.

1928   Synchro-mesh transmission introduced by Cadillac.

       Studebaker acquires Pierce-Arrow.

       Shatterproof glass standard equipment on Ford. Model A starts.

       Coast-to-coast bus service begins.

       Chrysler offers Plymouth and De Soto.

1929   Total production passes five million.

       Over 90 per cent of passenger cars now have closed bodies.

       Automobile radios appear.

       Foot-controlled dimmer switches are introduced.

       Ford raises wage scale to $7 a day minimum.

1930   Passenger car production drops below three million.

       Cadillac offers V-12 and V-16.

Freewheeling introduced.

Several cars come wired for radio.

Prowl cars equipped with radio.

1931   Passenger car production drops below two million.

Freewheeling available on models of seventeen makers.

The 50-millionth U.S. motor vehicle produced.

Only four new makes of cars offered. None survives.

1932   Passenger car production drops to slightly over one million.

Ford supplants Model A with V-8.

Graham puts skirts on fenders.

Outside visors move inside.

Two new makers start business. Short lived.

1933   Production for year less than two million.

Parts and replacements for year exceed 200 million.

"No draft" ventilation introduced.

M. E. Coyle becomes president of Chevrolet succeeding W. S. Knudsen.

Introduction of independent wheel suspension.

Only one new make of car this year—Continental.

1934   Passenger car production rises above two million.

Gearshift lever appears on dashboard.

Radio controls are seen on instrument panel.

Lafayette is only new make of car launched.

1935   Passenger car production for year passes three million.

Sales of replacement parts passes 300 million.

Motorist now pays one of every eight tax dollars.

All-steel "turret top" introduced.

One new make this year—Stout Scarab.

1936   Replacement parts sales pass 454 million dollars.

Government announces 54 per cent of United States families now own cars.

Diamond T offers Diesel-powered truck.

Nineteen makes of house trailers displayed at National Automobile Show.

1937   Passenger car production just misses four million.

Replacement parts exceed 461 million dollars.

Steering column gearshift introduced.

New make this year—Bantam.

1938 Passenger car production tumbles to two million.
      Parts production drops 21 per cent.
      Chrysler offers "fluid drive."
      Only new car—Mercury.

1939 Hood lock under dash appears.
      Hydra-Matic Drive offered by Olds.
      Lincoln Zephyr omits running boards.
      Knee action arrives.

1940 Sales of replacement parts passes 500 million.
      Total production of motor vehicles for year passes 4½ million.
      Knudsen goes to Washington on production job.
      Motorcar factories turn to aviation for duration of war.

1941 Production of passenger cars near four million for year.
      Production of trucks and buses passes one million.
      Mauri Rose wins at Indianapolis at 115.117 miles per hour.
      The 29-millionth Ford comes off assembly line.

1942 Wartime production of only 222,862 passenger cars, but
           818,662 buses and trucks.
      Production of civilian cars halted February 9.
      National speed limit cut to 35 miles per hour.
      Gasoline rationing effective December 1.

1943 Passenger car production for year, 139; trucks and buses, 669,-
           689.
      Gasoline ration books delivered to 25,000,000 motorists.
      Employment in motorcar plants reaches wartime peak. Value of
           war products made passes thirteen billion dollars.

1944 Passenger car production for year 610 units.
      Basic gasoline ration reduced to two gallons a week.
      Government reveals passenger cars now being scrapped at 4,000
           a day.

1945 Passenger car production for year 69,532.
      Value of replacement parts passes one billion dollars.
      Reconversion to civilian production of passenger cars July 1.
      Ford resumes civilian production July 6.

1946 Passenger car production again touches two million, with trucks
           and buses over 940,000, and the value of replacement parts
           over one billion dollars.
      Stout 46, a car with Fiberglas body, is shown.

Indianapolis Sweepstakes revived.

Vacuum-operated windows introduced.

Radio telephone for motorcar introduced.

1947 Total production for year, 4,797,820. Value of replacement parts two billion three hundred million dollars.

Deaths during year, William C. Durant and Henry Ford.

Outside sun visors again appear.

The Davis, a three-wheeler, displayed in Los Angeles.

Driving courses taught in many high schools.

1948 Total production exceeds five million.

Tubeless tires introduced.

Tucker Corporation displays first models.

One-hundred-millionth American motorcar produced somewhere in the country.

Value of replacement parts reaches new record of 2½ billion dollars.

Passenger car registrations pass 33 million.

Motorists paid in taxes $3,360,000,000.

1949 Self-energizing disc brakes introduced.

Compression ratio of motors rises as high as 7.5 to 1.

Hard-top convertibles in popular favor.

1950 Small cars again become popular with introduction of Rambler and Henry J.

1951 Power steering and hemispherical combustion chamber introduced by Chrysler.

1952 Cadillac raises horsepower to 190.

Electric-eye headlight beam deflector introduced.

Index

A

Adams, Frederick Upham, 11
Ainsley, Charles, first Ford buyer, 33
Albany, road signs to, 73
"All outdoors" found in Nebraska, 162
Amen Corner, 50
American Automobile Association
    (AAA), 79–83
    Contest Board of, 87, 88, 142
    emergency service of, 210, 211
    first meeting of, 83
    "Good Roads" promotion of, 185
    organization of, 79
    reliability run to St. Louis, 88–98
    School Safety Patrol, 211
    sponsorship activities of, 86, 87
    Travel Department of, 210
American Motor League, 50
American Motorist launched, 185
Andrews, Gen. Avery D., 51
Anti-theft Act, 211
Ardsley Country Club, 25
Arents, George, 125
Association of Licensed Automobile
    Manufacturers (A.L.A.M.), 70
Astor, Col. John Jacob, 25, 67, 76
Automobile camping, 194, 195
Automobile Club of America (A.C.A.),
    51
    Bridgeport club run, 75
    Buffalo reliability run, 77
    disbanded, 140
    first Auto Show of, 63
    Long Island road race, 75
    organization of, 50, 51
    Philadelphia reliability run, 75
    second Auto Show of, 69
    takes interest in "Good Roads" move-
        ment, 74

Automobile Club of Southern Cali-
    fornia, 178
Automobile Clubs, federation of, 80
Automobile factories, increase of, 41, 42
Automobile Manufacturers Association,
    32
Automobile shows, 63–70
    at Chicago, 63, 64
    at Grand Central Palace, 80
    at Madison Square Garden, 39, 40

B

Bad Lands, driving across, 164
Barber, Amzi, 60
Barnum, Phineas T., 64
Barnum & Bailey, 25
Bay Shore, 74
Beecroft, David, 115
Bell, Alexander Graham, 28
Benz, Carl, 2, 3
Benz car, 15
Blacksmith, low charges of, 157, 158
    as repairman, 153
Block and tackle as equipment, 165
Bloom, Mr. and Mrs. Roy, 165, 166,
    167
Blue Book, 155
    passing of, 196
Bonneville Flats, Utah, 140
Bonnyriggs Four Corners, 154
Boston Automobile Club, 52
Brayton, George, inventor, 2
Bridgeport Automobile Club, 73
Brooklyn, winter club run of, 74
Bruce, Robert, 154
"Buckskin Ed," 194
Buffalo, road signs to, 73
Buffalo Automobile Club, blackboard
    of, 156
    formation of, 52

229